BAC PRO

Première
et Terminale

CONFORME AU CECRL

PRO GOAL plus

Patrick Aubriet
Professeur de Lycée professionnel, formateur IUFM

Annick Billaud
Professeur de Lycée professionnel

Marie-Thérèse Kowalczyk
Professeur de Lycée professionnel, formatrice IUFM

Béatrice Léonori
Professeur de Lycée professionnel, formatrice IUFM

FOUCHER

Les compétences du CECRL

Pour chaque activité proposée dans le manuel, vous trouverez un pictogramme indiquant la compétence traitée avec l'indication du niveau du CECRL (de A2 à B2) permettant ainsi d'évaluer la difficulté de chaque exercice et d'adapter votre démarche.

	Écouter
	Lire
	Parler / Prendre part à une conversation
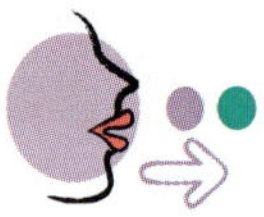	Parler / Prise de parole en continu
	Écrire

ISBN 978-2-216-10633-2

Sommaire

dialogue enregistré (compréhension orale) — support rédigé (compréhension écrite) — support illustré

sommaire

dialogue enregistré (compréhension orale) support rédigé (compréhension écrite) support illustré.

unit 1

Getting in touch

contact

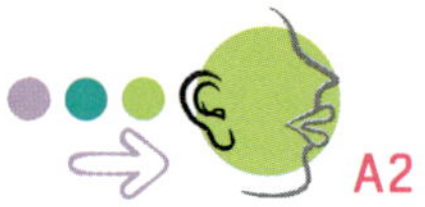

1 Listen to the first part of the dialogue and find the right solution.

a. What (are you doing / do you do) today?
b. Right now (I work / I'm working) in the garage.
c. Later this afternoon, I (install / 'm installing) brand new computers.
d. What (does she do / is she doing)?
e. She (directs / is directing) customers and (answers / is answering) the phone.
f. She (wears / is wearing) a nice new uniform.

2 Complete with the correct present tense. Then listen again and check your answers.

a. .... you clean........ the manager's car ? No, I'm not.
b. We .... wear........ uniforms in the offices.
c. No, I'm not. I .... chang........ all the plugs *(prises)* for new equipment.
d. She .... visit........ our new store with me.
e. We .... always show........ trainees our newest stores.
f. This month, I .... start........ French.

fOcus

Usually, she works at the reception desk.
Today, she is helping Tina in the perfume department.
Tomorrow we're going to Dover together.

- *Quels sont les deux temps utilisés dans ces énoncés ? Rappelez leur conjugaison.*
- *Quel type d'activité expriment-ils respectivement ? (en cours, habituelle, future ?)*
- *Dans ces énoncés, quel marqueur de temps exprime une action en cours, habituelle, future ? Quels autres marqueurs de temps pourrait-on également utiliser ?*

Action

1 Turn the verbs into the positive form of the simple present or –ING present tense. Underline the tense marker.

a. Usually, I (eat) a salad at the cafeteria, but today I (have) lunch in a restaurant with my boss. Tonight I (go) to a Chinese restaurant with my friend.
b. Salesgirls often (do) very different tasks* *(tâches)*. At the moment, Tina and Marion display* *(mettre en rayon)* articles but this afternoon Tina (work) at the till* *(la caisse)*.
c. Normally chefs (cook) hot meals. Here, the trainee (prepare) fish for dinner. In fact, he (take) his exam on Tuesday and he (practise).
d. We (travel) to Dover by train today because it (snow). Tonight we (stay) at a hotel near the port.

A2

2 Listen to the end of the conversation. Complete the questions with the present form you hear.

a. How (you / like) your job at Tesco?
b. What (you / do) today?
c. How much (you / earn) as a trainee?
d. (you / stay) at a student hostel?
e. What (you / do) on Saturday evening?
f. (you / work) overtime next Sunday?

3 Find the right information about the different people.

a. Marion thinks the people (speak / eat) (too slowly / too quickly).
b. Today Marion is (selling / labelling) (cosmetics / perfume).
c. Dave usually (installs and repairs / sells and delivers) all sorts of equipment.
d. Marion earns (59 / 95) pounds (per a week / per weekend).
e. Marion is staying (at a hostel / in a flat / with a family).
f. Flo is working overtime (on Saturday / all Sundays / on Sunday) this week.

Chatitime

A2

You are student A (Sam). You answer student B's questions. Then you interview Peter or Jane (student B). Student B is on Appendix page 148.

Name	Sam Broote	Peter ...	Jane ...
Age	19		
Occupation	shop assistant		
Company / school / department	Marks & Spencer in the furniture dept.		
Job / studies	sell furniture / display articles / advise people		
Present activity	clean a table		
Opinion about job	+ : rather pleasant / meet people		
Salary	£ 180 / week		
Work overtime	sometimes / at Christmas time		
Home	with parents / rent a house in the suburbs		
Tonight	go to the cinema / see my girl / boyfriend		

A2

Tell about Sam, Peter or Jane

unit 1

B1

"Working at McDonald's... I'm lovin'it !"

I work at a McDonald's store in Sydney, Australia. I'm seventeen and this is my third job in food, but this is by far my best.

I am still at high school but times are flexible and adapted to my school timetable. It sometimes clashes with the work shifts*, but as managers are very understanding, I am not forced to work at a time when I can't.

Our management team is really great and the crew get along very well. I believe managers work ten times harder than any of the crew, sorting out* problems and helping where it is needed. Being in a teenage workplace, they look out for* the younger crew, because the older, more experienced crew have a tendency to treat them badly.

The pay here is OK. I started at $8.50 nine months ago and I am currently* earning $9.07. It's not bad as I'm part time and I get sick leave, annual leave, etc.

As a crew trainer I look after the new employees and teach them everything in the job from making fries to working at the front counter or dealing with* customers. Being a crew trainer is cool because we get some extra benefits; for example we're getting a pizza party soon, just for us. We are also the first to try the new menu items, like the Asian salad that is coming later this month.

Our uniforms are washed, dried and pressed and waiting for us when we get to work. Some people complain because we don't always get the right size but here we don't have to pay for it.

Our store also supports community events and donates to good causes. Our managers love to do stuff for the kids. For Easter* we are giving out a special gift* to each child, and at the end of each shift, the crew will get one too.

There are so many bad rumours about McDonalds, but I can tell you that here they are 99% not true. Our store owner is strict and a perfectionist. Because of that I think, he owns one of the best McDonalds' in Sydney, committed* to hygiene, safety, great customer service and teamwork.

It may sound idealistic but it's possible. I know, I see it every time I go to work.

Mike Scott

adapted from *Aboutmyjob.com*

help

work shifts *plages de travail*
sort out *résoudre*
currently *actuellement*
look out for *faire attention à*
deal with *se comporter avec*
Easter *Pâques*
a gift *un cadeau*
committed to *impliqué / engagé dans*

Anticip

Compr

ph

d. faire des « trucs » pour les gosses (§6)

5 What's the French for...?

a. crew trainer (§4)
b. a teenage workplace (§2)
c. making fries (§4)
d. ...are washed, dried and pressed (§5)

6 Answer these questions about the document.

a. Is it the first time he works in a restaurant?
b. What does he think of his managers?
c. How much does he earn?
d. Does he work full time or part time? Why?
e. What food is he trying at the moment?
f. What sort of problem do the crew have with their uniforms?

fOcus

I believe they work ...
Our managers love to stuff ...
I think he owns one of ...
I know, I see it ...

- *À quel temps du présent sont ces verbes ?*
- *Quels verbes expriment un sentiment, une opinion, la possession ?*
- *Retrouvez l'exception à usage publicitaire dans le document.*

>> Training n°2 et 5

7 Right or wrong? Justify your answer.

a. Mike sometimes doesn't go to school because of his job.
b. The employees buy their uniforms.
c. The restaurant is serving pizza very soon.
d. The store and the manager are not very generous.
e. His store is very clean.

nOw in French

8 Répondez en français à ces questions.

a. Pourquoi les managers sont-ils particulièrement vigilants envers les jeunes récemment recrutés ?
b. En quoi consiste l'activité de formateur de Mike ?
c. Quels sont les avantages exclusifs accordés aux formateurs?
d. Quelle est son opinion sur le propriétaire de son établissement ?

Writing

B1

9 Introduce yourself (name, age, town...). Tell about your studies (what? where?).
Do you have a job? Tell about it.
Say if you like what you do or not, and why?

unit 1

B1

Young workers

1 SATISFIED

I am a twenty-three-year-old college student and while I am not attending school I can be found at work. I work on the weekends and whenever I can find the time during the week.

I have been working as a parking-lot attendant for a year. My job consists of gassing* and washing cars after they are sold, keeping keys and moving cars from the storage areas onto the lot.

The positive aspect of my work situation is that it's close to home, simple, and flexible, with my own schedule. The down side is that I am surrounded by lazy* people: salesmen.

The car-dealer where I work sells new vehicles so I feel cool when I 'm driving around in $50,000 cars. My boss is a completely chill guy who respects me and my schedule. He lets me choose my hours and tries to calm me down when I come in to work stressed out. He agrees with me that the salesmen can be lazy but he relies on* them for his business.

A lot of my friends say, 'So, you're still cleaning cars?' and that makes me sad. It's a lot more than "cleaning cars" and I don't like them to think I have a small job. This job fits perfectly into my life right now. I know that the jobs I have during college are just a passing phase in my life. I am attending school to become a commercial photographer and I know I will lead a successful life.

Sarah parking-lot attendant,
adapted from Aboutmyjob.com

*gassing = filling up with gasoline (US) / petrol (GB)
lazy *fainéants* – rely on *compter sur.*

1. Does Sarah have much free time?
2. Can you describe the sorts of things she does?
3. Can you explain why she does not like the salesmen.
4. What is a small job? In her opinion, why doesn't she have a small job?

2 ANGRY

B1

I'm seventeen-years-old, I work at McDonalds and I hate it. Well, I need money and a job. But the fact that they make people fat with their greasy, dirty food and spread* their propaganda makes me sick. After six months, I still work in the back making sandwiches. I'll just describe to you some of the good things and some of the bad ones:

– My friends work there and I chat and have fun while I'm working.

– You get good long breaks (20 minute and 30 minute breaks in an 8 hour shift).

– You get minimum wage – $5.05 – and unpaid breaks.

– They have about 100 people working there, but it's usually understaffed.

– It's extremely unsanitary. We make the food with our bare* hands, yet we hardly ever wash them. Nobody ever cleans anything and the place often looks disgusting.

– Over half of our crew is VERY new, because a lot of people quit there. So, the more experienced people do all of the work and are overworked*.

– Managers scream at* you even when you've done nothing wrong.

– Promotions are a joke. It's not about hard work, speed and good communication. It's just a popularity contest.

To conclude, McDonalds has done nothing for me but cause serious stress, exhaustion, anger and a lousy* pay sheet.

Gary, Wisconsin, adapted from
Aboutmyjob.com

*spread *étaler* – bare *nu* – overworked *surchargé de travail* – scream at *crier après* – lousy *"nul"*.

5. Why does Gary have this job?
6. What does he think of McDonald's in general?
7. Sort out the good and bad sides of his job.
8. Why do so many crew quit their job?
9. Compare the two McDonald's stories.

outlook

B1

3 FORGOTTEN

10. Do these children work to finance their studies?

11. What is appalling about their living and working conditions?

12. What is a slave? Why is Nasib a slave?

In Indonesia, thousands of children work in conditions of appalling* deprivation on fishing platforms whose deck* is hardly three metres above the ocean. According to an Indonesian humanitarian foundation, they are the sites of the worst child slave-labour in the region. About 75 per cent of employees are boys and a third of them are under the age of 14. They fish, 'teri', an anchovy-like fish. The fish is sold IR35,000 (Indonesian Rupiahs) – about £1.60 a kilo. Here is Nasib's testimony:

"My name is Nasib. I work on Ben Ciong jermal, it is 8 miles from the coast. Everyday I work twelve or thirteen hours, sometimes twenty; it is long. We fish 'teri', a small-fish, then we sort them, boil and dry them. Boiling is very difficult. The cauldron-room is very hot and drinking water is limited. It is very dangerous when the sea is bad ; we have no life boat… I sleep in the dormitory with the other boys, only the supervisor has a bed… I see my parents in the village every three months and give them my salary. It is 45,000 rupiahs a month. I am fourteen…"

adapted from *Focus n°95*, October 2000

*appalling *épouvantable* – the deck *le pont* – to sort *trier*.

hot line

A2

Enrolling for the students'union

1. Listen to the conversation and complete it with the missing information.

Secretary	Enrolling student
1. Students' Union Galway, ...?	Yes, I'm phoning to .... the .... Is it .... by ....?
2. Yes, it is. Welcome. Can ....?	Yes, ...
3. Can ...., please?	It's ....
4. Thank you. And .... in Ireland?	It's .... In Galway ....
5. Sorry .... the name of.................	Sure, ...
6. And ....?	I .... at ....
7. .... card number?	Yes, just a moment. Yes, it's ....
8. ....?	....
9. Now .... choose a P....... I....... N.......? It's .... letters and .... numbers.	OK. Well ....
10. .... Good. Now you can come and get your ...... But don't forget .... Good bye. See you soon.	....

B1

2. Practise more dialogues. Other students' role-cards are on appendix page 148.

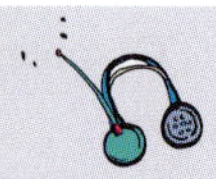

say it

a. Retrouvez les intrus dans ces lettres de l'alphabet regroupées selon leur prononciation. Puis écoutez et vérifiez.

[eɪ] like eight: A E H I J K
[i:] like three: B C D E G J P S T V
[e] like egg: F L K M N R S X Z
[aɪ] like why: I Y J
[ju:] like you: Q O U W
[əu] like open: O U
[ɑ:] like are: A R

b. Notez l'élément épelé. Quelle question précise a été posée pour l'obtenir ?

a. My name's Simon ...
b. I live at 5 ... Street.
c. I'm Welsh, I'm from ...
d. I work at ...'s pub in Galway.

1 Complétez par une forme conjuguée de *be* ou *have*.

a. How old ... you?
b. How many brothers ... you got?
c. We ... from Paris.
d. Sam ... a good job.
e. Do they ... a good salary?
f. She ... a daughter who ... about my age.
g. ... you in a youth hostel?
h. He ... his own room.
i. We ... 3 breaks a day.
j. You ... welcome.
k. I ... Saturday off.

2 Mettez les verbes aux formes demandées du présent simple.

a. (You / learn) electronics? No, (I / not study) that subject; (I / study) cooking.
b. Where (Sandra / work)? (She / work) in the accounts dept. (She / not sell) clothes.
c. (Pam / enjoy) her job? No, (she / not like) it. (She / think) it's boring.
d. (they / own) their house? No (they / rent) it. (They / pay) a £350 rent a month.

3 Mettez les verbes aux formes demandées du présent en *-ING*.

a. What (the new trainee / do) today? (He / help) in the sports dept. (He / label) new articles.
b. John! (you / drive) to London soon? No, (I / not visit) clients this week. (I / stay) at the office.
c. Loic, this is the cafeteria staff. The chefs, (Peter and Mary / cook) the hot meals for lunch, (Pat / cut) tomatoes and (Maria / clean) the dishes.
d. (You / come) to the pub with me? No, (we / go) to the bowling alley. (Our friends / wait) for us.

4 Dites leur métier, ce qu'ils font habituellement (a), ce qu'ils font aujourd'hui (b), et ce qu'ils ont prévu de faire ce soir (c).

a b c

5 Formez les questions au présent simple ou en *-ING*, puis répondez en utilisant toujours des verbes conjugués à une forme négative.

a. (Trainees / get) a salary in France? No, they ... . Companies (not pay) them.
b. How much (your brother / earn)? He (not earn) much because he (not have) a qualification.
c. (You / work) overtime tomorrow? No, I ... . I (not like) working on Sundays.
d. (Your parents / own) their house? No, they ... . They (not get) a big salary, you see.
e. (Sandra / live) with her parents? No, she ... because they (not live) in the same town.
f. (Loic / go) to Lea's party on Saturday? No, he ... because he (not know) her address.

remember

Pour exprimer des actions ou des activités habituelles, on emploie le présent simple avec des adverbes et des indicateurs de fréquence (voir Unit 3 p. 29).

I start at 8 every day You live in ... He / she / it work**s** ... We study ... They earn ...	**Do I start** at 8? Yes, I do / No, I don't Do you live...? Yes, I do / No, I don't **Does** he / she / it work ? Yes, he does / No, he doesn't Do we study...? Yes, we do / No, we don't Do they earn ...? Yes, they do / No, they don't	**I don't start** at 8 every day. You don't finish ... He / she / it **doesn't** go... We don't like ... They don't want ...

Le **'s'** de la troisième personne du singulier devient **'es'** (prononcé [iz]) pour les verbes terminés par **ch, s, sh, x, z** ou par la lettre **'o'**: She watch**es**, he go**es**.
Le **'y'** terminal d'un verbe en 'y' précédé d'une consonne devient **'ies'** : I try → she **tries**.
I study → he stud**ies** mais You stay → he stays.
Certains verbes s'emploient habituellement au présent simple quand ils expriment :
- **des sentiments ou la volonté** : like, love, hate, wish, want.
- **des opinions** : believe, think, understand, suppose, know, remember, imagine, prefer, realize.
- **la possession** : belong, own, have, possess.

Pour décrire ou parler d'une action en cours, d'une situation momentanée, temporaire, on utilise le présent en *–ING*. Il se forme avec *be* et le verbe en *–ING*.

I am working He, she, it **is** coming You, we, they **are** studying	Am I working? yes, **I am** / no, **I'm not** **Is** he, she, it coming? Yes, he **is** / No, he **isn't** **Are** you, we, they studying? Yes, we **are** / No, we **aren't**	I am not working He, she, it **is not** coming you, we, they **are not** studying

- **Il peut souvent se traduire par « être en train de », en français.**

→ I am peeling potatoes. *Je suis en train d'éplucher des pommes de terre.*
→ This year, she is studying in Ireland. *Cette année, elle étudie en Irlande.*
→ As it's snowing, all the representatives are working at the office.
Comme il neige tous les commerciaux travaillent au bureau.

- **Ces marqueurs de temps servent à exprimer une action en cours :**

Now, at present, at the moment, currently, today, here..., this afternoon (morning)

Pour exprimer une activité prévue dans le futur, on peut utiliser le présent en *–ING*

→ What are you doing tonight? I'm going out to dinner.
Que fais-tu ce soir ? Je sors au restaurant.

- **Les marqueurs de temps du futur servent à exprimer une action prévue :**

Soon, tonight, next..., tomorrow.

Vocabulary

Verbs / verbes
attend *fréquenter*
be* off *être en congé*
check *vérifier*
display *mettre en rayon, présenter*
earn *gagner (salaire)*
fit * *convenir*
label *étiqueter* (a label) *une étiquette*
own *posséder*
rely on *compter sur (quelqu'un)*
rent *louer* (a rent *un loyer*)
scream *crier*
suit *convenir*
train *former*
work overtime *faire des heures supplémentaires*

Nouns / noms
an attendant *un employé, gardien*
a bill / an invoice *une facture*
a break *une pause*
a counter /a till / *une caisse*
a crew *une équipe / un employé*
a day off *un jour de congé*
a department *un service, rayon*
an employee *un employé*
an employer *un employeur*
a paysheet *une fiche de paye*
a pay / a salary /wage(s) *un salaire / une paye*
a parking lot (US) a car park (GB) *un parking*
a schedule *un emploi du temps*
a shift *une plage horaire / un poste de travail*
the staff *le personnel*
a team *une équipe*
a trainee *un stagiaire*
a trainer *un formateur*

Adjectives / adjectifs
appalling *épouvantable*
cool, chill *'cool', décontracté*
lazy *fainéant*

unit 2

Describing attitudes

contact

SECURITY INFORMATION

No sharp objects, no weapons, no liquids and gels are permitted in your hand luggage.

Make sure you have a valid passport and visas with you for your trip.

Don't forget ...
All coats are placed through the X-ray machines. Please assist us by placing all wallets*, mobile phones and keys in your hand luggage.

*wallet *portefeuille*

A2

1 **Look at the pictures and listen to the dialogue (Part 1). Then answer the questions.**

a. Where are Carla and Kyle? Where will they go? Why?
b. What time is their plane? What time do they have to go through the security controls?
c. What is not permitted in your hand luggage?

2 **Listen again and answer the questions.**

a. What is not permitted at the airport?
b. Where are Carla's wallet and passport? What should she do?
c. Where did Carla pack her scissors and cosmetics?
d. What will they do before going through the security controls?

3 **Listen again and complete the following sentences.**

a. Let's ... out.
b. ... at the board.
c. ... make sure you are ready.
d. You ... keep your wallet in your backpack.
e. You ... be more careful.
f. ... be so nervous.
g. ... worry.
h. I checked my ... .
i. We ... plenty of time.
j. Let ... offer you a drink.

fOcus

Put them into your secure pocket.
Don't smoke here.
Let me help you.
Let's go to the cafeteria.

- *Parmi ces énoncés, lesquels expriment plutôt une interdiction, une suggestion, un ordre ou un conseil ?*
- *Quelles sont les deux constructions possibles ? Quel mot 's remplace-t-il dans le dernier énoncé ?*
- *Comment traduire les énoncés ?*
Peut-on toujours traduire le verbe par un impératif en français ?
Quelle autre traduction est possible ?

Action

1 **Turn these sentences into the negative or affirmative form to give good advice before leaving.**

a. Pack your credit card in your backpack.
b. Don't place your money in your secure pocket.
c. Don't let me put your keys in your luggage.
d. Never check your luggage.
e. Don't let's hurry.
f. Let him forget his passport.

2 **Turn these tips (advice) into orders.**

a. You shouldn't smoke in the car.
b. You should stop every two hours.
c. You shouldn't telephone when driving.
d. You should always wear a seatbelt.
e. You shouldn't let them drive so fast.
f. You should never let him drink and drive.

A2

3 **Listen to the end of the dialogue (Part 2) and answer the questions.**

a. Where will they work as volunteers?
b. What will they repair and install?
c. Where is the camp?
d. Who is responsible for the camp? What's her attitude?
e. What are the local people's attitudes?
f. How could Carla learn about their traditions?

4 **Listen again and write down the advice Kyle gives Carla. Use two different verbal forms as in the example.**

Ex: *about the job (worry)* ➡ *Don't worry. You shouldn't worry.*

a. to help volunteers (try)
b. if you have a special need (ask)
c. in the sun (work)
d. in the evening (wear)
e. With local people (be respectful)
f. When it's time to go (let / talk)

Chat time

You are Student A. Explain your problems (pictures a, b, c, d) and ask student B to advise you. Student B (see p. 149) will give you tips to help you. Note down the 3 tips he gives you.

A2

Ex: **A:** *I'm always late at school. What can I do? Can you advise me?...*
B: *Always get up early. You should ... / Be careful. Don't ...*

help

e. ask a friend to introduce you – be impatient – invite him / her at a party – send a love letter...
f. exercise – jog – eat pop corn/ fresh fruit and vegetables – drink soda / water – watch TV...
g. spend more / less money – buy magazines / clothes / drinks – find a job to earn money ...
h. make new efforts – talk during classes – learn your lessons – do your homework ...

a

You are always late.

b

You feel depressed.

c

You smoke too much.

d

Your English is bad.

Then change roles. Listen to student B and give him / her minimum 3 tips.

unit 2

B1

Don't buy it!

Help fight the black market of counterfeiting*. Prefer genuine* products.

BAD BAG

The maker

You favour the exploitation of people who work 10 to 15 hours a day, 7 days a week in conditions that compromise health and safety for very low wages. Thousands of workers are children 3 to 14 years of age.

The tourist

Yours for €15 plus a €10,000 fine*. The counterfeit is illegal. For example, in Italy, if you buy one of these products, you will risk a fine up to €10,000.

The boss

You support organized crime that produces and trades* counterfeit products* and takes advantage of millions of people in an inhumane way. Some counterfeiters* use the money they make to buy and sell drugs and guns.

The seller

You favour illegal jobs. For many it is the only possible job because they are illegal immigrants. These workers are continuously exposed to fines and confiscation of goods that must be repaid.

BE CAUTIOUS. Check that the product you are buying is not counterfeit. Counterfeit goods look so much like the real* product that it is difficult to tell that they are fake* when you are buying them. They cover a wide range of items from designer clothing to computer games and perfumes.

Beware* of goods sold through the Internet. Take extra care at street markets, pubs, or in other situations where it would be difficult to get in touch with the trader* if anything was wrong.

Examine the quality of the items. Look carefully at the labels and packaging. "Cheap" goods often mean "cheap" quality. Some fake goods are dangerous. When the product you are buying has an unrealistically low price, carries a logotype that is identical to a famous brand*, it could be counterfeit.

Don't buy it. Don't risk a fine. Prefer genuine* products.

REMEMBER that if you buy counterfeit goods, you will contribute to child labour and exploitation of immigrants. Local workers may lose their jobs because people are buying the counterfeit goods and not the real ones. Genuine manufacturers can't compete. In the European Union, it is thought that 100,000 jobs per year are lost as a result of counterfeiting. If people were more cautious, they wouldn't contribute by buying counterfeit goods.

Don't buy it. Help fight the black market of counterfeiting goods.

No COUNTERFEITING

help

trade / a trader *commercialiser / un vendeur*
counterfeit products / fake goods / fakes *des contrefaçons/des faux*
counterfeiting *la contrefaçon*
a counterfeiter *un faussaire*
a fine *une amende*
Beware of... *faites attention à ...*
genuine / real *authentique / véritable*
a brand *une marque*

Adapted from consavari.com and www.gov.im /2006

Anticipating

1 Look at the pictures and the logo . Read the title and subtitles of the text. Then answer the questions.

a. Who is the document aimed at *(destiné à)*? The maker? The boss? The tourist or the seller?
b. Select the two words which could be the general title of the document.
c. What is a 'bad bag'?

Comprehension

2 Read the document and answer the questions.

a. How old are the children who make counterfeit bags?
b. What are the makers' working conditions?
c. Are they well-paid?
d. Why is the boss a criminal?
e. Who are the sellers? What do they risk?
f. What will you risk if you buy one of these bags?

3 Find more details about counterfeit goods.

a. What do counterfeit goods look like?
b. What sort of goods can be counterfeit?
c. Where can you buy them?
d. What sort of logo do they carry?
e. What about the price?
f. What about the quality?

4 What's the English for...?

a. la santé et la sécurité (l.1-6)
b. qui doivent être remboursés (l. 18-23)
c. Soyez prudents (l. 24-27)

5 What's the French for...?

a. a wide range of items (l. 27-29)
b. labels and packaging (l. 34-36)
c. child labour (l. 41-43)

6 Right or wrong? Justify your answer.

a. Fake bags are cheaper than genuine ones.
b. It is easy to recognize counterfeit products.
c. You should take care when you buy through the Internet.
d. You should be cautious when you buy goods outside a real shop.
e. Fakes are often poor quality products.
f. If you buy counterfeit products, you will help local economy.
g. Genuine manufacturers don't want to make cheap products.

fOcus

If you buy one, you will risk a fine.
If people were more cautious, they wouldn't contribute by buying counterfeit goods.

- *À quels temps sont les verbes après if ?*
- *Quels modaux sont utilisés dans la deuxième partie des énoncés ? À quels temps correspondent-ils ?*
- *Traduisez les deux énoncés et comparez avec les temps employés en français.*
- *Quel énoncé exprime une hypothèse ? Lequel exprime une réalité ?*

>> Training n°5 et 6

nOw in French

7 Répondez en français aux questions suivantes.

a. En quoi le marché de la contrefaçon favorise-t-il l'exploitation humaine ?
b. Relevez et traduisez trois conseils qui permettent d'éviter d'acheter une contrefaçon.
c. Quels sont les risques par rapport au produit, par rapport au coût ?
d. Quelles sont les conséquences pour l'emploi en Europe ? Pourquoi ?

Writing

B1

8 Give your opinion about the document.

What would you do if you saw beautiful sports shoes at a very low price? Why? Give 2 or 3 reasons. In your opinion, what are the advantages and the drawbacks of buying counterfeit goods?

9 Choose a type of product you like buying: clothes, shoes, DVDs, computer games... Then give 5 tips to buy a good quality product without paying too much.

Cultural differences

GUIDE TO STUDYING IN THE USA

1. Read the titles and the introduction. Tell what the document is about and who it is aimed at.
2. Read the paragraph entitled 'Demeanor'. Try and guess the meaning of this word. Give 2 other words which have the same meaning.
3. Choose one paragraph and explain the differences between the American culture and your own culture. Then tell what the two cultures have in common.
4. Your friend is going to study / work in the USA. What is it essential to be aware of? Write 5 pieces of advice for him / her.

1

There are a lot of nuances to life in the US that you can only learn by living here. Nevertheless, we will try to introduce you to some of the more important cultural differences.

Good manners

Americans tend to be more informal than people from other countries. It is common for Americans to wear casual clothing to school and to greet professors by first name. Nevertheless, good manners and politeness are always appropriate. If you are courteous and polite, and dress a little more formally than your American friends, it will only reflect well on you. When smiling, it is normal to bare* your teeth, so long as the facial expression still looks like a smile, not a grimace.

Personal space

Americans tend to require more personal space than in other cultures. Try to avoid physical contact while you are speaking. So don't put your arm around their shoulder, touch their face, or hold their hand. Shaking hands when you initially meet or part is acceptable, but this is only momentary. Don't kiss on the cheek someone you see for the first time.

Demeanor

In an interview, talk about your goals and accomplishments. Be direct. Put your best foot forward.

Eye contact is important. It is not a sign of disrespect, but instead an indication of openness, honesty, and enthusiasm.

Business Visits

Business visits tend to be extremely punctual. If you arrive late to a business appointment, it will reflect badly on you. So try to arrive on time, or even a little early. If you know that you will be arriving late, you should telephone ahead to let them know of the delay. When businessmen or businesswomen meet, they usually introduce themselves by shaking right hands.

Smoking

Smoking has become socially unacceptable in the US, in part due to the health risks. Smoking is prohibited in government and public buildings, and many businesses, especially restaurants. Your school probably has a ban on smoking within campus buildings or near building entrances. Tobacco products may not be sold to anyone under 18 years old, and federal law requires stores to ask to see a photo ID for anyone under 27 years old.

www.eduPASS.org, July 2002

* bare *dénuder, montrer*

outlook

2

A2

THE PERFECT EUROPEAN

5. Write down the names of the countries where these European people live.
6. Find in the document the opposite of these adjectives: 'busy / clumsy / impatient / mean / messy / mute / noisy / proud / sad / stressed / thirsty / tolerant / unknown'
7. Choose 2 pictures. Describe what the people on the pictures are doing.
8. Choose among the adjectives your 3 qualities and your 3 defects. (Tell what you are and what you should be.)

hot line

A2

Asking for information about a foreign country

1. Listen to the telephone conversation and complete the chart below.

What the travel agent says when he picks up the phone:	Good morning Lisa .... Can I ....?
What Karen is asking for:	I'd like ....
Places to visit: What would you .... me to visit?	1 .... 2 .... 3 ....
Other activities: What else ....?	4 .... 5 ....
Climate: What's the climate ....?	6 .... 7 ....
Food: .... the food?	....
Special events: Are there special events which ....?	The Melbourne Cup. It's a .... It takes place in ....

A2

2. Now work with your partner. You telephone a tourist office to ask for information about Florida, Scotland, Spain or a place where you'd like to spend your holidays. The employee (your partner) answers your questions and gives you tips. You can use the grid page 149. Then change roles.

say it

La consonne 'th' se prononce :
- soit [θ], le son sourd de *health* ou *think*,
- soit [ð], le son sonore de *this* ou *breathe*.

a. Écoutez les mots suivants et classez-les dans le tableau ci-dessous.

then – something – thanks – weather – them – their – through – nevertheless – mouth – teeth – than – enthusiasm – that – clothing – there

[θ]: health, think	[ð]: this, breathe

b. Écoutez pour vérifier et répétez.

1 Formulez ces interdictions différemment en utilisant la structure : *Don't* + V

Ex: *No bicycles* ➡ *Don't ride your bicycle on a motorway / highway.*

a. No bicycles

b. No parking

c. No dogs

d. Please stay off the grass

e. No smoking

f. No cooking

2 Remplacez les mots soulignés par le pronom personnel qui convient.

a. Let your mother come with you. Your mother would like to be with you.
b. Don't let Frank drive. Frank is too tired.
c. Your friends are too early. Let your friends wait a moment.
d. You and I are late. Let ...... hurry up.

3 Vous souhaitez aider un ami. Incitez-le à accepter votre aide.

Ex: *She wants to help you.* ➡ *Let her help you.*

a. I can drive you to the station.
b. They want to carry your bags.
c. He wants to buy a sandwich for you.
d. They don't want to go away.
e. We can wait together for the train.

4 Remettez les mots dans l'ordre pour indiquer comment se tenir à table aux États-Unis.

a. smoke / at / table / never / dinner.
b. bread / on / always / your / a plate / put
c. talk / chewing / don't / while
d. hands / keep / on / don't / the table / your
e. taste / food / when / a little / always / it's offered

5 Mettez les verbes entre parenthèses au temps qui convient pour formuler ce que vous ferez / feriez si...

a. If you are late for school, you (apologize) when you enter the classroom.
b. If you (be) in the USA, you wouldn't smoke in the schoolyard.
c. If your friend (invite) you for dinner, you will offer to share the bill.
d. If your neighbours play music very loud at night, you (ask) them politely to turn down the music.
e. If you found a €100 on the street, you (pick) it up and ...

6 Complétez les phrases ci-dessous.

a. If I have enough money next summer, ...
b. If I have time this week, ...
c. If a stranger asked me for money, ...
d. If someone offered me a very expensive gift, ...
e. If someone lighted a cigarette in my home without asking for permission, ...

7 Mots cachés : retrouvez 18 adjectifs pour qualifier un bon conducteur automobile.

R	E	S	P	E	C	T	F	U	L	Q	U	C
E	G	O	O	D	C	A	R	E	F	U	L	H
S	S	N	L	R	E	N	I	C	E	I	X	E
P	A	T	I	E	N	T	E	A	L	C	R	L
O	F	A	T	B	R	O	N	L	A	K	E	P
N	E	R	E	F	W	Y	D	M	O	R	L	F
S	O	B	E	R	O	N	L	O	U	F	A	U
I	S	E	C	U	R	E	Y	R	L	I	X	L
B	C	O	N	C	E	N	T	R	A	T	E	D
L	C	A	U	T	I	O	U	S	B	U	D	H
E	Y	O	U	C	O	U	R	T	E	O	U	S

8 Rédigez 5 conseils à donner à un jeune conducteur.

remember

Pour exprimer un ordre, une interdiction ou plus simplement un conseil, une recommandation, une suggestion, on utilise les structures suivantes :

- ***V / Don't + V* :** si on s'adresse directement à *YOU* (un ou plusieurs interlocuteurs) :
  → Be careful ! *Fais attention* / Don't take too much money. *Ne prends pas trop d'argent.*
- ***Let's + V (Let us + V) / Don't let's + V* :** si on s'adresse à *WE* (un groupe dont on fait partie).
  → Let's go. *Allons-y* . / Don't let's panic. *Ne paniquons pas.*
- ***Let me + V / Don't let me + V* :** si vous souhaitez que votre interlocuteur vous autorise, vous laisse faire quelque chose.
  → Let me help you. *Laisse-moi t'aider* / Don't let me go. *Ne me laisse pas partir.*

- On utilise la structure ci-contre si des ordres sont donnés à l'attention d'autres personnes.
  → Let him carry your luggage. *Qu'il porte votre bagage.*
  → Don't let them come in. *Ne les laissez pas entrer.*

Let Don't let	him her them	+ V

Pour parler d'une situation possible et décrire son résultat, on construit une phrase sur le modèle suivant : *If* + verbe au présent, ...*will / won't* + V (base verbale)

→ If you **arrive** late to a business appointment, it **will reflect** (it'll reflect) badly on you.
Si vous arrivez en retard à un rendez-vous d'affaire, vous ferez mauvaise impression.

→ If you **are** rude, it **won't reflect** well on you. *Si vous êtes impoli, vous ne ferez pas bonne impression.*

Pour parler d'une situation irréelle ou imaginaire, on construit une phrase sur le modèle suivant : *If* + verbe au prétérit, ...*would / wouldn't* + V (base verbale)

→ If you **were** my friend, you **would respect** (you'd respect) my right not to smoke.
Si tu étais vraiment mon ami, tu respecterais mon droit de ne pas fumer.

→ If you **studied** in the USA, you **wouldn't smoke** on campus.
Si vous étiez étudiant aux États-Unis, vous ne fumeriez pas sur le campus.

Pour donner des conseils, on peut également employer : *should / shouldn't + V*

→ You **should be** more polite. *Tu devrais être plus poli.*
→ You **shouldn't arrive** late. *Tu ne devrais pas arriver en retard.*

Vocabulary

Verbs / verbes

advise *conseiller*
be careful *faire attention*
make sure *s'assurer, vérifier*
manage *gérer, réussir*
pack *emballer, faire ses bagages*
share *partager*
stay out of trouble *éviter les ennuis*
take care *faire attention*
worry *s'inquiéter, se tracasser*

Nouns / noms

advice (a piece of advice) *des conseils (un conseil)*
an attitude, a behaviour, a demeanour (US: a behavior, demeanor) *une attitude, un comportement*
a backpack *un sac à dos*
a belt *une ceinture*
clothing (an article of clothing) *des vêtements (un vêtement)*
an item *un article, un produit*
luggage (a piece of luggage) *des bagages (un bagage)*
manners *les manières* / **good manners** *les bonnes manières*
table manners *les règles de bonne conduite à table*
safety / security *sécurité*
a secure pocket *un petit sac, une pochette de sécurité*
a tip *un truc, un conseil*
a wallet *un portefeuille*

Adjectives / adjectifs

available *disponible*
cautious *prudent*
courteous *courtois, poli*
discreet *discret*
flexible *souple*
helpful *serviable*
polite *poli*
rude *impoli, grossier*
safe *sûr, sans danger*

unit 3

Travelling

contact

A2

1 Listen to part 1 of the dialogue. Complete the questions, and reorder Wendy's answers.

Job / Place of work	What ... you ... and where ... you ... ?	I / work / a secretary / and / I / at / London / 'm / HMV / in
Distance from home	How far ... ... ?	it 's / from / twelve / home / miles
Transport	How ... ... get ... work ?	tube / I / by / go / I / walk / and
Time for journey	How long ... it ... you ?	takes / me / it / one / about / hour
Cost of journey	How much ... it ... you ?	It / a month / me / pounds / costs /150 /

2 Listen again and find the right information.

a. HMV is a big (department / music) store in Oxford (Street / Station).
b. Her journey to work is about (eighty / eighteen) kilometres.
c. Travelling by car is too (long / expensive) and by bus it is too (expensive / long).
d. Wendy has a (weekly / monthly) pass.
e. Her friend Brett (rides / drives) to work. He is a (representative / reporter).

focus

How long does it take you?
Usually, it takes me one or two minutes only.
How much does it cost him?
Last week it cost him £70 in petrol only.

- *Quel est le sujet de ces énoncés ? Représente-t-il quelqu'un ?*
- *Traduisez les énoncés. Les pronoms* you, me, him *sont-ils sujet ou complément ? Citez-en d'autres.*
- *À quels temps sont les différents énoncés ?*

Action

1 **Ask and answer questions about duration and cost.**

Ex: *I go to work by tube. (20 minutes – €6.00 / day).*

➡ *How long does it take you to go to work ? It takes me twenty minutes.*

➡ *How much does it cost you? It costs me €6 a day.*

a. I go to school by bus (1/4 hr – €10 / month

b. I cycle to school. (1/4 hr – £00 = nothing)

c. She drives to work. (1/2 hr – £35 / week)

d. They fly to London. (3/4 hr – €120)

e. We sailed to Calais. (1.1/2 hr – £30)

f. He will go to Paris by Eurostar. (2.1/2 hr – £ 90)

2 **Listen and take notes (name, job, place of work or destination, transport, duration, cost). Then write a paragraph (he, she, they...).**

Transport	I walk	I cycle	I go by car / bus / train / tube / bike		I fly	I sail
Time for journey	1/4 hr a quarter of an hour	1/2 hr half an hour	3/4 hr three quarters of an hour		1.1/2 h hr one and a half hour	2.1/2 hr two and a half hours
Distance	800 m = 1/2 half a mile	1.6 km = 1 1 mile	2.4 km = 1.1/2 one and a half mile	4 km = 2.1/2 two and a half miles	16 km = 10 ten miles	30 km = 20 twenty miles
Places of work	factory	office	building site	shop / store	hospital	company

A2

3 **Telling the time. Listen and note down the times.**

a .... b .... c .... d .... e .... f .... g .... h ....

4 **Listen to part 2 of the interview. Find more details about Wendy's work days. Find the times when she:**

a. gets up: ...

b. leaves home: ...

c. takes the tube: ...

d. arrives at work: ...

e. starts work: ...

f. has a break: ...

g. finishes work: ...

h. comes back home: ...

Chat time

A2

1. Ask and answer about these people's journeys to work.

A2

2. Now talk about your journeys to school.

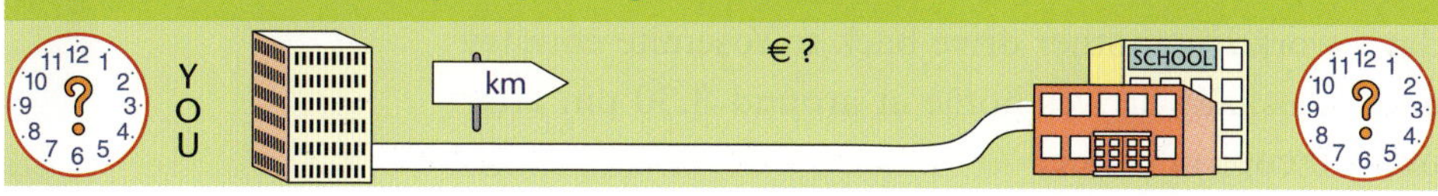

B1

"America's longest commute" contest

"How far are you willing* to drive to work? For Dave Givens of Mariposa, Calif., the answer is 186 miles – one way – good enough to take first place in Midas search for America's Longest Commute."

As the winner of the first prize, Dave Givens receives $10,000 in gas* money as well as a range of maintenance services and products from Midas® plus free coffee.

Midas ® is one of the world's largest providers of automotive service, offering brake, exhaust, maintenance, tires, and suspension services at 2,600 Midas shops in 19 countries.

Givens, an electrical engineer with Cisco Systems, in San Jose, California, drives a 186-mile one-way commute, a round-trip journey of 372 miles that takes him a total of seven hours. He has been making the lengthy commute since 1989.

"I have a great job and my family loves the ranch where we live on the edge* of Yosemite National Park. We could live a bit closer but it would cost us more and wouldn't be as beautiful. So this is the only solution". He said in explaining why he commutes five days a week.

Five times a week, with his family still sleeping, Givens leaves home at about 4.30 am. "What do you do during the trip?" – "I listen to the radio or to audio books and keep my eyes on the road," he says. "I also drink about nine cups of coffee every morning...". Then after his day's work it's another drive back to Yosemite country and he usually arrives home at around 8.30 pm after over 30 cups of coffee.

The "America's Longest Commute" Contest, in honour of Midas' 50th anniversary, drew* about 3,000 entries nationwide. "The second place winner was Jeffrey Haussy of Georgetown, Illinois, who drives a 175 miles to his job with American Airlines at Chicago O'Hare International Airport. The third place winner was Kay Phillips with 164 miles to her job at the Adolescent Pregnancy* Prevention Center in North Carolina.

Participants had to report the mileage of their current daily commute, defined as the most direct route, one way, in miles, from their place of residence to their place of employment. They had to drive a minimum of four days a week, each week of the month. Motorcycles, delivery trucks, and all forms of public transportation were not considered a daily commute.

April 12, 2006 abridged from *www.midas.com*

help

willing *prêt / disposé à*
gas gasoline *(US)*, petrol *(GB)*
brake *frein / freinage*
exhaust *échappement*
the edge *le bord / la bordure*
drew *a attiré*
pregnancy *grossesse*

Anticipating

1 Look at the picture.

Where does it take place? Why?

2 Read the title and the introduction.

a. What is the French for contest: *'contestation'*, *'constat'* or *'concours'*?
b. What sort of contest is it?
c. Who is its organizer? Its winner?
d. How far is he willing to drive to work?

Comprehension

3 Find details about the winner (introduction and paragraphs 1 to 3).

first name: .... surname: ....
residence: .... state: ....
job: .... company: ....
city: .... state: ....
distance to work: ....
time for journey (one way): ....

4 Read the text. Match these titles with the different paragraphs.

- The other winners: § ...
- Dave's day: § ...
- The rules of the contest: § ...
- The contest's organizers: § ...
- Reason of the choice: § ...
- Dave's commute: § ...
- The big prize: § ...

5 What's the English for...?

a. voyage(r) pour aller au travail (intro)
b. inscriptions (§6)
c. (un) concours (§6)
d. camions de livraison (§7)

6 What's the French for... ?

a. a range of maintenance services (§1)
b. a round trip journey (§3)
c. the Adolescent Pregnancy Prevention Centre (§6)
d. mileage (§7)

7 Right or Wrong? Justify your answers.

a. Dave works at Midas.
b. Living near San José is more expensive than in Mariposa.
c. He reads a lot during his trips
d. Commuting by train, coach or bike was not accepted for the contest.

fOcus

I always listen to the radio.
He usually arrives home at around 8.30 pm.
Five times a week, Givens leaves home at about 4.30 am.
I also drink about nine cups of coffee every morning.

- *Dans les deux premiers énoncés, qu'expriment les éléments soulignés ?*
- *Comment s'appellent-ils ? Où sont-ils placés ? En connaissez-vous d'autres ?*
- *Dans les deux dernières phrases, quelles expressions indiquent la fréquence ? Où sont-elles placées ?*
- *Retrouvez-en d'autres dans le texte.*

>> Training n°5, 6 et 7

nOw in French

8 Répondez en français à ces questions.

a. Qu'a reçu le gagnant du 1er prix ?
b. Qui a organisé ce concours ? Quel est son champ d'activité ?
c. Pour quelles raisons Dave ne voudrait-il pas déménager ?
d. Que fait-il durant ses longs trajets ?
e. Quelles étaient les conditions pour pouvoir participer au concours ?

Writing

B1

9 Use these questions to write a paragraph about Dave's journeys to work.

a. How does Dave go to work?
b. How far is it from Dave's ranch to his work in San Jose?
c. How often does he commute to San Jose?
d. How long does it take him to drive to work?
e. How long does he spend in his car each day?
f. How much a week does it probably cost him?
g. What do the two other winners do?

10 Tell about your daily journey to work (to school). Do you enjoy it? Why (not)?

unit 3

Reasons for travelling

B1

1 FROM WASHINGTON TO MOSCOW

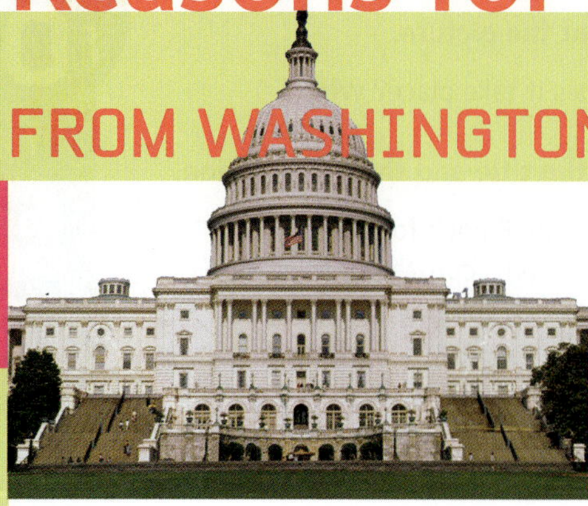

1. Why did he leave the USA?
2. How long did it take him to go to work? And now?
3. Is the traffic better in Moscow?
4. How does he commute now?
5. How much does it cost him?
6. Why is he satisfied?

I used to live in Carroll County, Maryland. But I got so tired of my 2 hours commute into Washington D.C., resulting from a 1 hour drive and another hour on the metro... that I moved* to Moscow, Russia. The traffic jams here are a lot worse and the drivers are crazier*. But there I do not drive. The metro goes anywhere you want to be and it costs only 4 roubles (15 cents) per trip, with unlimited transfers and no higher prices for longer trips. But I do not even pay for that. By buying a monthly pass for 120 roubles (just under five dollars) I can travel all I want, all month long, for the cost of a round-trip in D.C. Thank you, Moscow!

Richard Smith

* move *déménager* – crazy *fou.*

www.washingtonpost.com./commutingsentences

2 BACK HOME TO INDIA

B1

We normally fly to Mumbai* using indirect flights as these are cheaper. Direct flights to Mumbai take about 9 hours. Indirect flights add another 3 hours to flying time. Most flights leave London early in the morning and reach Mumbai around midnight. We normally go there once a year for a relaxing holiday in a warmer climate.

Everything is different in India when compared to the UK. The temperature is also much higher. In April, it was around 35 deg. C. As the seasons are more well defined in India, you can plan day-out picnics much better. One thing that hits you most in India is the noise. Due to hot climate, you need to keep windows open as long as possible, which means noise from traffic and people can be heard continuously. Indian drivers do not have the road discipline we see in Europe. Cars overtake from either side, left or right, which is very dangerous and frightening. Most cities have motorised rickshaws, which give off a lot of pollution and are very noisy. The attraction of this transport is that rickshaws are cheaper than taxis. Cities like Mumbai, Delhi and Calcutta have a lot of traffic jams because more and more people can afford cars.

When we go, we usually stay for 3 weeks, as a few days are needed to get used to* the heat and noise. Besides, we have lots of relations and we like to meet everyone.

Hema and Badresh Patak, Southampton.

* Mumbai *Bombay* – get used to *s'habituer à.*

7. Look at the picture. Where does it take place? Which different transports do you see?
8. Where do Hema and her husband live? Where do they usually go on holiday? Why?
9. Ask and answer more questions about their holidays. Use: where, how, how long, why, how often.
10. Would you like to live in this country? Why (not)? What else, do you think is different?

outlook

B1

3 HEALTHY COMMUTING

11. Ask questions about his commute to work (use how, how long, how much, what time,..).

12. Why does he enjoy so much cycling to work?

I used to be an everyday slave to public transportation, until I realized that cycling to and from work would take me just as much time.

I live in Washington DC, and every day I get up early in the morning to bike to work, I ride along the G.W Parkway and through Old Town. Everyday is a beautiful experience no matter what the weather is like.

As I ride along the parkway I can see some of the frustrated and often angry* faces of drivers who are stuck* in traffic. The only stress I have from commuting comes from negligent drivers who do not share* the road, and who think they own the road because they are on a 4,000 lb* vehicle while I am on 20 lb one.

My commute takes about half an hour to the office at 1300 New York Ave. where I usually arrive at 8 o'clock to exercise at the company's gym, have breakfast and be on my desk by 9 - 9:15. Then at 5 pm I commute back home.

I think more people should opt for this type of commute as riding your bike is absolutely healthier and you never get stuck in traffic jams. Moreover, I save $6.55 every day for not using the metro and parking.

Augusto D. Clavijo

www.washingtonpost.com./commutingsentences

* angry *en colère* – stuck *bloqué* – share *partager*
2 lb = 2 pounds = about 1 kilo.

hot line

B1

Booking a trip

1. Listen to the conversation and complete it with the missing information.

Travel agent	Client
Suntrips Travel Agency! Can I help you?	Hello! Yes, I'd like to go to .... for ....
When would you like .... there ?	On .... the .... in the ....
Yes, now how would you like to	I'd rather travel by ....
By ....Can you hold on for a moment?	....
Yes. There is a .... from .... at	At .... Good. When does it arrive?
It arrives at ...... at .... local time.	So, how long .... ?
It takes	And how much does it cost for a ....?
A ...... class .... ticket costs	All right, I'd like to book ...... seats. .... will come .....
No problem. What is the name?	...... It's ...... / ...... /...... / ......
Thank you M. .... See you	Good ....

2. Practise more dialogues. The travel agent's schedules are on appendix page 150.

B1

a. You want to go to Paris for your holiday: July 21st /afternoon – by Eurostar – standard class return: 3 seats. You will come tomorrow afternoon. Note the details of your trip.

b. You want to go to Madrid for your business : April 30th / morning – by plane – economy class return: 1 seat. Your secretary will come on Monday. Note the details of your trip.

say it

DIFFÉRENTES PRONONCIATIONS DE LA LETTRE A.
Écoutez les mots suivants et classez-les dans le tableau.
central – far – parking – half – quarter – station – walk – usual – pass – company – secretary – past – around – arrive – start – apple – based – save.

[ɑː] comme dans **car**	....
[æ] comme dans **cat**	....
[ei] comme dans **ate**	....
[ɔː] comme dans **call**	....
[ə] comme l'article **a**	....

1 Écrivez ces horaires « digitaux » puis transformez-les en « horaires traditionnels ».

a. 05:30 am
b. 06:55 am
c. 11:10 am
d. 02:15 pm
e. 03:25 pm
f. 06:45 pm
g. 10:40 pm
h. 11:20 pm.
i. 02:05 am.

2 Calculez le temps mis pour réaliser ces actions. Formulez-le en une seule phrase.

a. I leave home at ten past seven and I arrive at school at twenty to eight.
b. Her tube leaves the station at quarter to eight and she arrives at her office at half past eight.
c. They take the ferry at quarter past twelve in Dover and they land in Calais at quarter to two.
d. Our plane took off from Paris at two-forty pm and landed at five-ten in Malta.

3 Faites des phrases pour exprimer la distance entre ces endroits.

a. Kate's office – her home : 1/2 mile.
b. My father's factory – our house: 3 1/2 km
c. Ben's building site – his flat : 13 km
d. My school – home : ...

4 Posez les questions sur les éléments soulignés.

a. It costs me £95 a month to get to work.
b. My school is half a mile from home.
c. They usually fly to New York.
d. It takes him ten minutes to cycle to his office.
e. Her plane will land at five-thirty pm.

5 Remettez ces phrases dans l'ordre

a. your / you / usually / do / travel / to / how / office / ?
b. I / a bus / often / don't / school. / to / take
c. to / fly / / businessmen / usually / London ? / do
d. my / times / goes / on / three / a / sister / year / holidays /
e. late / not / for / often / work / I'm
f. we / a / year / usually / training period / have / twice

6 Complétez logiquement par des adverbes de fréquence ou des indicateurs de fréquence différents à chaque fois.

a. We are on holiday on December 25th.
b. We have school holidays.
c. It doesn't rain in Algeria.
d. We finish school at 3: 30 pm.
e. Our school has an open day.
f. I miss Monday morning classes.

7 Selma est secrétaire à Virgin. Dites ce qu'elle fait et à quelle fréquence.

Retrouvez les questions concernant la fréquence ayant apporté ces réponses.

a. I get up at 6:30 four times a week.
b. No, my parents never travel by plane.
c. Yes, I'm often tired on Monday mornings.
d. No, not always. I sometimes take the bus.
e. Last year my boss flew to the USA twice.
f. Twice a day.

remember

Pour interroger sur une caractéristique le plus souvent chiffrée on utilise un interrogatif composé de : *HOW* + adverbe ou adjectif.

Pour interroger sur:	interrogatif	exemples
la fréquence	How often	How often do you take the tube?
le prix	How much	How much does it cost by plane?
la distance	How far	How far is it (from home)?
la durée	How long	How long did you stay?
le nombre de ...	How many + nom	How many times did you see that film?

Pour interroger ou s'exprimer sur le prix ou la durée d'une action, on peut utiliser des tournures impersonnelles.

→ How long does **it** take you to drive to work? **It** takes me twenty minutes.
Combien de temps te faut-il pour / mets-tu pour...? Il me faut.../ Je mets...

→ How much will **it** cost your sister to fly to Spain? **It**'ll cost her £250.
Combien cela coûtera-t-il à ta sœur pour aller en Espagne en avion ? Cela lui coûtera £250.

Pour exprimer des mesures fractionnées de durée, distance, capacité, on utilise:

1/4	A quarter of (**an** hour / **a** mile / a litre)
1/2	Half (a mile / a kilometre / an hour / a litre)
3/4	Three quarters of (a mile /a kilometre / **an** hour)
1.1/4	One and a quarter hour
1.1/2	one and a half (mile / hour / litre / kilometre)
2.1/2	Two and a half (miles / hours / kilometres / litres)

Pour indiquer la fréquence d'une action, on utilise les adverbes et les indicateurs de fréquence.

- **Les adverbes de fréquence : never:** *jamais*, **hardly ever:** *presque jamais*, **rarely:** *rarement*, **occasionally:** *de temps en temps*, **sometimes:** *quelquefois / parfois*, **often:** *souvent*, **usually:** *habituellement*, **always:** *toujours*. Ils se placent toujours **avant le verbe** mais **après 'be'**.

→ What time do you usually take the train? *À quelle heure prends-tu habituellement le train?*
→ I sometimes travel by bus. *Je prends parfois le bus.*
→ She doesn't often go to England. *Elle ne va pas souvent en Angleterre.*
→ The tube is always late, it is never on time. *Le métro est toujours en retard, il n'est jamais à l'heure.*

- **Les indicateurs de fréquence : everyday:** *tous les jours*, **each day :** *chaque jour*, **every morning / month:** *tous les matins/ mois*, **once a week:** *une fois par semaine*, **twice a day:** *deux fois par jour*, **four times a year:** *quatre fois par an*, **five days a week:** *cinq jours par semaine*. **Ils se placent au début ou à la fin de la phrase ou de la proposition.**

→ What time do you take the bus every morning? I travel by train once a week.

Vocabulary

Verbs / verbes

bike *aller à moto / à vélo*
commute *faire le trajet maison-travail*
cycle *aller à vélo*
drive* *aller en auto / conduire*
fly* *voyager par avion*
sail *aller en bateau*
hit* *frapper*
overtake* *dépasser*
share *partager*
spend* *passer, dépenser*

Nouns / noms

a brake *un frein*
a building site *un chantier*
a commute *un trajet (travail)*
a commuter *une personne qui fait des trajets journaliers*
a contest *un concours*
a delay *un retard*
exhaust *échappement*
a flight *un vol / avion*
gas /gasoline (US) *essence*
a (traffic) jam *un bouchon*
a journey / a trip *un voyage*
a prize *un prix (concours)*
a tube (UK) *un métro*
a tire (US) tyre (UK) *un pneu*

Adjectives / adjectifs

angry *en colère*
healthy *bon pour la santé*

unit 4

Describing places

contact

A2

1 **A new employee, Hannah Hill, is being told where the different offices are in her new firm. Listen to the first part of the conversation, look at the plan and name the places shown with a number.**

Use the words: restaurant – marketing manager – secretary – conference room – general manager.

1 = 2= 3=

4= 5=

2 **Listen again and answer the following questions:**

a. What are the names of the Personnel Manager and the guide?
b. What time does the Personnel Manager say he will see the new employee?
c. Where will the new employee be working?
d. Which floor is it?
e. Where is the company restaurant?

fOcus

Mr Wood, who is not in at the moment, is our general manager. The restaurant, which is in the other building, is only open at lunchtime. This is where you will be working.
There are vending machines where you can get all sorts of drinks. There are days when he is very demanding.

- *Relevez les pronoms relatifs dans les trois premiers énoncés ; traduisez-les. Dites si les antécédents sont humains ou non.*
- *Traduisez les deux derniers énoncés. Quel relatif est employé en français, en anglais ? Pourquoi ?*
- *Quels autres pronoms relatifs anglais expriment la raison (pour lequel, pour laquelle...), l'appartenance (dont le, dont la...) ?*

Action

1 Complete with 'who', 'which', 'where', 'when'.

a. Ruth is the accountant ... can solve all the problems.
b. This office, ... is in the right aisle, is the engineer's office.
c. This is the moment ... all the gates are closed.
d. Henry, ... intends to work late tonight, is always late in the morning.
e. The village ... I live has no facilities.
f. Henry will never forget the time ... he was a trainee.

A2

2 Listen to the end of the conversation and fill in the blanks with some of the following words: lift – reception – warehouses – cafeteria – which – marketing – sales – corridor – department – stairs – workshop – records

Hannah: What about this door?
Mandy: Here we are, in the (...) department. Here is your office. Over there, you have the (...), the stationery, next to the (...). Toilets of course. Another vending machine. On the left, there is the R'n D (...) where I work. And the (...) room... Look! Can you see the buildings over there?
Hannah: Yes. What are they?
Mandy: Well, this is the (...) with the production department and the two (...). The old warehouse (...) is at the far end is going to be enlarged. But we will go and visit the place later on. ...
Hannah: I didn't know the company was so big...

3 Complete with 'why' or 'whose'.

a. The customers ... orders got mixed up, were very angry.
b. This is the reason ... I applied for this training period.
c. The students ... CVs are very good will be accepted for a training period.

4 Link the sentences with 'whose' as in the example.

Ex: *This man is the team coach. His daughter is the new regional champion.*
➡ *This man whose daughter is the new regional champion is the team coach.*
a. The man is an inspector. His car is parked in front of the workshop.
b. Mrs Smith is going to retire next September. Her husband works abroad.

Chat time

You are student A. 1. You ask questions to your partner to complete your plan. You will also answer his / her questions to complete his / her plan. Be as precise as possible. (Student B: see page 150.)

A2

You must find the location of:
– the conference room,
– the transport manager's office,
– the marketing department,
– the purchase manager's office,
– the accounts manager's office,
– the reception,
– the personnel manager's office.

GROUND FLOOR

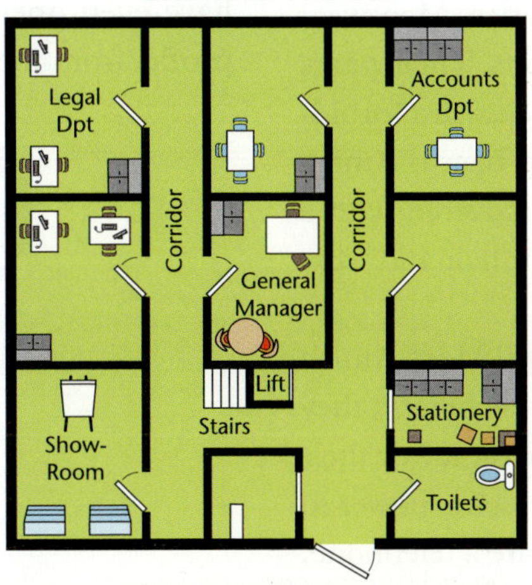

FIRST FLOOR

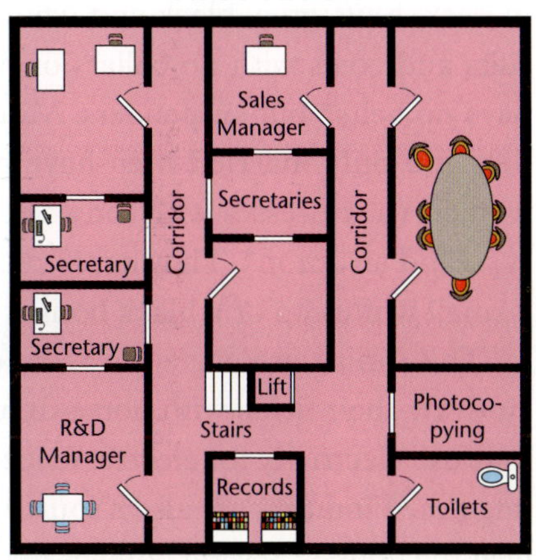

2. Then choose a position *(un poste)* or a room and tell how to go there. Student B must find where it is.

unit 4

B1

Amish country

The Amish people, an old religious group from Europe (who are in favour of adult baptism, not infant baptism) arrived in America around 1730. They have settled in 24 states, Canada and Central America. Today, 80% live in Pennsylvania, Ohio and Indiana.

All aspects of Amish life – from clothes to farming techniques – are dictated by written or oral rules* called "Ordnung". Ordnung varies from community to community, which explains why you see some Amish riding automobiles and others who don't even accept the use of battery-powered lights!

The home is the centre of Amish life. Houses are usually painted white. The kitchen is the centre of activity with its big stove*. The bedrooms are decorated with colourful quilts*, simple furniture and clothes hanged on the walls. There is running water, from a cistern. When electricity is needed for washing laundry, the family starts a gasoline-powered generator. At night, kerosene lanterns are used.

Amish dress is very simple. Clothing is made at home, in dark, blue, grey, black and white fabrics. Men wear suits and coats with no collars or pockets. Their pants have no belts* but suspenders. Moustaches are forbidden and only married men have got a beard. Amish women wear dresses with long sleeves, covered with a cape and an apron*. They never cut their hair and wear a small white cap or a black bonnet.

The Amish are averse to technology. Most Amish cultivate their fields with horse-drawn machinery; they may use electricity for electric fences for cattle* or their buggies. Windmills are also a source of electric power to heat the houses. Several families may share a telephone, which is located outside the houses. But they use barbecue grills or cell phones... which is not specifically prohibited by Ordnung!

The Amish provide education till the eighth grade* only in their private schools where children learn basic reading, writing, maths and Amish history. The US law has exempted Amish children from attending school after the eight grade.

What reinforces the links in the Amish groups is community life: families help one another. They have often got seven to ten children. The man, who usually works on the farm, is considered the head of the household while* the wife does the washing, cleaning, cooking... A German dialect is spoken at home and children learn English at school. Marriages are only permitted in the community.

The Amish are private people that avoid* contact with strangers and the "outside world" for religious and cultural reasons. However, most have accepted tourism as something they cannot change. Some Amish families have even opened small shops and are now realizing profits from the tourists.

help

rules *règles, lois*
a stove *un poêle*
a quilt *un couvre-lit*
belts *des ceintures*
an apron *un tablier*
cattle *du bétail*
while *tandis que*
avoid *éviter*
eight grade *la classe de quatrième*

Anticipating

1 Look at the photos, the title and read the introduction to the text. Answer the questions.

a. What is the text about?
b. Where do these people live?

Comprehension

2 Read the text completely and match each paragraph with a title.

a. Family life
b. Technology
c. The Rule
d. Private people
e. Education
f. Clothing
g. Home

3 Answer the questions.

a. Who are the Amish?
b. Why is the number of Amish people growing rapidly?
c. When do men wear a beard?
d. What type of education do Amish children have?
e. What do Amish use electricity for?

4 What's the English for...?

a. fournissent, procurent (§5)
b. des bretelles (§4)
c. le foyer (§6)

5 What's the French for...?

a. baptism (intro)
b. settled (intro)
c. strangers (§7)

6 Correct these statements with elements from the text.

a. The Amish settled in America in the sixteenth century.
b. The Amish clothes have got a lot of ornementation.
c. They can drive automobiles.
d. Children learn plenty of different subjects at school.
e. The Amish like to be looked at by visitors.

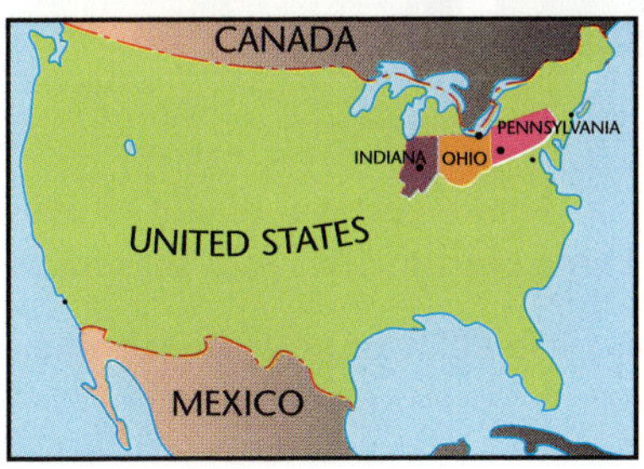

now in French

7 Répondez en français aux questions suivantes :

a. Qu'est-ce que l'Ordnung ?
b. Par quel moyen les Amish fabriquent-ils leur électricité ? Quel usage en font-ils ?
c. Pourquoi ont-ils la permission d'utiliser des barbecues ou des téléphones portables ?
d. Pourquoi les enfants peuvent-ils arrêter l'école très tôt ?
e. Pour quelle(s) raison(s) les Amish évitent-ils le contact avec les autres populations ?

fOcus

The Amish are private people that avoid contact with strangers and the 'outside world'.
Ordnung varies from community to community, which explains why...
What reinforces the links in the Amish groups is community life.

- *Dans la première phrase, par quel pronom relatif pourrait-on remplacer* that *?*
- *Peut-on supprimer* that *dans cette phrase (= relatif Ø) ? Pourquoi ?*
- *Traduisez les deux derniers énoncés. Que remarquez-vous concernant les mots soulignés ?*
- *Quand emploie-t-on* which *? Quand emploie-t-on* what *?*

>> Training n°3 et 5

Writing

B1

8 Finish up the sentences to produce a summary of the text.

a. The Amish people originally came ...
b. Today the majority live ...
c. Ordnung dictates ...
d. The Amish houses are ...
e. The dress code is strict. Men wear ...
f. The Amish don't like ...
g. At school, children learn ...
h. Family life and commmunity life are ...

9 Describe your village or district (location, housing...) OR describe a company you know: either the company where you have already been on a training period, or the company you have worked in for a summer job.

unit 4

Places to live...

A CAPSULE APARTMENT

1

B1

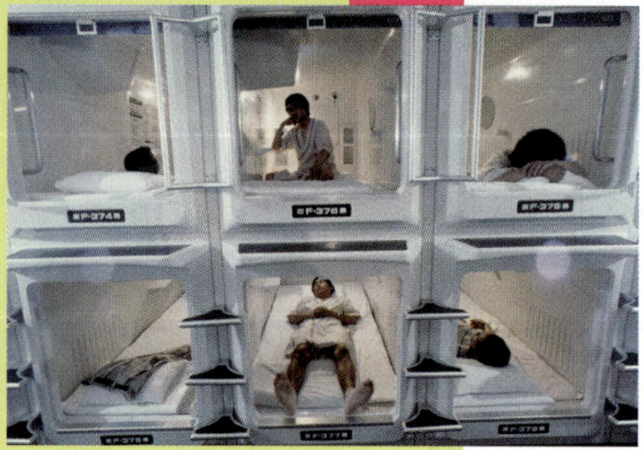

1. In what country is this small apartment located? Say why apartments are so small over there.
2. List the elements of equipment in the flat.
3. Would you like to live in such a place or another unusual place? Explain why or why not.

Akira Sakazaki (...) lives alone in a tall modern apartment block. He is able to afford this accommodation because it is extremely restricted in space. In fact he cannot actually stand up in it, and (...) is obliged to crawl, rather than step, inside.

The apartment, or living unit, is like a very luxurious padded cell*. About four metres long, three metres wide and one and a half metre high, its walls, floor and ceiling are lined with a carpet of soft, synthetic fibre. A low recessed* shelf along one wall acts as a sofa by day, a bed by night. Shelves and cupboards are mounted above it. Recessed or fitted flush* into the opposite wall are a stainless steel sink, refrigerator, microwave oven, electric kettle, colour television, hi-fi system and telephone. A low table sits on the floor before the window. (...) The window cannot be opened. The room is air-conditioned, temperature-controlled and soundproof.

Four hundred identical cells are stacked and interlocked in this building like a tower of eggboxes. It is a new development, an upmarket version of the "capsule" hotels situated near the main railway termini that have proved so popular with Japanese workers in recent years.

There is a small hatch* in one wall that gives access to a tiny windowless bathroom, with a small chair-shaped tub* just big enough to sit in, and a toilet. (...)

From *Small World* by David Lodge, published by Secker & Warburg. Reprinted by permission of the Random House Group Ltd.

* a padded cell *une cellule capitonnée* – recessed *encastré(e)* – fitted flush *integré(e)* – a hatch *une écoutille* – a tub *une baignoire*

2

A2

IMAGINE YOUR HOUSE

4. Write a sentence for each photo.
5. Choose the place where you would like to live among these three places. Give your reasons.
6. Describe your house / flat or your ideal home in a paragraph.

outlook

A SCOTTISH FRIEND 3

A2

Dear friends,

(...) I live in Oban, a busy working port in the West Highlands. It's a small picturesque city dominated by McCaig's Tower, a coliseum-style monument which celebrated its centenary in 1997. It was built by a wealthy banker to help lower unemployment in the area. A good idea, wasn't it?
Oban is also a popular holiday resort with a full range of attractions. Its distillery, where a pure malt whisky is produced, attracts visitors who also like the fascinating exhibits of "a World in Miniature". At Caithness Glass, you can learn about the skills of glass blowing.
I like sports very much and I am lucky: there are many sports facilities, such as a leisure centre where anyone can practice numerous sports.
On week ends, I go to bars, cafes and restaurants. There are plenty. We also have different shops and stores, from small craft shops to modern centres packed with all the top retail stores and brands. As for cultural facilities, the top one is Highland Theatre Cinemas.
And if you go to Oban in August, you will be able to attend Argyllshire gatherings, with piping competitions and Highland Games. Well, it's a nice place to live in! (...)

Ian Mac Gregor

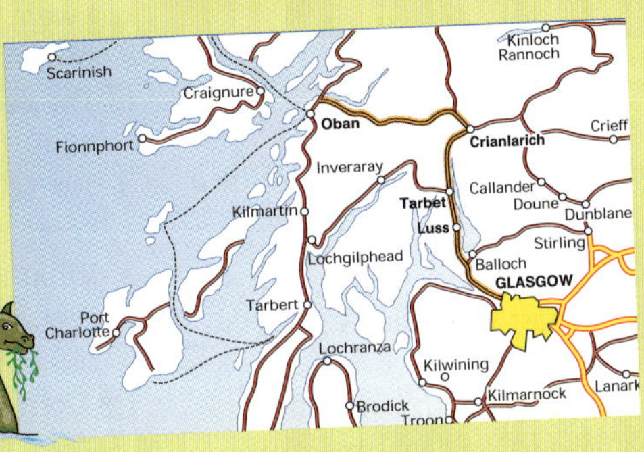

7. List the facilities of Oban and classify them in categories. (essential, sports...)
8. Look at the map and tell the way from Glasgow to Oban.
9. Write a paragraph about your town or village (location, facilities...)

hot line

A2

Telling the way

1. Listen to this conversation between a trainee and the receptionist of Bradford Waters and locate the company on the street map of Bradford.

A2

2. Now work with your partner. You are the receptionist at Birchwood's, who tells the new trainee how to go to your company in John Street. Your partner is the trainee.

say it

« w » or « v » ? **a. Complétez par « v » ou « w ».**

/-ait / -oyage / -allet / mo-e / -isit / -ant / -ho / sand-ich / dri-e / -ear / -ork / shi-er / beha-e / in-ite / -omen / -intage / -atch / -inter / -hich / -alue / -inegar /

b. Écoutez, vérifiez et répétez les mots.

c. Prononcez les mots suivants et vérifiez avec l'enregistrement.

whose – very – victim – wonder – vest – vehicle – why – wood – vanilla – whom

1 Complétez les informations suivantes par le relatif qui convient (*who, which, why, where, when* ou *that*).

a. The place ... they work is Kube, an American-run company.
b. The workers ... were on strike last week didn't gain anything,
c. The day... the new boss will give in hasn't arrived yet !
d. The store... is next to the production department will be enlarged.
e. The reason ... the new trainee can't start tomorrow is ridiculous.
f. Anna Bell is the lady ... is going to manage the new department.

2 Complétez la définition de ces métiers, lieux ou objets en utilisant le pronom relatif qui convient.

a. A pharmacist is a person ...
b. A bakery is a place ...
c. A computer is a device ...
d. A joiner is a person ...

3 Supprimez le pronom relatif *that* quand cela est possible.

a. One of the places that I have always wanted to visit in New York is the MOMA.
b. The book that he lent you is his secretary's.
c. Finnish, that is very different from other European languages, is difficult to learn.
d. The secretary that has just arrived is fluent in Russian.
e. The Californian managers that I know do a lot for charities.

4 Reliez les énoncés entre eux par le pronom relatif donné.

a. Yesterday, I met a new supplier. He was very nice. (who)
b. I went to the new store. It had a wide range of items. (which)
c. The delivery man wanted to leave early. He was in a hurry. (who)
d. The sales representative phoned me this morning. His company sells office equipment. (whose)
e. What was the name of the car? It won the Car of the Year Award. (that)

5 Complétez par *which* ou *what*.

a. (...) I prefer in my new job is flexitime.
b. Brian couldn't succeed in this deal, (...) was obvious from the start.
c. Mrs Brown, the accountant, gave John some money, (...) she regretted later.
d. (...) she likes in her job is its variety.

6 Reliez les prépositions de lieux à l'illustration qui convient.

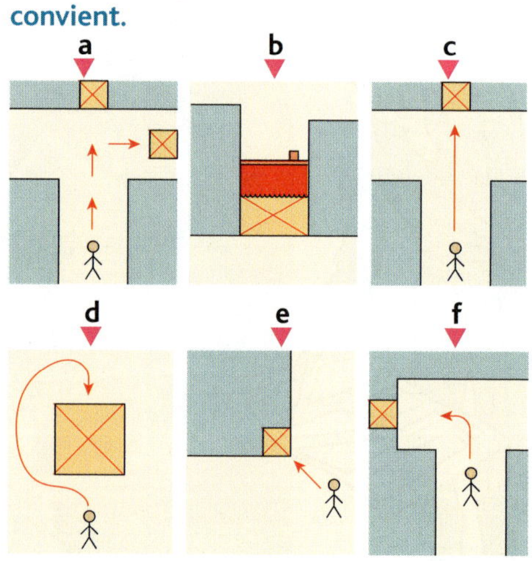

between – behind – on the corner of – in front of – opposite / on the right – next to / on the left

7 Quel est l'itinéraire permettant d'aller de Wool Exchange à Rawson Market, à Bradford.

remember

La proposition relative sert à compléter un groupe nominal ou une phrase. Elle est reliée à la proposition principale par un pronom relatif qui dépend de son antécédent et de sa fonction.

Antécédent humain	Antécédent non humain	Appartenance	lieu	moment	raison
who, that *(qui, que)*	**which, that** *(qui, que)*	**whose** *(dont le, la, l')*	**where** *(où)*	**when** *(où)*	**why** *(pour laquelle)*
The child **who** plays in the film is very young.	The shoe shop **which** is round the corner has just closed down.	Andrew, **whose** life has inspired novelists, is now a star himself.	I wonder **where** this boy lives.	The moment **when** he will regret it hasn't arrived yet.	This is the reason **why** he stopped his business.

- **Dans le langage formel, à l'écrit notamment, on trouve *whom* à la place de *who* quand il est complément.**
  → The lady whom I met at the reception desk is a millionaire. *La femme que j'ai rencontrée à l'accueil est millionnaire.*

- **Il existe deux types de propositions relatives :**

1. → I haven't seen the film (that) he mentioned. *Je n'ai pas vu le film dont il a parlé.*
La relative permet d'identifier l'objet dont on parle : c'est une **relative déterminative**

2. → His last film, which was shot in Australia, is a great success. *Son dernier film, qui a été tourné en Australie, a beaucoup de succès.*
La relative apporte une précision non indispensable : c'est une **relative non déterminative.** Celle-ci est toujours entourée de virgules.

- **Dans les relatives déterminatives, lorsque le pronom est complément, on utilise *that* ou Ø.**
  → Here is all the money (that) I have. *Voilà tout l'argent que j'ai.* This is one of the boys (that) I can't stand. *C'est l'un des garçons que je ne peux pas supporter.*

- **Ce que, ce qui :**

What annonce quelque chose qui va être précisé.
→ What I like best is Indian cooking. *Ce que je préfère, c'est la cuisine indienne.*
Which reprend ce qui précède.
→ Mary was late, which surprised me a lot. *Mary était en retard, ce qui m'a surpris.*

Vocabulary

Verbs / verbes

attend *assister*
forbid* *interdire*
locate *situer*
provide *fournir, procurer*
settle *s'installer, s'établir*

Nouns / noms

accountancy *comptabilité*
a baptism *un baptême*
a belt *une ceinture*
bookkeeping *la comptabilité*
a department *un service*
a floor *un étage*
gasoline *l'essence (US)*
a household *un foyer*
a lift *un ascenseur*
photocopying *la photocopie*
records *les archives*
a rule *une règle, une loi*
the staff *le personnel*
stationery *papeterie, petit matériel*
a stove *un poêle*
a suspender *une bretelle*
a vending machine *un distributeur*
a warehouse *un entrepôt*
a windmill *un moulin à vent*
a workshop *un atelier*

Prepositions / prépositions

above *au dessus*
against *contre*
along *le long de*
at *à*
behind *derrière*
below *au dessous de*
between *entre*
by / near *près de*
close to *tout près de*
in *dans*
into *dans (avec mouvement)*
in front of *devant*
inside *à l'intérieur*
next to *à côté de*
on *sur*
opposite *en face de*
out of *hors de*
outside *à l'extérieur de*
through *à travers*
to *à (mouvement)*
under *sous*

unit 5

Beginning to work

contact

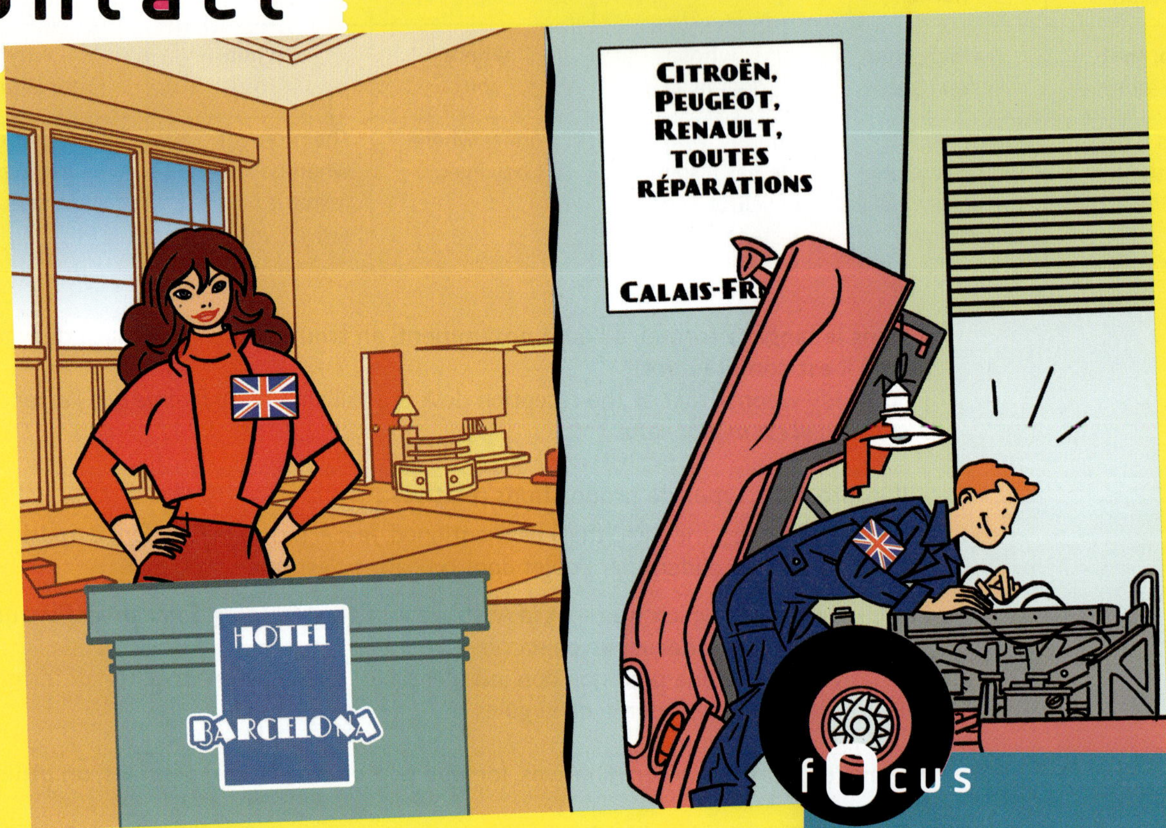

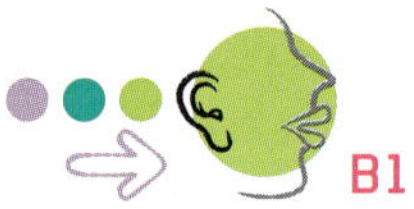

1 Listen to the conversation and fill in the blanks with 'was / wasn't / were / weren't'.

a. My training period ... great!
b. I know that you ... in Spain, where ... you exactly?
c. I ... in Barcelona, in the north of Spain.
d. There ... many tourists who ... always easy-going.
e. I ... very busy.
f. It ... difficult for me.
g. I ... happy at all.

2 Listen again and put the words from the list in the right place.

understood – stayed – spoke – worked – went – did – didn't.

a. I ... in a big hotel.
b. I ... for six weeks at the reception desk.
c. I ... go to Spain.
d. Where ... you go?
e. I ... to Calais.
f. Many people ... and ... English.

focus

It was much better last week when we were on our work placement. There was a lot of work.
I arrived two days ago. I came back yesterday morning. I travelled by plane.
When did you come back? How did you travel? I didn't speak much French.

- *Dans les 2 premières phrases, quelle est la base verbale de* was *et* were *?*
- *À quel temps ce verbe est-il conjugué ? Pourquoi ?*
- *Que deviennent* it was, we were, there was *dans une question et dans une négation ?*
- *Dans les phrases suivantes, retrouvez la base verbale des verbes soulignés.*
- *Comment a-t-on obtenu le prétérit ?*
- *Comment construit-on la forme interrogative et la forme négative ?*
- *Relevez les marqueurs de temps du passé. En connaissez-vous d'autres ?*

Action

1 Listen to the sentences and complete the chart.

	a	b	c	d	e	f	g	h	i	j
Verbes réguliers	*worked*									
Verbes irréguliers										
Base verbale	*work*									

2 Reorder the words to make correct sentences.

a. many / were / tourists / there / ?
b. it / enjoy / did / she / ?
c. improve / Spanish / her / didn't /.
d. she / arrive / when / did / ?
e. do / did / Dylan / where / training / period / his / ?

3 Turn the verbs into the past simple and classify them into: regular / irregular verbs: **start – begin – finish – work – be – go out – welcome – cash – learn – give.**

4 Answer the questions personally.

a. How long ago did you begin learning English?
b. What time did school finish last Monday?
c. How often did you go out at night last summer?
d. When was your last training period?

A2

Name	Alison	Dylan
Accommodation	*hotel*	
Working hours		
Day-off		*Saturday*
Leisures		
Friends		
Tasks		

5 Listen to the conversation (part 2) and put the following information in the chart. **hotel, Thursday, 9-12 am / 1-5 pm, Alex, cafés, discos, bowling alleys, host family, 8-11 am / 5-9 pm, Saturday, welcome guests, oil changes, deal with bookings, services, visits, beach, cash payments, Melinda.**

6 Listen again to Alison and Dylan. Then answer the questions.

a. Was Alison accommodated in a hotel?
b. What time did she begin in the morning?
c. What time did Dylan start after lunch?
d. Did he finish late?
e. Did Alison work on Thursdays?
f. When was Dylan's day-off?
g. Did Alison welcome the guests at the hotel?
h. What did she cash?

Chat time

When did you first... ? When did you last... ?
Utilisez les vignettes pour réaliser des mini-dialogues avec votre partenaire.

A2

Ex: **Student A:** *When did you first type on a computer?*
Student B: *The first time I typed on a computer was five years ago.*

First

Last

Time markers

last (week / month / year / Friday / night...)
yesterday (morning / evening...)
the day before yesterday (in the afternoon / at night...)
two / five / ten ... (days / years...) **ago**
a long time **ago**
in (2005 / July...)
on (Tuesday / September 20th...)
when I was (twelve / a child / younger / in Greece...)

unit 5

Students' odd jobs

B1

Testimonies from Mercury Club players (Phoenix, Arizona). Some girls of the basketball team remember their first job experiences which were very far from professional sport.

Phoenix Mercury forward Belinda Snell (12).

"My first real odd job came in my first year of college*. I worked at Footlocker from October to June. It was cool because I loved sneakers and I could buy prestigious brand names at a very low price. I also had a 10% commission on every pair I sold and it made a nice pay check to bring home. I used to work from 10 am to 8 pm on the weekends but most days, it was part time."

Mercury Guard Cappie Pondexter

"When I was 16, I had a summer job in a ranch for one month. I worked in the fields and I did all that is possible to do on a farm. I got $15 per day and two free meals but it was an exhausting job."

Mercury Forward Kate Christensen

" I had my first casual job three years ago. I did secretarial work on Saturdays for the wildlife Park. I stayed there for nine months, but as they didn't pay me very well ($3 an hour), I left. Then, I found a job at Lunch Box. It was a hamburger stand and I worked there as a waitress. I earned $1.50 more than in the previous place and the working hours were totally different. I opened at 6 pm and closed at 9, except for Sunday evening which was my day-off."

Mercury Guard Ann Strother

" I was thirteen when I started in my auntie's milk bar. She used to sell milk, lollies*, ice cream ... I made four bucks* an hour. I came straight there from school in my uniform and I wore a nice blue apron on it. My aunt used to give me a big milkshake before I started, I could eat as much candy as I wished. Then, I found a weekend job at Big Bill's Pizza. Big Bill used to coach basketball players and there were often sports fans coming in. I got paid $6 per hour and it was great."

Mercury Forward Belinda Snell

"I began working in a hot dog stand in New Jersey. I was 17 and kept the job for two summers. It was the worst job ever! I used to stay in the sun for hours, sweating* the whole time and I stank* like hot dogs when I went home. The only consolation was the good wage – $8 an hour whereas my schoolmates used to get half of it."

Mercury Guard Jennifer Janik

Adapted from
www.wnba.com/mercury/news/girl-thing-first-jobs.html,
June 2006

help

a college (US) *une faculté*
lollies *des sucettes*
a buck (fam.) *un dollar*
sweat *transpirer*
stink (fam.) *puer*

Anticipating

1 Look at the opposite page and answer the questions.

a. What are the people doing in the photos?
b. What is the document about?

Comprehension

2 Read the text and find information about each player.

Player's first name ....
Place(s) of work ....
Duration ....
Salary per hour ....

3 Write full sentences containing the information above.

Ex: *Cappie first worked at ... .*
She kept the job for ... .
She earned ... per hour.

4 What's the English for...?

a. petits boulots d'étudiant (§1)
b. un travail épuisant (§2)
c. mon premier petit boulot (§3)
d. ce fut le pire de mes emplois (§5)

5 What's the French for...?

a. it made a nice pay check (§1)
b. it was part time (§1)
c. I came there straight from school (§4)
d. the good wage (§5)

6 Answer the questions.

a. Did Cappie work full time or part time?
b. How many hours did she work at weekends?
c. How old was Kate when she started?
d. Did Ann work every day in her first job? Was it the same at Lunch Box? What were her working hours?
e. Did Belinda work at the milk bar on Saturdays? What about her second job?
f. How old was Jennifer when she left her job?

now in French

7 Répondez en français aux questions suivantes.

a. Quel est le point commun entre les diverses narratrices ?
b. En quoi consistait le travail de Kate et de Ann ?
c. Comment était rémunérée Cappie ?
d. De quels avantages en nature bénéficiaient Kate et Belinda ?
e. Quel était l'emploi le plus pénible ? Pourquoi ?

fOcus

I used to work from 10 am to 8 pm.
She used to sell milk.
My aunt used to give me a big milkshake.

- *Quelle expression exprime l'habitude dans le passé ? Comment est-elle construite ?*
- *Traduisez les énoncés ci-dessus.*

>> Training n°6 et 7

Writing

A2

8 Use the information below to relate Sandra's first work experience.

– her first odd job / 2 years ago / find;
– 18 / be;
– video shop / after school / 6 pm -8 pm / work;
– Saturdays / 2 pm-9pm / open / close;
– $5.25 / earn.

9 Write a paragraph about the casual job Eddy had last summer.

Livreur de pizzas (pizza boy), juillet / août. Tous les soirs, 19-22h sauf lundi. €3.50 / h plus 10% sur pizzas livrées (*delivered*). Travail fatiguant mais achat d'une nouvelle console (*games console*).

B1

10 Write 10 lines about one of your work placements or casual work. Say what you used to do, what you enjoyed and what you hated.

unit 5

First experiences

IT WASN'T REAL WORK...

B1

1

"I learnt to hustle for money* at an early age and this attitude set me up for life.

I remember that when I was little, maybe 10 or 11, my mom took a job in China and after school, I used to dance in the streets or do some karate demonstrations for money. The passers-by were generous, they probably thought I was really in need. In fact, I spent all the coins* I earned on ice cream and candy. My mother was ashamed and used to reprimand me: 'How can you ask for cash* from the poor Chinese people?'. To be honest, I found it very entertaining and I never thought I was doing something wrong."

Kanye West,
American rapper and hip-hop artist.
Adapted from
www.femalefirst.co.uk/celebrity/79412004.htm

* hustle for money *se démener pour de l'argent* – a coin *une pièce (de monnaie)* – cash *l'argent.*

2

A2

ODD JOBS AREN'T ALL ROSES...

A few stars remember they had to cope with the average person's life before becoming famous...We asked them to tell about their most terrible jobs.

1. What nationality is Kanye West? Where did he live when he was a child? What did he use to do after school? How did he spend what he earned?
2. Did Tom Delonge need his brain in his work? When did his job become easier? Did it last long?
3. How did Brian Mc Fayden bear the odd job he had ?
4. Which one of the three jobs would you accept / refuse? Give your reasons.

"When I was seventeen or eighteen, I delivered concrete*. It was the most horrible thing ever. I had to lift heavy bags off a giant truck in disgusting hot weather. They let me use a forklift* for a while but I fooled around with it and I junked* it. Then I had to go back to delivering it all by hand.

Tom Delonge
(Californian singer)

* concrete *ciment* – forklift *chariot élévateur* – junk (fam) *esquinter* – collect *ramasser* – poop *crotte.*

" In my senior year of high school, I worked at a pig farm. My job consisted in scooping the pig poop*. That wasn't so pleasant but the owner also restored antique cars and I helped him out. I learnt so much about cars that summer that I forgot all about the bad sides of the job."

Brian McFayden, MTV
(Irish pop singer)

outlook

LUCKY PEOPLE EXIST

B1

3

5. Where did Nathalie go on work placement? How long? What sort of company was it?

6. Why did she enjoy it so much?

'In my first year at business school, I spent six weeks in Terre Haute, Indiana, doing an internship* in a small printing company. I took it as a golden opportunity to travel to the US and improve my English. When I first arrived, the staff manager arranged for me to stay at a hotel for a week and the rest of the time, I stayed with a colleague.

Working for a small firm meant that my tasks were very varied. I had a lot of contacts with the customers. The other advantage was that I learnt how the company functioned on every level*, from accounting to the manufacturing process. I was paid $110 a week by cheque which I could cash directly at the bank, without having an account.

Everyone in the office, as well as* in the workshop was friendly, and the climate was great. I enjoyed myself so much, that I've decided to go back for a holiday as soon as I can afford * it.'

Nathalie, 20.

adapted from *Today in English*
© Alexandra Zagalsky

* internship *stage* – level *niveau* – as well as *de même que* – afford *avoir les moyens*

hot line

A2

Making an appointment

1. Listen to the telephone conversation and fill in the blanks with the right words.

Sonia	Mister Thomas
I wonder if I could ....? (take / make / shake / an appointment / an allotment / a payment.)	Which day would ....you? (cube / mute / suit)
Monday morning is already .... (fully booked / nearly cooked / surely hooked.)	Any other moment will be .... (consequent / confident / convenient)

2. Listen again and say if the following statements are right or wrong. Justify your answers.

a. Sonia is calling a friend.
b. She needs information about a product.
c. She read an ad offering a permanent job.
d. She is speaking with the store manager.
e. She asks for an appointment.
f. She is the only applicant.
g. Mr Thomas is available on Monday morning only.
h. They will meet at 2 pm on Tuesday.
i. She must bring a CV.

B1

3. Use the following suggestions with your partner in order to phone for an appointment for an odd job. Reasons for calling: an ad offering a job as a / domestic help / car cleaner / babysitter / mechanic assistant / pizza boy / etc.

training

say it

a. Observez les signes phonétiques puis écoutez et répétez :

[ju:] comme dans 'used', [ʌ] comme dans 'umbrella'.

b. Écoutez et cochez la bonne colonne.

	[ju:]	[ʌ]		[ju:]	[ʌ]
universe			ultra		
unable			unhappy		
usual			unsatisfied		
useful			unit		
us			USA		
union			up		

1 Complétez les phrases avec le prétérit des verbes suivants.

be – drive – have – live – look after – stay

a. The Norton family ... in a West suburb of London.
b. Mike Norton ... born in 1960. He ... a small factory near the city.
d. Every morning, he ... to work in his van. His wife Monica ... at home and ... their two sons.

2 Posez les questions correspondant aux éléments soulignés.

a. No, Shelley didn't receive any wages.
b. She got a job at the library.
c. Tom had to lift heavy bags.
d. Mark walked around for five hours with golfers.
e. Players gave good tips if they were in a good mood.

3 Parmi les verbes soulignés, repérez les actions qui se produisaient régulièrement dans le passé et utilisez *used to*.

a. When we were children, we visited our grandparents once a week.
b. There, we had lunch at 12, never earlier nor later.
c. Three years ago, my parents and I drove to Scotland. It took us two days.
d. In my last holiday in Austria, I went skiing and I sprained my left knee.
e. When my cousin Liz lived in Switzerland, she went skiing every weekend in winter.
f. My father hates tobacco, but when he was young, he smoked very much.

4 Construisez des phrases au prétérit en utilisant A + B et en les reliant par *and*.

Ex: *Alison was in Barcelona and she worked in a big hotel.*

A

a. ***Alison (be) in Barcelona***
b. Dylan (go) to France
c. Alison (begin) at 8
d. Dylan (start) at 1
e. Alison (deal) with the bookings
f. The customers (be) happy

B

g. He (finish) at 5.
h. They (give) Dylan good tips.
i. ***She (work) in a big hotel.***
j. He (do) his training period in a garage.
k. She (cash) the clients payments.
l. She (stop) at 11.

5 Terminez chaque phrase de manière personnelle.

a. On my last birthday...
b. Last night...
c. Ten years ago...

6 Comparez Arthur jeune et Arthur maintenant.

Ex: *When he was young, Arthur used to play tennis. Now he sits in an armchair all the time.*

remember

Pour exprimer une action ou une succession de situations et de faits passés et terminés on utilise le prétérit simple (*simple past*).

- **En français, le prétérit simple peut se traduire par le passé composé, le passé simple ou l'imparfait.**

→ Last night, I **watched** TV. *Hier soir, j'ai regardé la télé.*
→ He **saw** a shadow and **ran** away. *Il vit une ombre et prit la fuite.*
→ The sky **was** blue, the flowers **were** beautiful. *Le ciel était bleu, les fleurs étaient belles.*

- **Les marqueurs de temps du passé, ou simplement le contexte, indiquent le moment où les événements se sont produits.**

3 weeks **ago** *(il y a 3 semaines)*, **last** year / month ... *(l'année dernière, le mois dernier...)*, **yesterday / the day before yesterday** *(hier / avant-hier)*, **in** 2001, **in** September, **on** June 1st, **when I was** 10 *(quand j'avais 10 ans)*.

- **Formation du prétérit simple :**

	Forme affirmative	Forme interrogative	Forme négative
verbe régulier	**S + V-*ed*** → Yesterday I played tennis.	***did* + S + V** → When did you play tennis?	**S + *didn't* + V** → I didn't play in the morning.
verbe irrégulier	*(voir liste sur rabats)* → Grandma gave me some money.	***did* + S + V ...?** → How much did she give you?	**S + *didn't* + V** → She didn't give me much.
be	I / she / he / it **was**. you / we / they **were**.	**Was** I / she / he / it? **Were** you / we / they?	I / she / he / it **wasn't** you / we / they **weren't**

Pour parler d'actions ou de situations qui étaient habituelles et qui ne le sont plus, on utilise *used to* + V.

→ I **used to see** her every weekend. *Je la voyais tous les week-ends.* When she was young,
→ Mary **used to jog** every morning. *Quand elle était jeune, Mary faisait un jogging tous les matins.* Things aren't what they **used to be**. *Les choses ne sont plus ce qu'elles étaient.*

- **Les formes interrogative et négative sont moins utilisées.**

→ How **did you use to spend** your summer holidays? *Comment passiez-vous les vacances d'été d'habitude?* Charlie **didn't use to smoke** before, but now he does. *Charlie ne fumait pas avant, maintenant si.*

Vocabulary

Verbs / verbes
be in need *être dans le besoin*
cash *encaisser*
earn *gagner (sa vie)*
get paid *être payé*
improve *progresser*
let *laisser*
spend *dépenser / passer (temps)*
stink *puer*
sweat *transpirer*

Nouns / noms
candy *les bonbons*
cash *de l'argent*
a casual job /casual work *un petit boulot*
a day-off *un jour de congé*
a host family *une famille d'accueil*
an odd job *un petit boulot*
a passer-by *un passant*
secretarial work *du secrétariat*
sneakers *des baskets*
a tip *un pourboire*
a training period / a work placement *un stage*
a work experience *une expérience professionnelle*

Adjectives / adjectifs
ashamed *honteux*
entertaining *amusant / distrayant*
exhausting *épuisant*
free *gratuit / libre*
low *bas*
tired *fatigué*
tiring *fatigant*

unit 6

Describing how it works

contact

New GPS (Global Positioning System) receivers are easy to use and give clear directions to your destination.

B1

1 Listen to the dialogue (Part 1) and answer the questions.

a. Why must Brenda be helped? Where must she go?
b. Where is the company located? What's the address?
c. What will Tony use to find the route?

2 Listen again and choose the right words.

a. A portable unit can be (taken / moved) from car to car.
b. It is (powered / connected) via the cigar lighter.
c. You simply enter your (code / destination).
d. Then the (route / map) appears on the screen.
e. The directions can also (be seen / be read) on the screen.
f. (Is it / Was it) connected to a satellite?
g. It (must / can) be connected to a minimum of 3 satellites to calculate your position.

fOcus

Then the route is calculated by the computer.
The directions are given by a computerized voice.
Brenda must be helped.
The GPS receiver can be used immediately.

- *Relevez les formes verbales de ces énoncés. Quels sont les éléments qui les composent ? Quel énoncé exprime une obligation ? une possibilité ?*
- *Dans ces énoncés, souhaite-t-on insister sur celui qui fait l'action ou celui qui subit l'action ? Pourquoi ? De quelle forme s'agit-il ?*
- *Qu'est-ce que le complément d'agent ? Par quel mot est-il introduit ? Est-il indispensable ?*

Action

1 **Complete the paragraph with the verb in the passive form (present tense).**

In-car sat nav: Press a small button. Then your in-car navigation-system ... (connect) to the control centre. The route ... (download) to your car and navigation begins. You ... (ask) where you want to go. Maps ... (not store) in the unit. So you are sure the very latest directions ... (give) by the control centre. You ... (guide) around traffic jams and road works.

2 **Explain what must be done and not done.**

Ex: *First, connect the GPS receiver* ➡ *First, the GPS receiver must be connected.*

a. Press the red button.
b. Don't forget the code.
c. Then choose the destination.
d. Don't give the exact address.

B1

3 **Listen to the end of the dialogue (part 2) and answer the questions.**

a. What must Brenda do to help Tony?
b. What happens when the red button is pressed?
c. Which directions are given by the computerized voice?
d. What is Brenda's opinion about the GPS receiver? What will she do?

4 **Turn the sentences into the passive voice. Then listen and check.**

Ex: *You enter the address.* ➡ *The address is entered.*

a. The GPS receiver places the car on the map.
b. The receiver stores the maps in the memory.
c. The receiver traces your route.
d. You can use it everywhere in Europe.
e. The GPS receiver can guide you.

Chat time

Student A: Look at the pictures. Choose the right order to proceed and explain a learner (student B) what must or can be done before driving off.
Ex: *First, the tyres must / can be checked. Then ...*

WHAT TO DO BEFORE DRIVING OFF

a. clean the windscreen

b. start the engine

c. switch off your phone

d. check the mirrors

e. adjust your seat

f. check the tyres

g. switch the car lights on

h. fasten your seatbelt

B1

Student B: Listen to the advice and write down the order to proceed. Then change roles (see page 151) and explain student A how to print photos.

unit 6

B1

How to create a TV show

***Lost* is an American drama television series that follows the survivors of a plane crash on a strange tropical island. It includes a number of mysterious or supernatural elements.**

Conception

In 2004, Lloyd Braun, then manager of ABC, contacted J. J. Abrams, creator of the TV series *Alias*, to write a script that was based on one of his ideas. *Lost*'s pilot episode was the most expensive in the network's history (between US$10 and 14 million). The show became one of the biggest successes with another new series *Desperate Housewives*. Yet, before it had even aired*, Lloyd Braun was fired* by executives at ABC's parent company, Disney, because he had approved such an expensive and risky project!

Filming location

Lost is filmed entirely on the Hawaiian island of Oahu. Various urban areas in and around Honolulu are used as stand-ins* for locations around the world, including Los Angeles, New York, Iowa, South Korea, Iraq, Nigeria, England, and Australia. For example, scenes set in a Sydney airport were actually filmed at the Hawaii Convention Center and a local bunker dating from World War II was used as an Iraqi Republican Guard installation.

Cast and Characters

Each season has about fifteen regular speaking roles. According* to producer Bryan Burk, it's more expensive to produce but you can benefit from more flexibility: "You can have more interactions between characters and create more diverse characters, more back stories, more love triangles."

Distribution

In April 2006, Disney announced that *Lost* would be available for free online, with advertising, on ABC's website (only for American people). The UK's Channel 4 and France's TF1 have also allowed access to the series online. Each episode is issued* online just after being broadcasted* on the channel.

Ratings* and critical response

The show was strongly advertised by ABC with many radio spots, special screenings and a large billboard* advertising campaign. The pilot episode debuted on September 22, 2004 and it was watched by 18.6 million viewers (ABC's strongest ratings* since 2000 when the US game show *Who Wants to Be a Millionaire?* initially aired).

For its first season, *Lost* averaged* 16 million viewers (mostly eighteen to forty-nine years olds). The second season premiere was even stronger than the first: over 23 million viewers watched this episode, which was a new record.

A survey of 20 countries by Informa Telecoms and Media in 2006 concluded that, next to CSI (Crime Scene Investigation), *Lost* was the second most popular TV show in the world.

help

air *diffuser*
fire *(ici) renvoyer / virer*
a stand-in *un remplacement*
according to *selon / d'après*
issue *sortir*
be broadcasted *être diffusé*
ratings *indices d'écoute*
billboard advertising *publicité sur panneaux*
average *atteindre la moyenne de*

Anticipating

1 Look at the photo and read the title and the introduction. Then answer the questions.

a. What sort of TV show is *Lost*? What is it about?
b. What is the general topic of the document?

Comprehension

2 Read the text and write the title of the paragraph where the following information can be found.

a. the number of actors
b. the number of viewers
c. how the series was created
d. how the episodes are issued online
e. where the series is filmed.

3 Find information about the series.

a. Who had the idea of the series?
b. Who was the script written by?
c. Is the series filmed in different locations around the world?
d. How many actors appear regularly in the series?
e. How was the series advertised by ABC?
f. How many viewers watched the first episode of the second season?

4 What's the English for...?

a. société / maison mère (l.7-12)
b. accueil de la critique (l.37-40)
c. disponible (l.30-35)

5 What's the French for...?

a. including (l.14-18)
b. for free (l.30-32)
c. special screenings (l.38-40)

6 Right or wrong? Justify your answer.

a. Lloyd Braun was fired by Disney because his project was not successful.
b. Some scenes set in New York were actually set in or near Honolulu.
c. Bryan Burk doesn't like a large cast because it's more expensive to produce.
d. *Lost*'s episodes could be seen on the channel's website before they aired.
e. Most viewers are aged between 28 and 59.
f. *Lost* was the most popular show in 2006. CSI was second.

fOcus

Lloyd Braun was fired by executives. All the scenes were filmed in Oahu. Over 23 million viewers watched this episode.

- *À quel temps et à quelle forme sont les verbes utilisés dans les deux premiers énoncés ? Pourquoi ?*
- *Transformez la dernière phrase pour insister sur l'épisode et non sur les téléspectateurs. Respectez le temps employé et utilisez* by.
- *Relevez dans le texte deux énoncés passés et deux énoncés présents qui sont construits à la forme passive.*

>> Training n°5 et 6

nOw in French

7 Répondez en français aux questions suivantes.

a. Quel a été le coût du premier épisode de *Lost* ? Quelles ont été les deux conséquences de ce coût ?
b. Donnez deux exemples de lieux de tournage utilisés en remplacement d'autres endroits ?
c. Pour quelles raisons les producteurs préfèrent-ils un casting avec de nombreux acteurs ?
d. Quelles sont les conditions de distribution des épisodes sur le site ABC ?

Writing

B1

8 Write a summary of the article and then give your opinion about *Lost*.

When was it created? Who was the series produced by? Where was it filmed? Do you like it? Why or why not? What is your favourite TV show? Why?

9 Write a paragraph about your favourite series.

unit 6

Recycling

B1

1 WHAT HAPPENS TO THE GLASS WE PUT IN THE GLASS BANK? WHERE DOES IT GO?

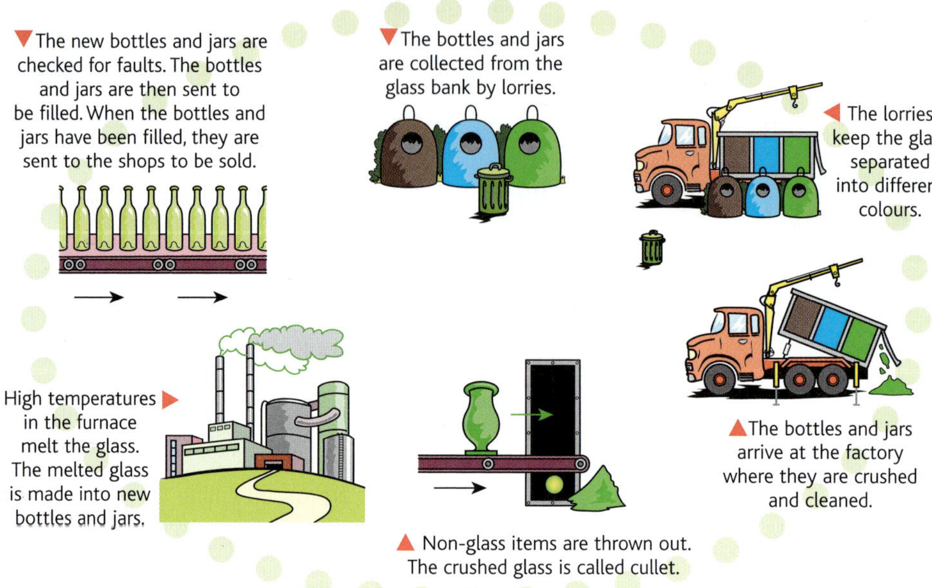

GLASS IS 100% RECYCLABLE

1. **Read the text and reorder the different steps of the recycling process: a. filling, b. collecting, c. checking, d. transport, e. sorting, f. glass melting, g. store shelf, h. cullet.**
2. **Is it important to recycle glass? Find at least 3 reasons in the document.**
3. **How can you help recycle glass? What can you do exactly?**

REASONS FOR RECYCLING GLASS

1. Melting anything in a furnace uses energy and affects the environment. Making glass by melting recycled glass in the furnace uses far less energy and reduces pollution.

2. To make glass, lots of materials are quarried and heated in a furnace (the major raw material is sand). The more glass we recycle, the less new ingredients we will need, and this means less quarrying in the countryside.

3. Waste disposal means getting rid of rubbish. Millions of pounds are spent each year hiding our rubbish in landfill sites (huge piles that can be the size of up 10 football pitches). 8% of our household rubbish is glass.
If we recycled this glass instead of throwing it into the bin, we could have less waste to get rid of, which would save the countryside and cost less money.

4. Everyone can help to look after the environment. Putting used bottles and jars in a glass bank is a small easy step we can all take to help clean up our earth.

2 B1 FROM PLASTIC BOTTLES TO PIPES

outlook

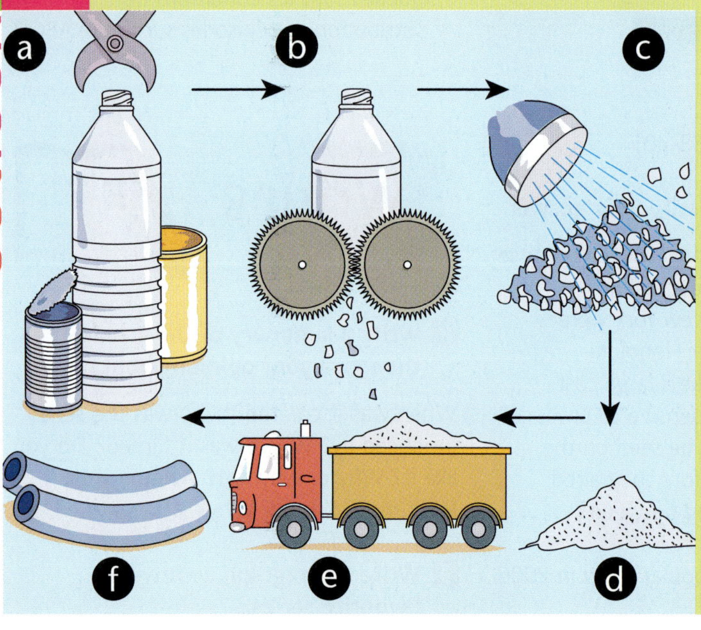

4. **Reorder the different stages of recycling.**
   - ❒ remoulding into tubes
   - ❒ washing
   - ❒ transporting
   - ❒ sorting
   - ❒ granulating into flakes
   - ❒ powdering
5. **Describe how a plastic bottle is recycled.**
   Ex: ***First the plastic bottle is sorted, then ...***
6. **Can you describe other processes of recycling (steel and aluminium cans, paper and cardboard...)?**

DO YOU KNOW WHAT TO THROW?

3

B1

HAZARDOUS MATERIAL & PAINT

Bring them to our drop-off sites (no charge!) Items accepted include: paints, oil, gas, pesticides and other chemicals from your home.

FACT
>> Over 90% of the items collected are recycled! Thousands of gallons of paint are put out for free reuse! Propane is locally recycled as a secondary fuel source.

APPLIANCES AND ELECTRONICS

Bring them to our drop-off sites or take them back to your retailer.

FACT
>> Electronics such as TVs and computer monitors may contain up to 8 pounds of lead, as well as other toxic chemicals.
>> Your old appliance can be taken back by your retailer.

TIRES

Take them to our drop-off sites or give them back to your local tire retailer.

FACT
>> Tires are recycled into items such as playground bases and doormats.

RECYCLABLES

Paper, cardboard, metal cans, glass jars and bottles, plastic bottles are picked up near your home.

FACT
>> Over 200 pounds per person are collected annually in Minnesota!

YARD WASTE

Bring your grass and leaves, tree waste and treated wood to our drop-off and compost sites. Yard waste must not be mixed with regular garbage.

FACT
>> Treated wood causes toxic smoke and ash when burnt.
>> Composting is a biological process in which fruits, vegetables, leaves and plant trimmings are converted into a soil-like material called humus. Compost can be used in your flower and vegetable gardens.

From *Your guide for recycling and disposal options* (Published by the Department of Public Health and Environment / Washington County, MINNESOTA, 2006). Reprinted with permission from Washington County Government, Stillwater, MN, USA.

7. **What can people do with some of their waste (instead of throwing it with their regular garbage)? Why?**

8. **What sort of waste is picked up near home? Which ones can be toxic for the environment? Which ones are recycled? Are these methods successful? Give 2 examples.**

hot line

B1

Telephoning the recycling office

1. Listen to the telephone conversation and choose the right letter to explain how each type of waste is collected in the City of York.

A. Take to a special container.
B. Put into a green bag and take to a composting site.
C. Place in a blue box and leave on the street on Monday.
D. Place in a grey box and leave on the street on Monday.
E. Tie in bundles and leave next to the grey box.

....

B1

2. Now work with your partner. You telephone the recycling office to ask how the types of waste are collected in your town. The secretary explains how it works in his / her town. Then change roles. (See help on appendix page 151).

training

say it

LES FORMES CONTRACTÉES DE *BE* CONJUGUÉ.

a. Écoutez les énoncés suivants et classez les différentes formes conjuguées de *BE* dans l'ordre.

won't be – isn't – weren't – 's – 'll be – aren't – 's been – can't be- 're – hasn't been – 'm – couldn't be

À quels temps correspondent ces différentes formes verbales?

b. Écoutez à nouveau pour vérifier et répétez.

1 Réécrivez ces énoncés en plaçant le mot souligné en début de phrase.

a. Thousands of people read *Time Magazine*.
b. They sell magazines all over the world.
c. They don't print them in the same country.
d. They publish an issue every week.
e. They don't write the articles in any other language than English.

2 Posez des questions au présent simple en mettant le verbe à la forme passive.

Ex: *Where / the materials / import from?*
➡ *Where are the materials imported from?*

a. Where / the company / locate?
b. Where / the products / make?
c. How / the machine / pack?
d. How / the products / transport?
e. How many products / export / every year?

3 Remettez les mots dans l'ordre pour indiquer ce qui peut être ou doit être fait.

a. recycled / some materials / by / be / other companies / can.
b. must / special agencies / be / the products / by / advertised.
c. different languages / be / the user guides / published / must / in.
d. repaired / a service company / can / by / the machines / be.
e. the net / sold / the new products / be / on / can.

4 Rédigez 5 énoncés à la forme passive pour expliquer comment se conduire en présence d'animaux sauvages.

a. Wild animals / must / see / from a distance.
b. Tourists / can / put in danger / when feeding animals.
c. Human food / shouldn't / give / to wild animals.
d. Animals / can / kill / by plastic bags or cans containing food.
e. Wild animals / must never / touch / by people.

5 Réécrivez l'histoire des hot dogs en plaçant le mot souligné en début de phrase. Ajoutez le complément d'agent si nécessaire.

a. In the 1860's, German immigrants sold sausages from carts in New York.
b. They put the sausage into a milk bun.
c. And they added mustard inside the bun.
d. In 1939, President Roosevelt served hot dogs to King George VI.
e. During last baseball season, fans bought 26 million hot dogs.

6 Vous souhaitez raconter l'histoire de la bicyclette en insistant sur les noms de ses créateurs. Remettez les phrases ci-dessous à la forme active.

a. In 1791, the first version of the bicycle was drawn and built by a French man, Comte de Sirac.
b. In 1816, a movable steering wheel was added by Baron de Sauerbrun in Germany.
c. In 1839, pedals were designed by Macmillan, a Scotsman.
d. In 1869, a bicycle with a large wheel and pedals was ridden by French carriage makers: Michaux and Lallement.
e. In the mid-1880s, the modern bicycles with two similar wheels and pedals between the wheels were manufactured by Englishman James Starley.

7 QUIZZ. Répondez à ces 5 questions en moins d'une minute.

a. Where is whisky made? Scotland / USA / Canada
b. Where is Melbourne located? New Zealand / Australia / the USA
c. Where was Bob Marley born? USA / Cuba / Jamaica
d. Who was President of the USA for 12 years? G. Washington / F. D. Roosevelt / G. W. Bush
e. What was Elvis Presley called? the Prince / the King / the Golden Boy.

Rédigez 5 questions du même type pour tester votre voisin.

remember

Pour dire qu'une action est faite par..., on utilise la forme passive.

La forme passive permet de présenter une action ou un événement d'un point de vue différent. Le sujet d'une phrase passive est celui qui subit l'action : → The car is repaired by the mechanic.

Alors que le sujet d'une phrase active est celui qui fait l'action : → The mechanic repairs the car.

- **Le passif se construit avec *be* conjugué au temps demandé + participe passé.**
La conjugaison de ***be*** détermine ainsi le temps du verbe au passif.

This car	**is** **was** **has been** **will be** **had been**	repaired	(by the mechanic)	*Présent simple* *Prétérit simple* *Present perfect* *Futur* *Past perfect*
These cars	**are** **were** **have been** **will be** **had been**			*Présent simple* *Prétérit simple* *Present perfect* *Futur* *Past perfect*

- **À la forme passive, *by* + complément d'agent (celui qui fait l'action) peut disparaître :**
– quand il est inconnu : → My car was stolen last week. *On a volé ma voiture la semaine dernière.*
– quand il n'est pas important : → This telephone was repaired. *Le telephone a été réparé.*
– quand on ne veut pas en parler : → Last night I was told about your new boyfriend. *On m'a parlé de ton nouveau petit ami hier soir.*

- **La forme passive est souvent utilisée avec un modal pour indiquer ce qui peut / doit / devrait être fait.**
→ Glass, metal and plastic **can be recycled**. *Le verre, le métal et le plastique peuvent être recyclés.*
→ The battery **must be charged**. *La batterie doit être chargée.*
→ Wild animals **should be protected**. *Les animaux sauvages devraient être protégés.*

Vocabulary

Verbs / verbes
advertise *promouvoir / faire de la publicité*
collect *ramasser, collecter*
connect *relier / raccorder / brancher*
deliver *livrer (à domicile)*
display *afficher (sur un écran)*
include *inclure / comprendre*
insert *insérer, introduire*
pack *emballer*
download *télécharger*
enter (data) *saisir / entrer (des données)*
move *déplacer / déménager*
power *fournir en énergie*
press (the button) *appuyer (sur le bouton)*
print *imprimer*
sort *trier (des déchets)*
support *soutenir*
store *stocker, mettre en réserve*
switch on / off *allumer / éteindre*
transport *transporter*
use *utiliser*
work *fonctionner / travailler*

Nouns / noms
a collection point (UK) / a drop-off site (US) *une déchetterie*
data *des données*
an executive *un cadre / responsable*
a network *un réseau*
the parent company *la société ou maison mère*
a provider *un fournisseur (d'accès)*
waste / rubbish /garbage *des déchets, des ordures*

Adjectives / adjectifs
available *disponible / accessible*
useful *utile*

unit 7

Giving instructions and advice

contact

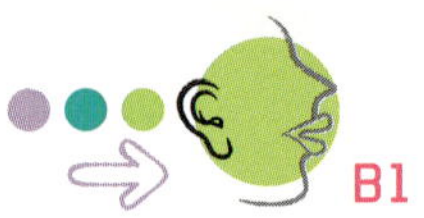

1 **Listen to the first part of the dialogue and tick what you hear. Then, underline examples of good behaviour at a job interview.**

a. ❑ wear jeans
b. ❑ put on a suit
c. ❑ wear a walkman
d. ❑ tie your hair up
e. ❑ be sitting properly
f. ❑ move your hands continually
g. ❑ look like a statue
h. ❑ show you are self-confident
i. ❑ express yourself calmly
j. ❑ take a pad and a pen
k. ❑ switch off your mobile
l. ❑ chew gum

2 **Listen again and complete with:** ***can't / 'd better / don't / have to / if I were you / must / should.***

a. You ... wear jeans.
b. You ... put on a suit.
c. Do I ... look like a statue?
d. You ... look your interlocutor straight in the eye.
e. What else ... I do?
f. ... forget to switch off your mobile.
g. ... I would have a warm bath.

fOcus

Tell me what I should do. You can't do that! You mustn't be late. You must show interest. You'd better have a good night sleep. If I were you, I would get there ten minutes early. You have to make a good impression.

- *Quels sont les énoncés qui expriment ce qu'il faut faire ? Ce qu'il ne faut pas faire ? Ce qu'il est conseillé de faire ?*
- *Comment appelle-t-on* can, must *et* should *? Quel est l'équivalent de* have to *? Comment traduisez-vous* you'd better *et* if I were you *?*

Action

A2

1 Listen and complete the sentences. Then put them in the chart.

a. You ... be there on time.
b. She ... dress properly.
c. He ... send his CV.
d. You ... move all the time.
e. ... chew gum.
f. ..., I would show interest and confidence.
g. ... interrupt your interlocutor.
h. I ... accept such conditions.
i. You ... take your school certificates with you.

	Advice	Obligations	Interdictions
a			
b			
c			
d			
e			
f			
g			
h			
i			

2 Choose the right modal verb.

a. You (must / can / can't) wear shorts at the office.
b. You (mustn't / 'd better / have to) show that you are afraid at a job interview.
c. We (can't / shouldn't / have to) arrive on time at the appointment.
d. My sister doesn't like her job, I think she (should / mustn't / had better not) look for another one.

3 Link the sentences that have the same meaning.

a. I think you should work near home.
b. You must be eighteen to take your driving license.
c. I have to get up early from Monday to Friday.
d. You'd better find a job in your town.
e. You can't become a motorist if you are fifteen years old.
f. I can't sleep late on weekdays.

B1

4 Listen to the dialogue 'Security visit' and choose the right element.

a. Debbie has found a job for (the summer / for one year / for six months).
b. The company manufactures (electrical appliances / electric razors / electric guitars).
c. The workshop where the dishwashers are made is (small / high / large).
d. The staff in the workshop must wear (earplugs because it's noisy / warm clothes because it's cold / gloves because it's dirty).
e. Working clothes protect (from the sun / from the grease / from the noise.
f. The staff (can smoke in the workshop / can smoke in the refectory / can't smoke anywhere).

Chat time

Student A: Ask your partner her / his opinion about the job applicants in pictures 1 and 2. Student B: Say what is wrong with the applicants and what they should or shouldn't do.Then change roles for pictures 3 and 4.

A2

Vocabulary

Too many piercings – shy – crazy hairstyle – smile – sunglasses – more self-confident – free and easy – chew – bring a dog – use a mobile – old fashioned – dress more normally – too relaxed – less scornful – bite her nails – look at her interlocutor

A: What / think / of the applicant number ...? B: She / he ...
A: What / think / she / he should do? B: She'd / he'd better / should / shouldn't...
A: What would you do if you were her / him? B: If I were her / him, I would...

unit 7

Snowboarder saved by mobile phone

Skiing and snowboarding are attracting more people each year, but as the popularity of these sports increases, the number of accidents is rising too.

Mirko Hausmann, a 28-year-old car sales representative from Hamburg, moved to Tyrol for professional reasons. He soon decided he would go snowboarding. As he had skied a few times when he was ten years younger, he thought everything would be easy. So on a sunny Sunday afternoon in October, he felt ready for a great time on the slopes. He was wearing his favourite jeans and sweater. His board was secondhand because he wanted to try this sport before investing more money. Mirko began with a few runs down easy slopes, but as there were too many people on his way, he chose to slide down* a closed area, despite* the signs and warnings.

About one hour later, as he was going faster and faster, feeling more and more self-assured, his snowboard suddenly snapped in two pieces and Mirko crashed into a tree head first. After the shock, he immediately knew that he had an ankle sprain and probably a wrist fracture. He managed to send a text message to a colleague, who alerted the mountain rescue services.

When they found him, it was already dark and Mirko was suffering from his ankle, wrist and also from slight* head injuries and minor bruising*. He was also very cold. He thanked the rescuers and told them everything was his fault: he should have bought new equipment, fitted for his weight and size, he should have worn a helmet and wrist guards, he should have put on ski pants, gloves and an anorak. The rescuers replied that first of all, he shouldn't have entered a prohibited area.

A study by the American Consumer Product Safety Commission estimates that each winter there are about 85,000 snowboarding injuries in the US. They also report that half of them would not happen if people wore helmets, wrist guards and knee pads. As for fatal accidents, 80% of them occur to risk-takers who ski or surf in prohibited areas.

help

slide down *descendre (en glissant)*
despite *malgré*
slight *léger*
bruising *des contusions*

Anticipating

1 Look at the title, the photo and the introduction, then choose the right statement.

a. The document tells about: (winter sports resorts / winter sports risks / winter sports costs).
b. Skiing holidays interest: (fewer and fewer people / as many people / more and more people every year).
c. The number of sports accidents is: (superior / equal / inferior / to what it was before).

2 Describe the photo. What is the man doing? What other sport does it make you think of?

Comprehension

3 Read the text and match each title with a paragraph.

a. Defective equipment.
b. Statistics and analysis.
c. A happy man.
d. Remorse and regrets.

4 What's the English for...?

a. augmenter (2 possibilités) (introduction)
b. une zone interdite (§1)
c. les blessures (§3)

5 What's the French for...?

a. a slope (§1)
b. snapped in two pieces (§2)
c. the mountain rescue services (§2)
d. new equipment, fitted for his weight and size (§3)

6 Answers the questions in English.

a. Was Mirko a real beginner?
b. Was he wearing appropriate clothes?
c. What sort of board did he buy?
d. Why did he ski off-limits?
e. Why did he lose control of his direction?
f. How were the rescuers alerted?

now in French

7 Répondez en français aux questions suivantes.

a. Quels éléments du texte montrent que Mirko est heureux et enthousiaste ?
b. Dans quel état les sauveteurs le trouvent-ils ?
c. Comment aurait-il pu éviter les problèmes ?
d. Peut-on considérer que Mirko a eu de la chance ? Pourquoi ?
e. L'accident de Mirko est-il un cas isolé ? Pourquoi ?
f. Que révèle l'étude menée aux USA ? Que représente le chiffre 80 % ?

fOcus

He should have worn a helmet.
He shouldn't have entered a prohibited area.

- *Quel auxiliaire suit le modal? À quelle forme sont les verbes* worn *et* entered *?*
- *Quelle est la bonne traduction du premier exemple ? « Il devrait porter » ou bien « Il aurait dû porter un casque » ?*

>> Training n°5, 6 et 7

Writing

B1

8 Write a summary of Mirko's story in about 8 lines. Use the following questions as a guide.

a. What do you know about Mirko's age / job / nationality?
b. Why did he leave his home town?
c. What did he decide to do one Sunday?
d. What about his clothing and equipment?
e. Why did he enter a prohibited area?
f. What happened while he was surfing off-limits?
g. What saved him?

9 Have you ever had problems that were your own fault? (In your family / with friends / with teachers). Tell your story and say what you should or shouldn't have done to avoid the trouble. (10 lines)

unit 7

Safety rules

HEALTHY EATING

B1

1

Developing healthy eating habits is sometimes difficult but small changes can help.

1. You should begin reading the labels of the foods you buy. Be careful with ' low fat' or 'light' labels. If a product is lower in fat, it is often higher in salt or sugar and vice versa.

2. Slowly replace high-calorie junk food* (crisps, candy bars, peanuts...) with three types of fruit per day (apples, grapes, oranges...).

3. Choose water rather than sweetened* drinks. It helps with digestion and weight loss and it improves the appearance of your skin.

4. Don't have much alcohol: one to two drinks per day for men and one for women. A drink equals 12 ounces* of beer or 4 ounces of wine.

5. Get a doggy bag* when you eat in a restaurant or a fast food. The portions they serve are often too big. Ask for a doggy bag when you order and pack up half your plate to enjoy the next day.

Adapted from http://health.eating.discovery.com/centers/nutritionfitness July 2006

* junk food *nourriture de mauvaise qualité* – sweetened *sucré* – an ounce *2,84 ml* – a doggy bag *petit sac pour emporter les restes après un repas au restaurant.*

1. Why should consumers be careful with light produce?
2. Can you give other examples of junk food? of fruit?
3. Why must you prefer water to alcoholic drinks or to sodas?
4. How can you eat less in an American or British restaurant?

2

B1

BE FIRE WISE* THIS SUMMER!

outlook

BARBECUES

1. Don't light fires when the wind is strong: you could cause millions of dollars damage and be liable* for it.
2. Take care with flammable liquids around barbecues. The fumes can ignite* and cause fire.
3. Extinguish your barbecue properly after use.

CARAVANS

1. Install a smoke alarm. Fires travel very quickly in a caravan and are often fatal at night-time.
2. Ensure the gas bottle and its hose* are in good condition.
3. Check the caravan power cord and plugs* and ensure the extinguisher on the inside is ready for use.
4. Make sure you perfectly know the fire service number wherever you are on holiday.

Adapted from 'The Tribune' (*Holiday Times* 2006) New Zealand

* wise *prudent* – liable *être tenu pour responsable* – ignite *s'enflammer* – a hose *un tuyau* – plugs *les prises de courant.*

5. What must you do to keep safe from fire?
6. Which equipments must be checked in a caravan?
7. Which liquids mustn't you use near a barbecue?
8. Why are caravan fires often fatal at night-time?
9. What number must you dial to call the fire services in France? Is it the same in every country?

BREAKDOWN GUIDE

3

B1

In case of a problem, you mustn't stop on the motorway itself, you must pull over onto the hard shoulder. Remember to use your warning lights.

Once you have parked, get out from the passenger side, open your bonnet to indicate you have broken down and lock the doors.

Use the emergency phones that are located every half mile. Calls are free and you will be put through to the police control, who will immediately know your location.

Keep away from the traffic and wait for assistance to arrive. You must not wait inside the vehicle.

It is illegal for anyone to offer help on the hard shoulder. Do not accept a lift.

At night, wear bright clothing and take a torch when walking to the emergency phone.

10. Why must you use the warning lights? / lock the doors? / stand away from the traffic?
11. Why should you call from an emergency phone rather than from your mobile?
12. Why shouldn't you accept anyone's help?

hot line

B1

Emergency call on the motorway

1. Listen to the telephone conversation and answer the questions.

a. Has Stan had a car breakdown?
b. Where did the problem happen?
c. Is anyone hurt?
d. What must the passengers do?
e. Where must they stand?
f. When will the police be there?

B1

2. Work with your partner to simulate an emergency call on the motorway.
Student A: Reorder the words to play the role of the police.
Student B: Go to page 152 to play the role of the caller.

Police	Caller
Emergency Service / I / help / you / can /?	....
what / it / sort of / is / breakdown /?	....
have / control / you / lost /?	....
is / your / where / car / parked /?	....
warning lights / are / on / your /?	....
anyone / there / is / inside / vehicle / your / ?	....
get out / they / must / of / car / the /.	....
and / keep away / they / traffic / must / from / the / .	....
is / car / what / your / make / the / of /?	....
the / will / there / breakdown service / be / 20 minutes / in /.	....

say it

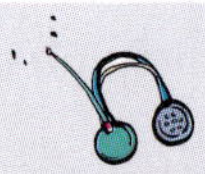

a. Écoutez la même phrase dite deux fois et notez si la voix monte ou descend en fin de lecture.

'Can you open your bag, please?'

b. Choisissez la bonne réponse:

c. Ecoutez et notez au bout de chaque exemple: ↗ D ou bien ↘ O.

a. Could you wait there?
b. Can you call me?
c. Can you answer my questions?
d. Can you show me your passport?
e. Can you give me your name?
f. Can you follow me?

1 Complétez le texte à l'aide de *must* ou *don't* en les associant aux verbes suivants: *call – close – open – use – try – get out*.

If a fire breaks out in your house, you ... all the doors. Before opening a door, you ... the back of your hand to touch it. If it feels warm, ... it. You ... as quickly as possible. ... to pick up valuables and possessions. You ... the number 999 from a neighbour's house or from your mobile once you are out of danger.

2 Donnez des conseils pour les situations suivantes.

Ex: *John has a very bad cold.* ➡ *I don't think he should go to work. / I think he should stay in bed.*

a. I put sausages in the fridge 3 weeks ago.
b. Tom is going to wear his yellow bermudas to his job interview.
c. I always arrive late at school.
d. Mark often drives at 90 mph on small roads.

3 Terminez les phrases de manière personnelle.

a. You can't smoke in a classroom, you must ...
b. I must wear something nice to the disco, I can't ...
c. He shouldn't eat so many sweets, he'd better ...
d. I have to get up early tomorrow, I can't ...
e. She shouldn't surf the Internet all night long, she should ...

4 En fonction des dessins, construisez des phrases exprimant une recommandation ou une interdiction.

Ex: *Don't drive over 35 mph. / You mustn't drive over 35 mph.*

Insert your money and take your receipt. / You must insert money and take a receipt.

helmet

drive and drink

goggles

safety gloves

5 Utilisez les suggestions pour indiquer ce que Mrs Ward n'aurait pas dû faire.

a. Mrs Ward, 75, slipped on the icy road. (go out)
b. Despite the pain in her knee, she walked to the shops. (continue).
c. Her bag was very heavy on her way back. (buy)
d. She sat down on a bank and caught a bad cold. (stop)

6 À votre avis, qu'aurait dû faire Mrs Ward ?

7 Lisez le paragraphe et dîtes comment Brian aurait dû se comporter.

Brian decided to go for a walk in the mountains. Although it was February, it was a beautiful sunny day. He didn't tell anyone at his hotel where he was going. He wore trainers, jeans and a jacket. He carried a packet of crisps, some chewing gum and a can of coca cola. Half way up, it started to snow. He decided to go on.

8 Write 8 lines about a bad experience in your life. (or in the life of someone you know well.)Say what you (she / he / they) should / shouldn't / could have done to avoid it.

remember

Pour donner et suivre des instructions, on utilise l'impératif ou bien les modaux *can't, mustn't, must*, et son équivalent *have to*.

- → **Don't take** photographs during the ceremony, take them later. *Ne faites pas de photos pendant la cérémonie, prenez-les après.*
- → Vehicles **mustn't run** on the hard shoulder. *Les véhicules ne doivent pas rouler sur la bande d'arrêt d'urgence.*
- → **You can't keep** this information secret : you must speak about it to your boss, it is essential. *Tu ne peux pas cacher cette information, tu dois en parler à ton patron, c'est capital.*
- → **I have to work** until 5:30 every day, it's in my contract. *Il faut que je travaille jusqu'à 5h 30 tous les jours, c'est dans mon contrat.*

Pour faire des recommandations ou donner des conseils, on emploie le plus souvent *should / shouldn't / had better / had better not / if I were you, I wouldn't…* .

- → I think you **should think** carefully before doing anything. *Je crois que tu devrais réfléchir avant d'agir.*
- → **You'd better not** interrupt him ; he would get mad. *Tu n'as pas intérêt à l'interrompre, il se fâcherait.*
- → **If I were you, I would** apply for this job. *À ta place (si j'étais toi), je postulerais pour cet emploi.*

Pour exprimer le regret ou la critique, d'une action ou d'une situation qui aurait dû ou n'aurait pas dû arriver, on emploie *should have* ou *shouldn't have* + V au participe passé.

- → He **should have got up** immediately when his alarm-clock rang. He **shouldn't have fallen** asleep again, now he is late. *Il aurait dû se lever tout de suite quand son réveil a sonné. Il n'aurait pas dû se rendormir, maintenant il est en retard.*

Vocabulary

Verbs / verbes

advise *conseiller*
ensure (that) / make sure (that) *s'assurer que*
extinguish *éteindre*
guess *deviner*
hide *cacher*
manufacture *fabriquer*
pull over *se garer sur le côté de la route*
sit properly *se tenir droit (assis)*
tie up *nouer / attacher*

Nouns / noms

an applicant *un candidat*
an arrow *une flèche*
an assembly point *une zone de regroupement*
a (car) breakdown *une panne*
the confidence *la confiance*
earplugs *boules Quiès ©*
a habit *une habitude*
the hard shoulder *la bande d'arrêt d'urgence*
an extinguisher *un extincteur*
an injury *une blessure*
a label *une étiquette*
a motorist *un automobiliste*
a motorway *une autoroute*
a pad *un bloc-notes*
a rescuer *un sauveteur*
safety rules *les règles de sécurité*
the skin *la peau*
a tyre *un pneu*
warning lights *les feux de détresse*
weight loss *perte de poids*

Adjectives / adjectifs

compulsory *obligatoire*
confident *confiant*
shy *timide*

Expressions / expressions

be self-confident *avoir confiance en soi*
don't accept a lift *refusez qu'on vous emmène*
I'm scared to death *je suis mort(e) de peur*
it was just a joke *c'était pour plaisanter*
straight in the eye *droit dans les yeux*

unit 8

Comparing facts and figures

contact

B1

1 **Listen to the first part of the radio broadcast and choose the right answers.**

a. Hema is: Thai – Indian – Chinese – Vietnamese.
b. Hong Gam is: Mexican – Indian – Japanese – Vietnamese.
c. Hema will prepare a recipe for: biryani – vegetable curry – chicken korma – chapatti.
d. For Hema, British food is: good – bland – blond – blended.

2 **Listen again and classify the adjectives you hear in the right comparative form.**

tasty – nice – excellent – hot – strong – rich – plain – colourful – fattening – varied

+	–	=

fOcus

Our breads have more flavour than the English ones.
Our food is hotter than English food.
But it is as varied as British food.
It is less rich and less fattening than yours.
In fact, it's better for your health.

- *Relevez les adjectifs des énoncés 2, 3 et 4 ainsi que les éléments qui permettent d'établir des comparaisons de supériorité, d'infériorité et d'égalité.*
- *Comment traduire* than *et* as *?*
- *Comment construit-on le comparatif de supériorité avec un nom?*
- *Quel adjectif est devenu* better *? Quels autres adjectifs ont un comparatif irrégulier ?*

Action

1 Use the different forms of comparatives : =, + or – .

a. Chinese food is ... German food. (– fattening)
b. Indian food is ... French food (= varied)
c. Continental breakfasts are ... English breakfast (not = healthy).
d. Whisky is ... beer (+ strong).

2 Compare traditional restaurants and fast food restaurants.

expensive – homelike – noisy – popular – comfortable – cheap – convenient – quick – impersonal – friendly

B1

3 Listen to Hong Gam's interview and write the comparative form of the adjectives you hear.

a. Do you think British food is (tasteless) Hema says...
b. And our nems are (crispy) an Indian poppadom!
c. I think catfish is (good) any fish you have here.
d. It's (healthy).

4 Give advice to your friend for a healthy diet.

Ex: *butter / olive oil* ➡ *You should use less butter and more olive oil.*

a. fruit / bread
b. ham / fish
c. red meat / chicken
d. Coca Cola / water
e. fruit juice / beer
f. potato / green vegetables
g. water / soft drinks

Chat time

1. You are going to share a flat with your friend.
Read the two adverts and compare the two flats with your friend.

B1

WEST END OF EDINBURGH NEW 2- BEDROOM FLAT,

Ground floor, fully furnished, TV, small kitchen, big bathroom with shower, one big lounge facing South Central heating, free private car park next to big shopping mall and bus stop

£408 per month, electricity included

tel 0131 313 1123

Edinburgh city centre, (off Princes Street)

2-bedroom flat, 2nd floor; old Victorian house, partly furnished. Large fitted kitchen, small bathroom with bath, fully carpeted lounge; stoves* + fire place*
Private entrance, within walking distance of all facilities. Parking space available (phone 0131 657 5194 for tariff)

£395 per month
tel 0131 667 6515

* a stove *un poêle* – a fire place *une cheminée.*

B1

2. Now, present the flat you have chosen to the class.

unit 8

B1

Harrods, a different world

Harrods in Knightsbridge, London, the greatest department store in the world, has more extravagant items for sale than any other store under the sun.

In the days before faxes and e-mails, Harrods had a cable address "Everything London". These two words summed up the magical philosophy of the world's most celebrated store.

Harrods is also a place for lovers of facts and figures: for example, 111,500 square meters with almost 74,000 square meters of selling space ! Up to 300,000 customers visit the store on certain days. The staff is composed of more than 5000 persons from over 50 different countries and 330 departments are spread on seven selling floors. A fleet of 47 delivery vehicles make up to 225,000 deliveries every year. 22 restaurants or places to eat offer a wider range of food than anywhere else, and 11,500 light bulbs turn Harrods into a Christmas tree each night… Harrods is the only department store to have started as a grocery shop (in 1849) and the Food Halls are still the heart and soul of the business. There, from the most humble potato to Italian white truffles at around £250 per 100g, Harrods can supply "everything, for everybody, everywhere."

From luxuries like the finest (and most expensive) jewellery, beauty treatment and interior design, to bizarre services like valet parking and dog-coat fitting, Harrods lives up to its world-wide reputation for providing "all things, for all people, everywhere".

Each floor has a variety of departments such as men's designer collections on the lower ground floor, antiques on the second floor or the customer accounts bureau on the fifth floor. There is also a travel agency and a lot of other services…

What can you get in Harrods? Everything! Here is Harrods's highly selective A to Z:

A could be for Aircraft (sold back in 1919) or Alligator (once bought here as a Christmas present), **B** for bookbinding* and **C** for carpets, **D** for Decoration, **E** could be for Everything or for Elephants (a baby elephant was bought at Harrods as a present for Ronald Reagan)… **L** for Ladies' Club, **M** for millions, **N** for Nursery, **O** for Orchestra, (because of the free concerts), **P** for Pipers, (the popular Harrods bagpipers* play in the store every day); **R** for Removals*, **T** for Tourism, **U** for Undertaking* (Sigmund Freud being one of the famous Harrods' embalmees'), **Y** for Yachts and **Z** for Zoo (live poultry in 1917 but any pet today, even the least common pets).

Harrods truly is a different world.

Adapted from
http://harrods-department-store.visit-london-england.com

help

bookbinding *la reliure*
bagpipers *joueurs de cornemuse*
removals *déménagements*
undertaking *les obsèques*

Anticipating

1 Look at the photo and the title and choose the right statement.

a. This text is about a historic castle in London.
b. It talks about a famous department store in London.
c. It presents a famous museum in London.

2 Describe the photo.

Comprehension

3 Read the text and complete the missing information.

	Surface of selling space
300,000	
	Number of employees
330	
	Number of restaurants
	Number of selling floors
	Number of deliveries a year
11,500	
	Price for 100g of Italian white truffles

4 What's the English for...?

a. un service de parking par voiturier (§3)
b. des ampoules électriques (§2)
c. des animaux familiers (§5)
d. des défunts (§5)

5 What's the French for...?

a. items (introduction)
b. the customer accounts bureau (§4)
c. its worldwide reputation (§3)
d. the heart and soul (§2)

6 Right or wrong? Justify all your answers with elements from the text.

a. The first store was a restaurant.
b. More than 300,000 customers visit the store every day.
c. You can buy anything in Harrods.
d. You can book a Mediterranean cruise at Harrods.
e. You can't buy animals there.
f. You can buy cheap items and expensive ones.

fOcus

Harrods, the greatest department store in the world...
... the finest and most expensive jewellery,
... even the least common ones (pets).

- *Comment appelle-t-on cette forme de comparaison ?*
- *Comment traduit-on « le plus » + un adjectif court, « le plus » + un adjectif long ?*
- *Comment traduit-on « le moins » ?*

>> Training n°5

nOw in French

7 Répondez en français aux questions suivantes.

a. Quelle surface totale occupe Harrods ?
b. Donnez trois exemples d'achats particuliers, possibles chez Harrods.
c. Citez cinq rayons en expliquant ce que le client peut y acheter.
d. Sur quel slogan Harrods a-t-il bâti sa réputation ? Relevez les deux manières de le dire.

Writing

B1

8 Answer the questions in order to write a summary of the text.

a. What is Harrods and where is it located?
b. How many people work there and how many departments can you find?
c. What type of items can you buy? Give some examples.
d. Why is Harrods truly different?

9 Compare Harrods with your favourite department store. (price, choice, service, quality, convenience...)

unit 8

More and more

TRANSPORT AND TRAVEL

B1

1

THE FASTEST MOTORCYCLE SPEED

Dave Campos, from America, riding a 7-m long streamliner named Easyriders, set an absolute speed record with an average speed of 518.450 km/h, at Bonneville Salt Flats, Utah, USA, on July 14, 1990. The Streamliner weighed 1133.9 kg (2,500 lb) and was powered by two 1,500 cc Harley-Davidson engines.

THE MOST VALUABLE CAR

The most remarkable of Ettore Bugatti's cars was the Type 41 Royale. This car is six-meter-long with a wheelbase of 4.3 meters and a 12.7-liter, eight-cylinder engine. It has a three-speed gearbox, reaching 145 km/h in second gear. Ettore had planned a series limited to 25 cars exclusively for royals but only six were built. All six Royales are very pricey*: $15 million each.

1. What do these figures correspond to: 1133.9? – 15? – 145? – 26?

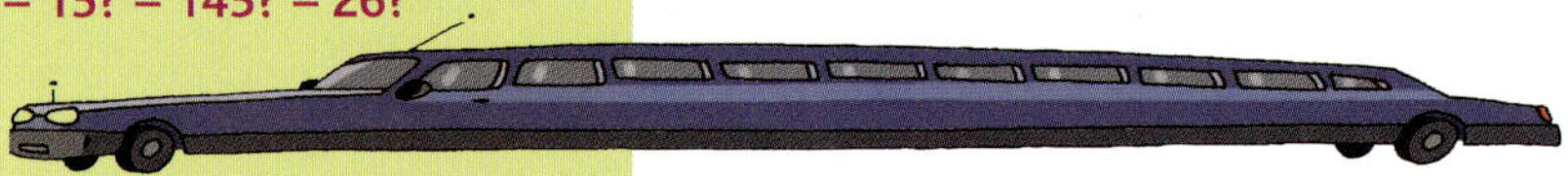

THE LONGEST CAR

The longest car is a 30.5-m long, 26-wheeled limousine, designed by Jay Ohrberg of Burbank, California, USA. Used mainly in films and exhibitions, it has got a swimming pool with diving board and a king-sized waterbed. People can drive it as a rigid vehicle, or it can be bent in the middle.

THE SMALLEST MOTORCYCLE

Tom Wiberg (Sweden) has built a motorcycle and rode it for a distance of more than 10 m in 2003. The micro machine has a wheelbase of 80 mm, a seat height of 65 mm and weighs 1.1 kg. Its top speed is 2 km/h.

Adapted from www.guinnessworldrecords.com/

2. Give information about the people's nationalities, the places and dates of records.
3. Which record is the most interesting for you? Why?

*pricey *onéreux*.

2

B1

NEW YORK'S LIGHTHOUSE

outlook

Considered as the most famous structure built by modern man, the 1,250-foot (381 meters) Empire State Building has dominated the New York City skyline since its completion on May 1, 1931. At that time, it was the most ambitious architectural project in the annals of the western world, the world's tallest skyscraper and New York's proudest achievement.

Though now surpassed in height, the building is America's most imposing National Historic Landmark and the best-known skyscraper in the world with about 4 million visitors every year. The most famous building of the 20th century has been visited by many of its famous people – from President Franklin Roosevelt, Winston Churchill, kings, queens and heads of states to entertainment icons like Paul Mac Cartney and... the legendary King Kong himself!

The most important figures about the Empire State Building: 6,500 windows – 1,860 steps – 73 elevators operating at speeds of up to 427 meters per minute – 60,000 tons of steel – weight: 365,000 tons...

It was completed in one year and 45 days, working seven days per week.

Adapted from an ESBO brochure

4. Pick up all the superlatives about the Empire State Building. Are they appreciative or depreciative?
5. When was it built? How long did it take to build it?
6. Where is it located?
7. Write the following figures into letters: 1,860 – 356,000.

B1

3

ANCHORAGE, THE NORTHERN-MOST BIG CITY IN THE US

8. Write the number of inhabitants of Anchorage in full letters.
9. How high is Mount McKinley? Convert it into metres.
10. What happened in 1964 in Alaska?
11. Why are there so many pilots in Alaska?
12. Write a similar paragraph about your home city or another important city. Use comparative and / or superlative forms.

Location

Anchorage sits at the base of the Chugach mountains in South-central Alaska. It is as far north as Helsinki, Finland and as far west as Honolulu, Hawaii.

Population

260,283. Anchorage is Alaska's largest city, with 41.5 percent of the state's population.

Aviation

Alaska has about one registered pilot for every 58 residents, six times as many pilots per capita and 14 times as many airplanes per capita as the rest of the USA.

Mountains

You can see the Chugach, Kenai, and Alaska ranges from Anchorage. Mount McKinley (20,320-foot) is the tallest mountain in North America.

Earthquake

On March 27, 1964, the Good Friday shook all South-central Alaska. It is the strongest ever recorded in North America (9.2 on the Richter Scale).

www.anchorage.net/11.cfm

hot line

B1

Comparing

1. Listen to the phone call between a shop assistant at John Lewis and a customer who wants some information about a new coffee maker for his / her office. Fill in the blanks.

Shop assistant	Customer
Hello, John Lewis, ...?	Yes, please, I would like more .... about the new .... you have just advertised.
What would you like to know exactly?	Well, what ....?
The Krups Nespresso is .... but contains a litre.	Is the Philips Senseo ....?
Well, it's only ...... of a litre but it has got a brewing	Which one is ....?
The Gaggia Cubika contains 2 litres.	OK. ....?
It's the Philips model: ...., 5 pounds less than the Krups. And the two other models are £139 each.	Right. Which one is .... to use?
They are all very .... to use.	Anyway, I'll come to the shop to have a look. Thank you very much.
And in the store we have other models. Good bye.	Good bye.

B1

2. Now you phone the local store to get information about their latest models: DVD recorders or LCD screens or motorbikes or..... Ask information to compare them. Your partner is the salesman / saleswoman. Then change roles.

say it

Le groupe de lettres « *est* » peut être accentué [est] comme dans « *the west* » ou non accentué [əst] comme dans « *the biggest* ».

a. Classez les mots suivants selon leur accentuation. Dites-les à voix haute, puis vérifiez avec l'enregistrement.
longest – harvest – warmest – richest – chest – highest – pest – nicest – greatest – arrest – nest – quest – fittest – youngest – crest – busiest – test.

b. À quelle catégorie appartiennent les mots non accentués ?

1 Réécrivez ces énoncés avec des adjectifs signifiant le contraire.

Ex: *England is smaller than France.*
➡ *France is larger than England.*

a. Villages are quieter than cities.
b. Forests are cleaner than villages.
c. Life in the countryside is cheaper than in big cities.
d. A job in a hospital is more difficult than a job in an office.

2 Complétez ces phrases à l'aide du comparatif de supériorité (+), d'infériorité (–) ou d'égalité (=).

a. The convolutions and nerve cells of the human brain are (– numerous) / the dolphin's.
b. The human brain is (– quick) / a computer at solving arithmetical operations.
c. After birth the brain continues to grow at a much (+ fast) rate / the rest of the body.

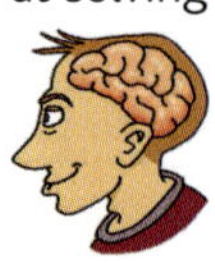

d. A neuron is (= complex) / an entire small computer.

3 Choisissez le comparatif (+, –, =) qui donnera du sens aux informations suivantes.

a. Heathrow Airport is (busy) Paris CDG.
b. Being self-employed is (interesting) working for a company.
c. A nurse's working day is (long) a secretary's.
d. A salesgirl is (well-paid) a manager.

4 Thomas Ross cherche à implanter une nouvelle usine de production, soit en Allemagne, soit en Espagne. Comparez les deux villes possibles à partir des informations du tableau.

	Valdepeñas (Spain)	Königswinter (Germany)
climate	warm	chilly
wages (per hour)	€11.15	€13.98
factory space	cheap	expensive
rate of unemployment	high	low
international airport	far	near

5 Retrouvez la forme de base des adjectifs soulignés.

David Bekham is not the most talented British player but he is one of the best. His last match wasn't his easiest victory; but he said his match at the World Cup was one of his worst ones. He and his wife Victoria are among the wealthiest people in Britain and Victoria is one of the sexiest mothers of three children in UK!

6 Écrivez les adjectifs de cet extrait d'article au superlatif ou au comparatif.

Official: Summer 2006 was the (long), (hot) continuous period experienced in Britain. The five months from May to September were (warm) than any equivalent summer since 1659. The temperature (16.2°C) was two degrees (high) than the average for this time of year. The (warm) month ever was July. The figures show that global warming is having a considerable impact on the British Isles.

Adapted from *The Observer*, October 15th, 2006

7 Complétez avec *as*, *than*, *of* ou *in*.

"Greenside Hotel" is under new management. The prices per night are as cheap ...... before but the breakfast menu is more balanced ...... last year; it's also less fattening ...... before. This place offers the best prices ...... the area and the most picturesque atmosphere ...... the moment.

8 Trouvez 9 adjectifs se rapportant à la nourriture dans la grille ; choisissez en deux pour parler de vos goûts.

S	V	T	G	O	O	D	T
S	R	P	L	A	I	N	A
P	V	A	R	I	E	D	S
I	R	I	C	H	H	O	T
C	H	E	A	L	T	H	Y
Y	O	W	B	L	A	N	D

remember

Pour comparer une personne ou une chose à une ou plusieurs autres, on utilise le comparatif. Il existe trois comparatifs : supériorité, infériorité et égalité.

- **Le comparatif de supériorité** : plus + adjectif + (que)
  - Adjectifs courts (une syllabe ou se terminant par « y ») : adjectif + *-er* + (*than*)
  - Adjectifs longs (deux syllabes et plus) : ***more*** + adjectif + (*than*)
  - → This office is nicer and more convenient than the other one. *Ce bureau est plus beau et plus pratique que l'autre.*

Remarque : **de plus en plus...** : adjectif + ***-er*** and adjectif + ***-er*** ou ***more and more*** + adjectif.
→ He works faster and faster. *Il travaille de plus en plus vite.* This job is getting more and more interesting. *Ce travail devient de plus en plus intéressant.*

- **Le comparatif d'infériorité** : moins + adjectif + (que) = ***less*** + adjectif + (*than*)
  → This company is less competitive than before. *L'entreprise est moins compétitive qu'auparavant.*

Pour un nom, on utilise ***more*** + nom + ***than*** (supériorité) ou ***less*** + nom + ***than*** (infériorité).

- **Le comparatif d'égalité** : aussi + adjectif + (que) = ***as*** + adjectif + ***as***

Dans les phrases négatives, on peut aussi utiliser : ***not so*** + adjectif + ***as***.
→ The new manager is not so demanding as the previous one. *Le nouveau manager n'est pas aussi exigeant que le précédent.*

Pour comparer une personne ou une chose à l'ensemble de sa catégorie, on utilise le superlatif. Il existe deux superlatifs : supériorité et infériorité.

Le complément est introduit par ***in*** s'il s'agit d'un lieu et par ***of*** dans les autres cas.

- **Le superlatif de supériorité** : le plus + adjectif (+ de)
  - Adjectifs courts : ***the*** + adjectif + ***-est***
  - → She is the nicest student in the class. *C'est l'étudiante la plus agréable de la classe.*
  - Adjectifs longs : ***the most*** + adjectif
  - → He is the most efficient worker in the company. *C'est l'employé le plus efficace de l'entreprise.*

- **Le superlatif d'infériorité** : le moins + adjectif = ***the least*** + adjectif
  → This is the least dangerous route. *C'est la route la moins dangereuse.*

Modifications orthographiques

- Adjectifs d'une seule syllabe avec consonne + voyelle + consonne → consonne finale doublée.
  big → **bigger** → the big**gest**
- Adjectifs terminés par « y » → -ier : happy → happ**ier** → the happ**iest**
- Irrégularités : good → better → the best ; bad → worse → the worst ; far → farther → the farthest ; northern → the northernmost

Vocabulary

Verbs / verbes
supply *fournir*
weigh *peser*

Nouns / noms
an earthquake *un tremblement de terre*
a bulb *une ampoule*
a delivery *une livraison*
flavour *du goût*
a lighthouse *un phare*
noodles *des nouilles*
a pet *un animal familier*
a recipe *une recette*
a skyscraper *un gratte-ciel*
weight *le poids*

Adjectives / adjectifs
bland *fade*
convenient *pratique*
efficient *efficace*
fattening *qui fait grossir*
healthy *sain*
homelike *accueillant*
hot (nourriture) *épicé*
leading *de pointe*
plain *ordinaire*
pricey *onéreux*
sharp *net, aigu*
spicy *épicé*
tasty *qui a du goût*
wide *large*

Cardinal numbers / nombres cardinaux
100 one hundred
101 one hundred and one
165 one hundred and sixty-five
500 five hundred
1,000 one thousand
1,400 one thousand four hundred
10,000 ten thousand
700,000 seven hundred thousand
1,000,000 one million
3,692,000 three million, six hundred and ninety-two thousand
one billion *un milliard*

unit 9 Shopping

contact

Department Store Guide

- **Ground floor:** Books, music and video, toys.
- **First floor:** Perfumery and cosmetics, ladies' fashion and shoes, accessories.
- **Second floor:** Men's fashion, sportswear.
- **Third floor:** Housewares, giftwares, cafeteria and toilets.

B1

1 Listen to the dialogue and answer the questions.

a. What are Jeff and Lizzie looking for? Why?
b. What size is Jeff?
c. What does the salesman offer Jeff?

2 Focus on their opinions.

a. Say what Jeff disagrees about: he doesn't like ...; he'd rather...
b. Say what the salesman agrees about: he thinks the purple jacket is ...
c. Say what Lizzie disagrees about: she thinks brand-name clothes are ...

3 Complete the chart with the information about the 4 items Jeff tries on.

Items	Size	Colour / pattern	Price	Qualities	Problems

focus

I don't think so.
Yes, I agree with you.
You are right.
For me, this jacket is nicer.
I disagree with you.

- *Relevez 2 expressions pour exprimer son accord et 2 expressions pour exprimer son désaccord.*
- *Traduisez l'énoncé « I agree with you » et comparez avec la structure employée en français.*
- *Relevez une expression synonyme de « In my opinion ».*

Action

1 Answer the salesperson and give your opinion as in the example.

	Ex: **Salesman:** This cap is a first-quality item. (**You:** Yes / nice) ➡ **You:** Yes, I agree with you / you are right. I think it's very nice. **S:** And it's not expensive at all for this design and quality. (**You:** No / expensive) ➡ **You:** No, I don't agree with you / I don't think so. For me, it's too expensive.		
	**S:** The price of this lipstick is sensational. (**You:** Yes / cheap). **S:** And the colour is really lovely! (**You:** No / ugly)		
	**S:** These sneakers are in fashion. (**You:** No / colourful). **S:** But they are comfortable! (**You:** No / tight)		

B1

2 Listen to dialogue n°2 and answer the questions.

a. What is Alison looking for? What size is she?
b. Which pair does she like? Does the pair fit? How much is it?
c. What does Alison prefer? What sort of fabric is it?
d. What does Alison agree about? How does she pay?

3 Reorder the sentences in two columns: what the salesperson says and what the customer says.

I'm looking for... Can I help you? I'm size ... What colour would you like? What size are you? I'd like ... .The fitting room is over there. I like this ... . How much is it? It's ... . Can I try it on? Yes, it fits well. How are you paying? By credit card. Does it fit? OK. I'll take it.

Chat time

Student A: You are a customer in a department store and you answer the salesperson's questions. Agree or disagree with him / her.
Student B: see page 152.

B1

Ex: *I'd like to buy.... / I prefer.... / I don't think so. / I think it's..... / I agree with you, but....*

Item			
Size	40	M	small
Colour, pattern	grey or black checked pattern	white with red or blue stripes	dark green or blue no pattern / plain
Price	?	?	?
Fitting	too tight	It fits well	/
Opinion	Yes, trendy but expensive	Yes, cheap but not a very good quality	Yes, convenient and large enough
Payment	by credit card	in cash	by cheque

unit 9

B1

Why don't you shop on-line?

I know you have your reasons. Yet, I shop on-line regularly and I can answer all your objections...

1. You say it isn't secure...

This one is the first objection. Fortunately, it is not accurate*. Most online shopping is highly secure and only getting better. Moreover, it's more secure than shopping in person because credit cards and receipts can be stolen in department stores by shoplifters* or dishonest employees.

Good online retailers* take security as seriously as you. After all, they want your business. Therefore, they protect your sensitive information by encrypting it and sending and receiving it over secure lines. So if there are no security policies* on your shopping site, don't shop there.

2. You think it's more expensive because you'll pay for shipping charges*...

Yes, you will, but there are "free shipping" offers. Usually, shipping charges are simply part of the cost of shopping on line. Just as you pay for gasoline, parking, and home delivery charges in conventional shopping. Yet you can save on shipping by purchasing more than one item with your order. Moreover when you search the Internet for the best price, you always save money.

3. You want more selection...

One nice thing about shopping on-line is that the selection is frequently greater than in a physical store. For example, there are not many bookstores which can have the space to display as many titles as Amazon.com.

4. You can't touch or try things on first...

But do you really need to? Obviously not with stuff like books and CDs. For clothes and items you want to see first, go to the local store and touch them or try them on. Then search the Internet, buy it on-line and find the best possible price.

5. You think it's hard to find stuff* on-line...

Anybody who's ever spent almost an hour trying to find something in a large store appreciates how easy the Internet makes finding products. Just enter the name of the item you are looking for into the search engine and you'll probably find hundreds of places to purchase it.

6. You enjoy getting out of the house to go shopping...

If you enjoy going to the mall or the supermarket, you enjoy it. But instead of enjoying fighting the crowds or searching endlessly for a parking space, you may equally enjoy browsing* on-line from the comfort of your favorite chair, your stereo on and a drink in your hand... No lines... No driving... Just imagine the possibilities.

Adapted from: *www.earthlink.net*

help

accurate *précis, exact*
a shoplifter *un(e) voleur(euse) à l'étalage*
a retailer *un détaillant / (commerce de) vente au détail*
security policies *procédures de sécurité*
shipping charges *frais de transport*
stuff *des choses, des trucs*
browse *flâner*

Anticipating

1 Look at the picture and read the title and the subtitles. Then answer the questions.

a. What is the general topic of the document? Who is supposed to be the author of the title and the subtitles?
b. In your opinion, what does the text aim at?

Comprehension

2 Read the text and find out which of the 6 paragraphs is about:

the large choice among many different goods (n°...) / the pleasure of shopping (n°...) / transport and its cost (n°...) / the risks of fraud (n°...) / the difficulty to surf the net (n°...) / the need to see the items before buying (n°...).

3 What's the English for...?

a. renseignements confidentiels (§1)
b. le commerce traditionnel (§2)
c. la livraison à domicile (§2)

4 What's the French for...?

a. encrypting (§1)
b. selection (§3)
c. the search engine (§5)

5 Find in the text what you should or shouldn't do when you shop on-line. Then translate into French.

a. You shouldn't shop at a site if.......
b. You should save on ....
c. You should search ...
d. You should browse online from...

6 Right or wrong? Justify your answer.

a. Online shopping is less secure than conventional shopping.
b. If you shop on-line, you pay for shipping charges but you save on gasoline and parking charges.
c. The selection of items is generally greater when you shop on-line.
d. *Amazon.com* is a physical store which sells books.
e. There are items you don't need to see before buying.
f. It is easier to find something on-line than in a large conventional store.
g. Everybody prefers staying at home instead of going to the mall.

fOcus

moreover (l. 6) **therefore (l. 10)**
but (l. 29, 44) **so (l. 12)**
yet (l. 20) **then (l. 32)**
instead of (l. 44)

- *À quoi servent ces mots ? Comment les appelle-t-on ?*
- *Quels mots expriment la conséquence ? l'opposition ?*
- *Comment construire le verbe qui suit* **instead of** *(paragraphe 6) ?*
- *Relevez, dans le premier paragraphe, 2 mots différents pour exprimer l'adjonction (par exemple* in addition*).*

>> Training Say it, ex. 5 et 6 p. 84

nOw in French

7 Répondez en français à ces questions.

a. Par quels moyens les fraudes sont-elles évitées lors du paiement par Internet ?
b. Comment économiser de l'argent lorsqu'on fait ses achats en ligne ?
c. Est-il facile de trouver sur le net l'article que l'on recherche ? Comment faire ?
d. Pourquoi est-il désagréable de sortir pour faire ses courses ? Citez 3 inconvénients.

Writing

B1

8 Complete the sentences to write a summary of the text.

a. This document tries to demonstrate that people's objections to online shopping are ...
b. The first objection is ... , however, ...
c. When shopping on-line, customers pay for shipping charges, yet they can save money if ... and if ...
d. Moreover, there are many advantages, for example: ... and ...
e. Therefore, shopping sites would like people to purchase items on the net instead of ...

9 Give your opinion.

Do you prefer online shopping or conventional shopping?
(Use 5 different linking words)

Where and when to shop

B1

WORLD'S LARGEST SHOPPING MALLS

1

China Builds Malls on Gigantic Scale

The South China Mall reproduces the look and feel of many of the world' greatest cities and tourist destinations. Here are some highlights of a rendering made by the mall's developer.

Venice
Gondola rides on a canal under bridges with a new Shangri-La Hotel on one bank.

Paris
A re-creation of the Champs-Elysées with a full-size reproduction of the Arc de Triomphe at its center.

Already, four shopping malls in China are larger than the Mall of America. Two, including the South China Mall, are bigger than the West Edmonton Mall in Alberta, which was the world's largest two months ago. And by 2010, China is expected to be home to at least 7 of the world's 10 largest malls.

For the moment, the world's biggest mall is the six-million-square-foot Golden Resources Mall, which opened last October in northwestern Beijing.

How big is six million square feet? That mall spans* the length of six football fields. It is a single, colossal five-story* building where 20,000 employees work – with rows* and rows of shops stacked* on top of more rows and rows of shops – so large that it is hard to navigate among the 1,000 stores and the thousands of shoppers.

In Dongguan, the South China Mall will offer seven million square feet of shopping space – over 1,500 shops – when completed*. It will be a $400 million fantasy land: 150 acres of palm-tree-lined shopping plazas, theme parks, hotels, water fountains, pyramids, bridges and giant windmills. It has a 1.3-mile artificial river circling the complex, which includes districts modeled on the world's seven "famous water cities", and an 85-foot replica of the Arc de Triomphe.

OTHER POINTS OF INTEREST

1. **Southern California**
A giant Imax theatre complex partially encircles this area of the mall which has a reproduction of the Hollywood sign.
2. A teletubbies theme park.
3. Obi, a giant German-based home improvement store.
4. Food court includes Mc Donald's and Pizza Hut restaurants.

* span *s'étendre sur* – five-story *de 5 étages* – rows *des rangées* – stacked *empilé* – completed *terminé*.

Adapted from David Barboza, *The Seoul Times*, Dec. 12, 2006.

1. Read the text and find the names of four large shopping malls. Where are they located?
2. Find details about the two Chinese malls: shopping space, number of shops, type of building. Which one is the largest in the world? Why?
3. Look at the picture. What is it exactly? List the different points of interest.
4. Would you like to shop in one of these huge shopping malls? Give advantages and disadvantages.

SUNDAY SHOPPING

2 your view

B1

5. Where is Nova Scotia? What has the province government just decided?
6. Look at the readers' opinions and tell who is for and who is against Sunday shopping.
7. In the readers' comments find 3 arguments for Sunday shopping and 3 arguments for Sunday rest.
8. Would you enjoy shopping on Sundays? Would you like to work on Sundays? Give your opinion.

CANADA: NOVA SCOTIA LIFTS SUNDAY SHOPPING BAN

Wednesday, October 4, 2006

Retail stores of all kinds can open on Sundays and other holidays, starting this weekend (the only exception is Remembrance Day). Nova Scotia was one of the last Canadian provinces to place Sunday restrictions on retailers.

DO YOU AGREE WITH SUNDAY SHOPPING?

THOMAS (Ottawa): "I absolutely support this ruling. After a day's work Mon to Fri, I simply want to get home – not go out and engage in shopping. Neither do I wish to squeeze in everything on Saturday, when everyone else is trying to do the same thing."

WADE (Halifax): "I've lived in Halifax for 35 years. I've always liked that the big shopping malls and supermarkets were closed on Sundays. Only restaurants, small stores and movie theaters were open. Sunday will no longer be a real day of relaxation anymore. Many people will be left without any leisure time. Are these the benefits of modern technology?"

PAUL (Hamilton): "If you want a 'day of rest' then simply do it. It's not that difficult. No one is forcing you to shop on Sundays."

TARA (Halifax): "I disagree with Sunday shopping as I have seen what happens to workers in Ontario. If you refuse to work Sundays you get less hours. Single mums are forced to work over the weekend when the children are at home."

CELINA (Ottawa): "Sunday shopping now means that store clerks have opportunity to earn more money."

ERIC (Halifax): "Stores are open six days a week, between eight and twelve hours a day. How much more can you possibly shop?"

CBC News: cbc.ca

hot line

B1

Ordering by phone

1. Listen to the dialogue and complete the chart.

Receptionist	Caller
The General Trading Company ....?	Yes, I'd like to ....
Of course. Just a moment. Right. What ....?	....
Can you give me the reference and the	Yes, it's .... Size ....
Is it a .... at £ ....?	Yes ....?
It's .... for postage and packing	When will it be delivered?
Within	OK. That's nice.
How ....?	By ....
Can you give me ...., please ?	Yes, it's 5923 2475 0012 9855 and I'm ....
What's the delivery address, please?	It's ....
Your order has been recorded.	Good.
Thanks for .... Goodbye.......... Have a nice day.	Thank you. Goodbye.

2. Practice more dialogues. You are the caller. If you are the receptionist, see p. 152.

Mail-order catalogue	The House of Bruar	The Green Shop	Home Collection	Liberty by post
Item	a sweatshirt	a compost bin	a lamp	a tie
Reference	HB325GW	CAL67X	54JL09	VU1213
Size	M	large	small	/

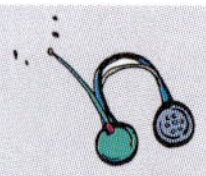

say it

Distinguez le son [e] comme dans *yes* ou *net* du son [ə] comme dans *sir* ou *search*.

a. Écoutez et entourez le son [e], puis soulignez le son [ə].

yet – however – therefore – never – moreover – instead – then – nevertheless – disagree – outlet – credit – department – website – supermarket.

b. Écoutez à nouveau pour vérifier et répétez.

1 Remettez ces mots dans l'ordre pour exprimer l'avis de Jeff.

a. think / nicer / I / brand-name clothes / are.
b. Lizzie / I / disagree / about / with / that.
c. But / right / she / is / says / when / she / it is too expensive.
d. a / buying / prefer / jacket / I / cheaper.
e. nicer / me / the D&G polo-shirt / is / for.

2 Complétez le dialogue.

S: Can ......?

C: Yes, I'd like ......
S: What colour would you like?
C:  or 
S: Plain or with a pattern?

C: With black or white ......
S: This one is very trendy.

C: No ......
S: What about ......?

C: Can I ...... ?
S: Yes, the fitting room is ......
(A moment later)

S: Does it ......?
C: No, ...
S: I agree ...... You need ......  Here it is.
(Later)

C: ....
I ....

3 Répondez en donnant votre avis.

a. I hate watching TV shopping channels.
b. I prefer ordering goods by telephone than by mail.
c. For me, department stores offer more choice than supermarkets.
d. I think brand name clothes are the best.
e. In my opinion, cheap clothes can be very nice too.

4 Complétez ces énoncés par *where / which / who*.

a. Consumers are the people ... purchase goods.
b. Retail outlets are any place ... consumers can buy goods.
c. The Internet has many shopping sites ... sell all types of products.
d. A mail-order catalogue is a book ... consumers can read at home. Then they can order what they like.
e. TV shopping channels employ presenters to show products to viewers ... order and pay by credit card.

5 Choisissez le mot de liaison qui convient pour relier les énoncés ci-dessous.

a. There are small shops near their home (because / yet) they don't buy a lot there.
b. They prefer going to the supermarket (as / however) it's less expensive.
c. The supermarket is two miles from their home; (therefore / moreover) they take the bus to go shopping.
d. At the supermarket, they can buy food. (As a result /In addition) they sometimes purchase clothes or other goods.
e. (However / Besides) the supermarket salespeople are not very friendly.

6 Utilisez *instead of* pour relier ces énoncés.

Ex: *I shouldn't spend a lot. I should save my money.*
➡ *Instead of spending a lot, I should save my money.*
a. I can pay by credit card. I mustn't pay cash.
b. I should shop on-line. I shouldn't go to the mall when it's crowded.
c. I don't like going to different shops for one special product. I prefer searching for it on the net.
d. I should save on shipping charges. I mustn't order only one item.

7 Complétez les phrases suivantes pour donner votre avis.

a. In my opinion, shopping channels are ... because .... However, I think ...
b. To my mind, home delivery is ... Moreover, ... Yet, I'm sure ...

remember

Pour exprimer son accord ou son désaccord, on peut utiliser:

agree / disagree with: → I agree with you. *Je suis d'accord avec toi.* / I disagree with you = I don't agree with you. *Je ne suis pas d'accord avec toi.*

be right / be wrong : → You are right. *Tu as raison.* / He is wrong. *Il a tort.*

Pour préciser ce que l'on pense, on peut utiliser les formes verbales suivantes :

I think **I find** **I believe** **I'm sure**	**that** **Ø**	they fit very well. *Je pense qu'ils/elles vont très bien.* it's too expensive. *Je trouve que c'est trop cher.* I lost the receipt. *Je crois que j'ai perdu la facture.* he'll change his mind. *Je suis sûr(e) qu'il va changer d'avis.*

Pour annoncer que l'on va donner son avis, on peut aussi utiliser les expressions suivantes :

For me *pour moi*
In my view *selon moi*
In my opinion *à mon avis*
To my mind *à mon avis, selon moi*

Pour relier les différents arguments, on utilise les liens logiques (ou mots de liaison).

Les liens logiques expriment plusieurs relations :

la cause (vise à expliquer)	**la conséquence** (vise à conclure)	**l'opposition** (vise à réfuter)	**l'adjonction** (vise à énumérer)	**la concession** (vise à concéder)
because *parce que* **for** *car* **as** *comme*	**so** *ainsi* **therefore / as a result** *par conséquent*	**but** *mais* / **yet** *pourtant* **however** *cependant* **though / although** *bien que* **instead of** (+V-ing) *au lieu de*	**and** *et* **moreover** *de plus* **besides** *d'ailleurs* **in addition** *de plus*	**after all** *après tout* **nevertheless** *néanmoins* **while** *tandis / alors que* **anyway** *de toute façon*

Vocabulary

Verbs / verbes

believe *croire*
deliver *livrer (à domicile)*
order *commander*
pay cash *payer comptant*
purchase / buy *acheter*
save *économiser (sauver)*
sell *vendre*
try on *essayer (des vêtements)*

Nouns / noms

charges *les frais*
a choice *un choix*
crowds *les foules*
a delivery *une livraison*
a department store *un grand magasin*
a fitting room *une cabine d'essayage*
a good *une marchandise*
a mall *un grand centre commercial*
a pattern *un motif*
a receipt *une facture*
a retail outlet *un point de vente*
a retailer / a shopkeeper *un commerçant*
a store / a shop *un magasin / une boutique*
a stripe *une rayure*

Adjectives / adjectifs

checked *à carreaux*
crowded *bondé*
plain *simple (sans motif)*
flowery *à fleurs*
striped *rayé*
tight *serré, étroit*
trendy *à la mode*

Expressions / expressions

pay by cheque *payer par chèque*
pay by credit card *payer par carte bancaire*
pay in cash *payer en espèces*
What size are you? *Quelle est votre taille ?*

unit 10

Telling about experiences

contact

B1

1 **Listen to Alison and her mother (dialogue 1) and complete the sentences with the correct form of the verb.**

a. Have you .... if there was any mail? (see – saw – seen)
b. Have you .... to become an actress? (decide – decided– decides)
c. I have .... for a scholarship. (apply – applying – applied)
d. You have not .... (speak – spoke – spoken)

2 **Listen to the dialogue again and fill in the blanks with the right adverb: *already – ever – just – never - yet.***

a. No Mum, I haven't been downstairs ....
b. I have .... had a shower.
c. I have .... heard about this agency.

fOcus

They have founded a partnership.
I have read in a magazine that ...
Have you ever heard about Tom Hanks or Tom Cruise? Yes, I have.
The postman has just brought the mail.

- *Quelles sont les deux parties d'un verbe conjugué au present perfect ?*
- *Comment se forme le participe passé ? Comment le distingue-t-on du prétérit ?*
- *Le present perfect exprime-t-il des événements datés dans le passé ou non datés ayant un rapport avec le moment où l'on parle ?*
- *Traduisez les trois premiers exemples. Quel est le temps employé en français ? Qu'en est-il pour le dernier énoncé ?*

Action

1 Complete the chart. Refer to the list (*rabats*) if necessary.

base verbale	prétérit	participe passé	base verbale	prétérit	participe passé
see				found	
	was / were			founded	
		decided	play		
hear about			apply		
		had			brought
speak				chose	

2 Write the verbs in the present perfect.

a. I . . . . . just . . . . . a long letter from my best friend but I . . . . . back yet. (receive – not write)
b. The agency . . . . . already . . . . . me and they . . . . . a lot of questions. (call – ask)
c. Tom Hanks and Tom Cruise . . . . . to help students. (choose)
d. . . . . . you ever . . . . . an interesting advertisement? (see)
e. Alex . . . . . never . . . . . any problems at school, he . . . . . always . . . . . a good student. (have – be).

3 Choose between the present perfect and the past simple, then translate the sentences.

a. My grandparents (have never been / never were) big travellers but last year, they (have spent / spent) a week in New York.
b. Yesterday, we (have heard / heard) about a new program for students.
c. Teddy, (have you ever seen / did you ever see) this film? Yes, I (have seen / saw) it two years ago when I (have been / was) at college.
d. Alison (has applied / applied) for a scholarship in January 2007 and three months later, she (has entered / entered) an art school in Los Angeles.
e. Manchester United (haven't lost / didn't lose) against Chelsea last Saturday, they (have drawn / drew) with Chelsea. *draw *faire match nul.*

B1

4 Listen to Alison and her mother (dialogue 2), then answer the questions.

a. What has Alison just received?
b. What have the actors founded?
c. What do the people from the 'Creative Artist Agency' think about Alison's project?

Chat time

Make dialogues with your partner. Use the example and the illustrations.

B1

A: Have you ever watched a marathon (on TV)?
B: Yes, I have.
A: When was it?
B: It was last year.
A: And er... have you ever run a marathon?
B: No, I haven't. I'm not athletic.

help

last ..., when I was..., ... ago, in ... I prefer badminton. There's no skating-rink here. I'm afraid to fall. Water scares me. It's too dangerous. The cord can break. I'd rather lie in the sun. I can't swim.

go surfing

play beach volley

go ice-skating

practise bungee-jumping

unit 10

B2

Businessman and adventurer on earth and in space

Richard Branson, the flamboyant British entrepreneur who has declared 'I want Virgin to be as well-known as Coca Cola' is a man with a many-sided personality.

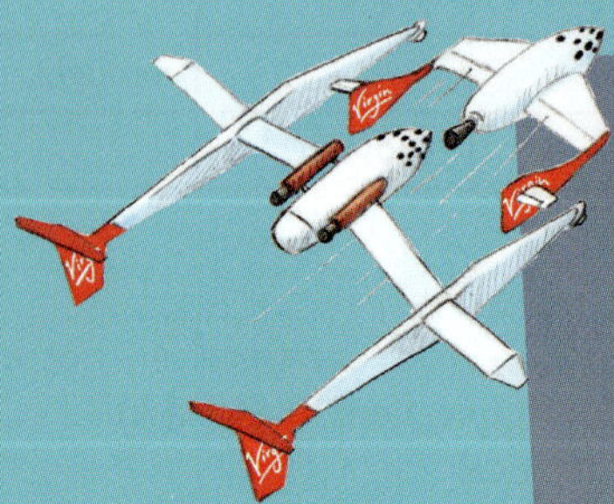

Born in 1950, Richard Branson grew up in a traditional family. He was only an average* student, however, at 20, he founded a mail-order record company. As he was virgin in business, he called it *Virgin*. Then he opened a music shop on Oxford Street, London. A few years later, he built a recording studio and started to sign contracts with the most famous singers and groups of the 1970s. Since 1984, he has built an empire of many successful companies estimated at £3bn*.

His group, under the *Virgin* banner, employs 25,000 people over three continents and includes multimedia stores, planes, trains, financial services, cinemas, cosmetics, wedding gowns*, cola, sports-centres, mobile phones and space tourism.

For the past 30 years, he has been one of the men Britons admire a lot for his simplicity and his involvement* in charities and in new technologies. In 2006, he donated a billion euros to research ecological fuels and the *Virgin* Group has announced plans to invest €3 bn in renewable energy. His fame is also due to his sports feats. In 1986, he broke the recorded time in sailing across* the Atlantic Ocean, and in 1987, he did the same thing aboard a hot air balloon. He repeated the exploit five years later over the Pacific Ocean, covering a distance of 6,700 miles.

Unfortunately, 'the entrepreneur in a sweater' as many people call him, has been meeting with difficulties for a few years. In 2001, he sold part of his record business and of *Virgin Atlantic Airlines*. But he is optimistic and says he has been taking risks since the age of 20 and will continue. Another airline, *Virgin America*, is planned in 2007. Since 2004, Branson and his team have been working with scientists on a commercial space program. The first passengers should fly aboard the *Virgin Galactic*, his space-cruiser, by the end of 2008.

SRB (Sir Richard Branson) often says: ' I have been working very hard since I was twenty and have had much success, but the most significant in my life are my wife and two children'.

Adapted from *Focus magazine*, Nov. 2006.

help

average *moyen*
bn (billion) *milliard*
a wedding gown *une robe de mariée*
involvement *participation, implication*
sailing across *en traversant à la voile*

Anticipating

1 Look at the photo. Read the title and the introduction. Then answer the questions.

a. What is the man like? What's his job?
b. Which word of the title can you match with the picture?
c. Which words in the introduction echo the title?

Comprehension

2 Read the document and pick out information about:

a. his beginnings in business.
b. his business success.
c. his business variety.
d. his human qualities.
e. his business problems.
f. his plans for the future.
g. his sporting life.
h. his family life.

3 What's the English for...?

a. une personnalité complexe (intro)
b. un marchand de disques par correspondance (§1)
c. la chose la plus importante (§5)

4 What's the French for...?

a. his fame is also due to (§3)
b. his sports feats (§3)
c. renewable energy (§3)

nOw in French

5 Répondez en français aux questions suivantes.

a. Quelles sont les trois premières entreprises créées par Branson ?
b. Quelle phrase montre le mieux l'ambition professionnelle de R. Branson ?
c. Pourquoi *Virgin* est-elle comparée à un empire ?
d. Comment justifiez-vous le terme « adventurer » dans le titre ?

fOcus

Since 1984, he has built an empire.
He has been meeting with difficulties for a few years.
I have been working very hard since I was twenty.

- *Quels mots veulent dire 'depuis' ? Lequel introduit la durée de l'action ? son commencement ?*
- *L'action exprimée par le verbe dure t-elle encore ou est-elle terminée ?*
- *Traduisez les exemples. Quel temps employez-vous en français ? Est-ce le même en anglais ?*
- *Quelles sont les deux constructions du* present perfect *employé avec* for *ou* since *?*
- *Transformez les exemples en questions commençant par* **how long**. *Traduisez.*

>> Training n°5, 6 et 7

Writing

B1

6 Write full sentences in combining A+B.

A

a. Richard Branson created *Virgin*...
b. Many music stars have recorded...
c. At 36, he won...
d. British people esteem Branson very highly because...
e. *Virgin*'s activity is...
f. The *Virgin* chairman has crossed...
g. Branson's business results have been...
h. But as he is optimistic...
i. The most important in his life has always been...

B

j. songs on *Virgin* records.
k. very diversified all over the world.
l. he doesn't look pretentious.
m. in 1970.
n. his first sailing trophy while crossing the Atlantic.
o. his wife and his children.
p. the Atlantic and the Pacific in a balloon.
q. less satisfactory for a few years.
r. he is very confident in his future.

7 Tell about a famous businessman / woman or a star: appearance, career, success, family life, problems (60 words minimum).

About brilliant careers and

B2

1 A RICH AND GENEROUS NOVELIST

1. What do you know about J. K. Rowling's family life?
2. Has she always lived in Scotland?
3. How many novels did she write? Were they successful?
4. In what way is she a 'generous novelist'?

Harry Potter has made J. K. Rowling an international author who has sold over 300 million copies of her fantasy novels so far*.

Joanne Kathleen*Rowling was born in 1965 in Yate, 12 miles northeast of Bristol. After studying French at the university, she spent a year in Paris and then worked as a bilingual secretary for Amnesty International in London. In 1992, she went to Portugal to teach English, married a journalist while there and divorced one year later, just after Jessica's birth.

How has she become a novelist? 'I have always wanted to be a writer, even when I was a child and I have been writing for most of my life' she says, 'I was starting *Harry Potter and the Philosopher Stone* when my mother died in 1990. I think her long battle against multiple sclerosis* has contributed to my fear*of death, which is an important theme in the *Harry Potter* seven novels.'

She has been staying in Scotland since 1994, first in a rented flat in Edinburgh and now in a luxurious 19th-century house in Perth, where she lives with her second husband, an anaesthetist, and David, born in 2003.

With a fortune estimated at €1bn, Joanne is generously involved in charity. She helps combating poverty across the globe and gives a lot of money to medical research and to the NGO* *Médecins Sans Frontières*. She is planning to publish an encyclopaedia of the Harry Potter world and she has already promised to donate all her profits to charity.

* so far *jusqu'à présent* – multiple sclerosis *sclérose en plaques* – the fear *la peur* – NGO non- governmental organization *une ONG.*

B2

2 A LARGE-HEARTED GENIUS

Born in 1955, William Henry Gates has always been a brilliant student. He co-founded the Microsoft Corporation in 1975. He has been its chairman* for years and has amassed a huge* fortune. In fact, he has been the richest person on earth since 1993.

In 1994, he married Melinda French and they have been living in Washington with their three children since then. Five years later, they created the Bill & Melinda Gates Foundation which is one of the largest charitable foundation in the world. The Gates have donated more than $29bn since the year 2000 for global* health and US education. The foundation helps American students who belong to ethnic minorities to pursue their university studies in mathematics, science, engineering and public health.

Bill thinks that it has become urgent to ameliorate the American education system. So, in the summer 2006, he decided that from July 2008, he would keep his post as Microsoft's chairman but would spend only 20 percent of his time there and would devote* the rest of his time and energy to the foundation. His goal is to promote school excellence and to permit students with financial needs to reach their fullest potential.

Adapted from *Newsweek* June 26, 2006 and *http://www.gatesfoundation.org/AboutUs/*

* a chairman *un président (entreprise)* – huge *énorme* – global *mondial* – devote to *consacrer à.*

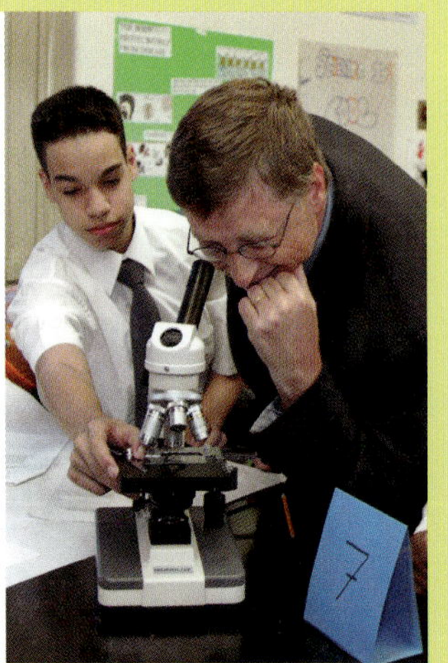

5. How did Bill Gates become famous?
6. What's the name of his foundation? Who can profit by it?

outlook

SPORTS CELEBRITIES HELPING ORDINARY PEOPLE

3

B1

7. Listen and fill in the chart with the information you hear.

Roger FEDERER	Tiger WOODS	Maria SHARAPOVA	Lance AMSTRONG
sport practised	sport practised	sport practised	sport practised ....
nationality	nationality	nationality	nationality ....
donation to...	donation to...	donation to...	donation to... ....

hot line

B1

Joining a new club

1. Listen to the dialogue and say if the statements are right or wrong. Justify your choice.

a. Brandon wants to join a swimming club.
b. He has never been a member of a club.
c. He has moved from Folkestone to Dover.
d. He runs in the junior category.
e. He is a sprinter.
f. There's a training session once a week.
g. The training session is at 5 pm.
h. Brandon will train on Mondays.

B1

2. Make dialogues with your partner. Student A: you are the receptionist of a sports club. Student B: You are Meg or Jack, who want to join a new club. (See page 153) Then change roles.

.... can I help you?	I am .... I'd like to join ....
How long .... practising ....?	For ....
Have you ever .... club?	Yes, I .... a member of .... in ....
Why do .... change?	Because I've just .... and I live in .... now.
The......... everyday, from ... to ... pm, which days .....?	I prefer .... and ....
Fine. See you next .... Good bye.	Thank .... Good ....

say it

Les lettres « ow » se prononcent [au] comme dans *how long* ou bien [əu] comme dans *snow*.

Classez les mots suivants puis écoutez et répétez.

no – now – how – show – slow – brown – down – grown – crown – blow – cow – know – clown – bowl.

1 Utilisez les éléments ci-dessous pour former des énoncés au *present perfect*.

a. Mike / play / rugby.
b. They / go / to the Olympic Games.
c. You / buy / sneakers?
d. No / she / jump / very high.
e. Their team / win / every match.
f. I / never / wear / tracksuits.

2 Employez l'un des adverbes suivants selon le sens de la phrase.
just – yet – never – already – ever

a. I have ... been to another continent because I'm afraid of flying.
b. Have you ... played basketball? No, I hate ball games.
c. I have ... watched polo on TV, but I have never seen cricket.
d. Is the match over? Yes, the referee has ... blown the final whistle.
e. Manchester United have not scored ..., they are going to lose.

3 Choisissez la forme verbale qui convient.

a. *Virgin* (made / has made) its name as a record label in the 70s.
b. Branson (created / has created) an enormous complex of companies.
c. *Virgin Entertainments* (closed / have closed) six stores in Europe in 2001.
d. Branson (published / has published) a magazine when he was 18.
e. He (became / has become) a millionaire.

4 Complétez par *for* ou *since*.

a. ... two years.
b. ... 1980.
c. ... six o'clock.
d. ... a few minutes.
e. ... last June.
f. ... Halloween.
g. ... a long time.
h. ... six hours.
i. ... yesterday morning.
j. ... their marriage.
k. ... four weeks.
l. ... his accident.

5 Pratiquez des mini-dialogues en vous inspirant de l'exemple.

Ex: *A: Have you ever gone rock-climbing?*
B: Yes, I have.
A: When was it?
B: It was last summer.

6 Associez les débuts et les fins de phrases.

a. Michael Schumacher has won ... .
b. The Vendée Globe race has existed...
c. Marion Jones has made ... .
d. I have been practising ... .
e. ... since 1989.
f. ... many TV appearances since the Olympics in Sydney.
g. ... more races than Alain Prost.
h. ... basketball for years, since I was 12.

7 Commencez vos questions par *how long* puis répondez en utilisant *for* ou *since*.

Ex: *play / in this club? / 2 years / last September.*
➡ *How long has Bob been playing in this club?*
➡ *He has been playing there for 2 years / since last September.*

a. Bob / do competition / last year.
b. Bob and his parents / live / in York / 1999.
c. He / go out with Karen / six months.
d. Bob and Karen / study / in a vocational school / 3 years.
e. he / work on weekends / as a waiter / his 19th birthday.

8 Rédigez un paragraphe évoquant vos expériences personnelles (scolaires, professionnelles, sportives...). Minimum 80 mots.

remember

Pour faire le bilan de ce que l'on a fait jusqu'à présent, on emploie le *present perfect*.

- **Construction**

Le verbe au *present perfect* se compose de *HAVE* + PARTICIPE PASSÉ.

→ They **have founded** a partnership. *Ils ont fondé un partenariat.*

→ The postman **hasn't brought** the mail. *Le facteur n'a pas apporté le courrier.*

- **Les adverbes de temps : *already, ever, never, just, not ...yet*, sont fréquemment employés avec le *present perfect*.**

→ You **have already asked** the same question. *Tu as déjà posé la même question.*

→ **Have** you **ever heard** about Tom Hanks? *As-tu déjà entendu parler de Tom Hanks ?*

→ I **have never heard** about this agency. *Je n'ai jamais entendu parler de cette agence.*

→ We **have just received** your letter. *Nous venons (juste) de recevoir votre lettre.*

→ The postman **has not been here yet**. *Le facteur n'est pas encore passé.*

Pour exprimer depuis combien de temps une action se déroule, on conjugue souvent le *present perfect* à la forme en *-ING*. *HAVE BEEN* + V *-ING*

→ The Bransons have been living in London since their marriage.
Les Branson vivent à Londres depuis leur mariage.

- **how long?** permet de demander **depuis combien de temps** l'action se déroule.

→ **How long** has she been swimming?
Elle nage depuis combien de temps ? / Cela fait combien de temps qu'elle nage ?

- **for** indique **la durée** en minutes, heures, jours, mois, années...

→ She has been swimming **for** half an hour.
Elle nage depuis une demi-heure. / Voilà une demi-heure qu'elle nage.

- **since** indique **quand l'action a commencé** : date, événement, période...

→ I have been practising judo **since** 1998 / since my 12th birthday / since last winter...
Je fais du judo depuis 1998 / depuis mon 12e anniversaire / depuis l'hiver dernier...

Vocabulary

Verbs / verbes
- apply for *postuler*
- be in need *être dans le besoin*
- create *créer*
- donate *faire don de*
- find *trouver*
- find out *découvrir*
- found *fonder*
- hear about *entendre parler de*
- need *avoir besoin de*
- promote *promouvoir*
- pursue *poursuivre*
- reach *atteindre*
- train *(s') entraîner*

Nouns / noms
- the ability *la capacité*
- an application form *un formulaire de candidature*
- a scholarship *une bourse*
- a donation *un don*
- a foundation *une fondation*
- health *la santé*
- medical research *la recherche médicale*
- the need *le besoin*
- an NGO *une ONG (Organisation Non Gouvernementale)*
- a partnership *un partenariat*
- poverty *la pauvreté*
- seriousness *le sérieux*
- a training session *une séance d'entraînement*

Adjectives / adjectifs
- large-hearted *au grand cœur*

unit 11

Relating success stories

contact

B1

1 Look at the picture and answer the questions.

a. What is this young man's job?
b. What does he sell?
c. How can his customers order?
d. What is he going to do?

2 Listen to the first part of the dialogue. Choose the right answer.

a. Tony has been nominated (the Young Gardener / the Young Entrepreneur) of the year.
b. As a child, after school he helped his (father / grandfather) in his (shop / garden).
c. At (15 / 16), he found a job as (a gardener / an apprentice) at Jenning's plant (nursery / factory).
d. He (was visiting / visited) the greenhouse when he (was reading / read) an advert.
e. They (looked at / were looking after / were looking for) an apprentice.
f. Two gardeners (were looking for / looked at / were looking after) flowers.

focus

My grandad was working in his garden from morning till evening. While my sister was doing her homework, I was reading gardening magazines. When I saw him, he was phoning.

- *À quelle situation répondent les énoncés : - Deux activités se déroulant au même moment ? – Une activité en cours lorsqu'un événement s'est produit ? Une activité se déroulant dans le passé ?*
- *Comment s'appelle ce temps, comment se construit-il ?*
- *Traduisez les énoncés. Quels sont les temps utilisés en français ?*

Action

1 **Complete this other interview of Tony with the simple or -ING form of the preterite.**

a. How (you / find) your job at Jenning's? I (visit) the nursery with my grandfather, we (look at) exotic plants, when I (hear) that Mr Jenning (look for) an apprentice. So I (go) to his office.

b. What (he / do) when you (arrive)? When I (enter) his office, he (call) a client. While I (wait), I (have a look) around the place; his secretary (send) some e-mails. Two gardeners (clean) the greenhouse.

c. Why (you / get) the job? Probably because I (explain) that I (help) my grandfather at weekends. I also (describe) the different jobs that I (do) during every season.

d. (you / like) your job immediately? Yes, I did. Because, there, I (work) with plants all day long.

B1

2 **Listen to the second part of the dialogue. Choose the verb form.**

a. I (watered / was watering) flowers when Mr Jenning (called / was calling) me.

b. Yes, he (was planting / had planted) too many vegetables, so I (gave / was giving) some to my neighbours.

c. I (saw / was seeing) my banker, I (borrowed / was borrowing) money and he (gave / was giving) me some good advice.

d. What (did you do / were you doing) when we (arrived / was arriving)?

e. I (packed / was packing) salads, cucumbers and green beans to deliver to restaurants nearby.

3 **Listen again to the whole dialogue. Find other details about Tony and his grandfather, Tony's studies, his jobs, his customers, his products.**

4 **Use the cartoon above to tell about Tony's story.**

Chat time

False interviews of famous people. Use the vocabulary box and the pictures to make similar dialogues.

A2

Mr GILLETTE
1895

THE SAFETY RAZOR

Mr LEVI STRAUSS
1850

JEANS

Mr IBUKA
SONY President 1979

THE WALKMAN

help

- shave – cut myself – bleed get the idea – safe.
- work – gold miner – wear torn trousers – tent canvas – use.
- play – listen to – heavy tape player – light cassette player – small earphones.

A: Mr ...... , What ...... invent?
B: I ...... the ......
A: What ...... you ...... when you ...... the idea?
B: I was ...... when / and ...... and ......
A: Then what ...... decide to ......
B: I ...... to ......
A: Thank you, Mr ...... It was a very good idea.

unit 11

B2

From Hum-Vees to Hummers

According to legend, AM General began making Hummers after Arnold Schwarzenegger had asked them to. Apparently, he had been impressed by a convoy of M998 Hum-Vees while he was filming *Kindergarten Cop* in 1990.

Hummers were originally built by AM General, the military vehicle division of American Motors, in its Mishawaka, Indiana assembly plant. Already in the late 1980s, AM General had planned to sell a civilian version of the famous Hum-Vee.

Then, in 1990, two Hummers were tested from London to Beijing over the rough roads of Central Europe and Asia. Their easy drive was broadcast on TV in the US. The following year the Hum-Vee was receiving its greatest advertising campaign for its service in Operation Desert Storm.

In 1991, AM General launched a civilian version of the Hum-Vee under the brand name "Hummer" H1. The H1 is basically a civilian Hum-Vee; with no armor or weapons. However, the drive-train*, chassis, body*, suspension, etc are exactly the same. It differs with its interior, including comfortable seats, stereo, and air conditioning as standard options.

In 1999, AM sold the brand name to General Motors. In the next few years, two new models were introduced: the H2 and H3. Since October, 2006, GM has been producing Hummers in South Africa for local consumption and for export. Hummers are now marketed in over 30 countries around the world.

Throughout the world, there are clubs of Hummer enthusiasts, who use their vehicles for off-road driving and recreation. However, because of their high fuel consumption, large size, and potentially-destructive use as off-road vehicles, Hummers have been depicted by environmentalists as excessively damaging to the environment, and as symbols of waste and destruction as well as icons of material excess and consumption.

California Governor Arnold Schwarzenegger who owns several Hummers responded to environmental critics that not only was he the first civilian to own a Hummer, but he had converted one of his Hummers into a hydrogen vehicle.

Hummers are now part of popular culture. H2s can be seen on *CSI: Miami**. For American rappers, Hummers represent a sign of status. As for Rock star Neil Young, he drives a Hummer that is run on biodiesel fuel. And even in *the Simpsons*, there is a character, a parody of Arnold Schwarzenegger, who owns a Hummer that is so big that it takes up 2 lanes; which causes other cars to crash.

help

the drive-train *la transmission*
the body *la carosserie*
Crime Scene Investigation: Miami *série 'Les experts Miami'*

Anticipating

1 Look at the pictures and the title.

a. What is the name of these vehicles?
b. Do their drivers have the same job?

2 Read the title and the introduction.

a. Who is it about?
b. Why is he mentioned?
c. Which vehicle is civilian? The Hum-Vee or the Hummer?

Comprehension

3 Choose a title for the introduction and each paragraph.

a. Expansion. §: ...
b. The manufacturer. §: ...
c. The first famous owner. §: ...
d. Hummer vs. Hum-Vee. §: ...
e. First appearance and war success. § : ...
f. VIPs and media users. §: ...
g. Fans and adversaries. §: ...
h. The original idea. §: ...

4 What's the English for...?

a. usine (§1)
b. armes (§3)
c. sortit / lança (§3)

5 What's the French for...?

a. convoy (intro.)
b. in the late 1980s (§1)
c. broadcast (§2)
d. consumption (§5)

6 Right or wrong? Justify your answer.

a. Arnold Schwarzenegger was driving a Hummer in the film *Kindergarten Cop*.
b. The first Hummers appeared before the Operation Desert Storm.
c. The H2 and H3 are made by AM General.
d. Hummer fans enjoy driving for fun in the country and forests.
e. Arnold Schwarzenegger owns an environment friendly Hummer.

now in French

7 Répondez en français à ces questions.

a. Pour quelles raisons A. Schwarzenegger serait–il à l'origine de la création des Hummers ?

fOcus

AM General began making Hummers after Arnold Schwarzenegger had asked them to. He responded that he had converted one of his hummers into a hydrogen vehicle.

- *Quel énoncé décrit des actions passées dont l'une est antérieure à l'autre ?*
- *Quelle est chronologiquement l'action la plus ancienne ? La plus récente ?*
- *Comment est construite la forme verbale évoquant l'action la plus ancienne ?*
- *À quel temps français fait-elle penser ? Quel est son nom ?*
- *L'autre énoncé rapporte-t-il des faits dans un contexte présent ou passé ?*

>> Training n°3 et 4

b. Quelles sont les similitudes entre le H1 et le Hum-Vee ?
c. Quelles sont leurs différences ?
d. De quels reproches les Hummers font-ils l'objet ?

Writing

B1

8 Answer these questions about the text.

a. What sort of vehicles does AM. General make? Where are they assembled?
b. Why were the first civilian Hummers tested in Central Europe and Asia?
c. Did AM General really advertise its Hum-Vees during Operation Desert Storm? Explain it.
d. When were the H2 and H3 launched?
e. Why are Hummer drivers criticized?
f. Who are Hummer users?

9 In your opinion, do vehicles like Hummers have a good image? Why (not)? Are they always necessary to their users?

unit 11

More success stories

B1

WRIGLEY'S: FROM SOAP TO CHEWING GUM

1

William Wrigley Jr. came to Chicago in the spring of 1891. He was 29 years old, had $32 in his pocket. He also had great talent as a salesman.

His father had a soap factory in Philadelphia, and his first job was naturally selling Wrigley's Soap. In order to boost his sales, William Jr. offered premiums*. He knew that the shopkeepers would buy Wrigley's soap if they received a little 'something for nothing'. One of these premiums was baking powder*. As baking powder was more popular than soap, he changed for that business.

Then one day in 1892, Mr. Wrigley got another idea. This time, he offered chewing gum with each can of baking powder. It was a big success. So he decided that chewing gum was the ideal product and he began marketing it under his own name. His first successful brands were 'Juicy Fruit' and Wrigley's 'Spearmint' in 1893. And so started the world's most popular and successful chewing gum business.

William was also a pioneer in the use of advertising. He informed the public about the benefits of his gums through newspapers, magazine ads, street posters and other forms of advertising. Then, more and more people began buying Wrigley's chewing gum.

The company was rapidly becoming an international business. After he had built the first factories in Canada (1910) and Australia, he expanded to Great Britain. Chewing gum was introduced to Continental Europe after the American soldiers had landed in June 1944. Later, new brands appeared, such as 'Freedent' (1975), and 'Winterfresh' in 1994. Today, all over the world people chew Wrigley's latest brands 'Airwaves' (1998) and 'X-cite' (2002) of that gum originally 'made in the USA'.

*premiums *primes, bonus* – baking powder *levure.*

1. **Which products did W. Wrigley sell successively?**
2. **Why was he a very talented salesman?**
3. **How did he boost his sales of chewing gums?**
4. **In what way did W. Wrigley Jr achieve the 'American Dream'?**

2

B1

FROM THE MIDDLE AGES TO NOWADAYS

5. **Reorder chronologically these means of communicating.**
6. **Describe the pictures. Give reasons why the people were /are communicating.**
7. **Which of these inventions do you still use? How often? What for? What are their advantages?**

outlook

RIP CURL: FROM SURFBOARDS TO SURFWEAR

outlook

3

B2

Back in 1967, two Australian friends – Brian Singer and Doug Warbrick – were living in the sleepy Australian coastal town of Torquay, Victoria, and decided they wanted to surf as much as possible. For that, they started a surfboard company, *Rip Curl* – in the surfing jargon, a synonym for the act of riding waves: 'rip the curl'.

In 1969, the pair made another decision. They had realized that there were too many surfboard companies but only one making wetsuit to keep their fellow surfers out of the cold.

So after *Rip Curl* had taken over an old house in Torquay and made a small investment in a pre-World War II sewing machine, the partners employed a few locals and went into production, cutting out the rubber on the floor and handing the pieces to an over-worked and underpaid machinist.

By today's standards, the first *Rip Curl* wetsuits were primitive, but they differed from others on the market in that they were made by surfers for surfers. The people who were running the company were – and still are – the test pilots.

Over the years since 1967, *Rip Curl* has grown from humble beginnings to an international surfing company with a range of innovative, functional, durable and stylish products available in more than 50 countries across the globe.

Along with surfboards and wetsuits, the *Rip Curl* product range has expanded to include surfwear (casual clothes for men and women), accessories (surf watches, travel bags, backpacks and wallets) and mountainwear (protective outerwear for snowboarding and skiing).

Like a wave, surfwear fashion has invaded streets, schoolyards and university campuses. Torquay is now a world centre for surfwear, with competing companies such as *Rip Curl*, *Quiksilver* and *Oakley*.

Adaped from triplecrownosurfing.com

8. **What is the common point between *Rip Curl's* creators and Tony the Gardener?**
9. **What were the different steps in *Rip Curl*'s growth?**
10. **What explained the success of *Rip Curl*'s wetsuits?**
11. **Do you have *Rip Curl* clothes or accessories? Why? Which ones?**

hot line

B1

A survey : advertising impact

1. Listen and complete the telephone conversation.

1. ....Hello!	2. Good .... Sarah Finay from ABC Advertising speaking.
3. Yes. What can I do for you?	4. Could you answer a few questions? It's for a survey.
5. Yes, what about?	6. About ....
7. All right, I'm ready.	8. What .... when you last .... our advert about ....
9. I	10. Yes, and ....it before?
11. Yes , I	12. Would you say you .... once, twice, a few times, many times?
13. Well, I................ it	14. Thank you. Last question. What .... when I ....you?
15. I	16. Thanks a lot. Have a nice day. Good bye!

2. Practise other surveys. The interviewer uses this page and asks:
- about street advertising posters for BIG BONE Dog food,
- about theTV advert for SUPERGUY Vitamin cocktail,
- about the radio advert for VAMPIRE Amusement Park.

The interviewee uses the information on Appendix page 153 to answer the questions.

say it

Comment se prononcent ces formes de verbes irréguliers ?
[ɔ:] comme *'walk'*, [əʊ] comme *'go'* ou [aʊ] comme *'round'* ?

a. Classez–les, puis écoutez et vérifiez.

	[ɔ:]	[əʊ]	[aʊ]		[ɔ:]	[əʊ]	[aʊ]
bought				grown			
blown				rewound			
brought				shown			
flown				sold			
found				thought			

1 Récrivez des mini-dialogues, d'après l'exemple.

Ex: *What (you / buy) when I (see) you at the clothes shop? (I / buy) a tie.*
➡ *What were you buying when I saw you at the clothes shop? I was buying a tie.*

a. Where (your sister / go) when we (meet) her at the station? (She / go) to London.
b. What (the boss / talk about) when I (hear) him in your office? (He / talk about) our best selling products.
c. Why (the people / drink) champagne when we (come) into the meeting room? Because (they / celebrate) our successful sales.
d. Who (you / speak to) when I (see) you at the reception desk? (We / speak) to a new customer.
e. What (you / do) when he (ring) you? (I / pack) some articles to deliver.

2 Famous stories. Complétez par des verbes au prétérit simple ou / et en *–ING*.

a. Mr Pemberton ... in a pharmacy in Alanta, Georgia, when he .... a new drink; his accountant ... it Coca Cola. (invent / call / work)
b. Mr Wilks ... the Land Rover when his boss ... him to conceive a utility vehicle like the old Jeep he ... in his free time. (drive / design / ask)
c. In July 1969, while Amstrong and Aldrin ... on the moon, Collins ... for them in the orbiting mother ship. (walk / wait)
d. Dr Martens ... when he .... and .... his foot. (fall / ski / start / hurt). So he ... to develop very comfortable shoes.

3 Complétez chaque élément de A par un élément de B afin d'obtenir une phrase logique.

Utilisez le prétérit simple ou le *past perfect*.

A

a. Levi Strauss (decide) to open a shop in San Francisco ...
b. Tony's vegetable business (expand) ...
c. Wrigley's (become) an international company ...
d. After he (join) the Renault Racing Team ...
e. Dr Marteens (develop) his famous shoes ...

B

f. ... because he (have) a skiing accident.
g. ... after he (advertise) his products.
h. ... F. Alonso (win) several world Championships.
i. ... before the American troops (come) to Europe.
j. ... after miners (find) gold in California.

4 D'après les vignettes et la préposition, inventez des phrases comportant un prétérit simple et un *past perfect*.

a.

b.

c.

d.

5 Racontez l'historique d'une entreprise que vous connaissez : sa création, ses produits, son expansion.

Utilisez les temps du passé étudiés ainsi que le *present perfect*. Indiquez les étapes successives à l'aide des marqueurs chronologiques (*first, after that, then, before, after, finally*).

remember

Pour raconter ou décrire des événements ou situations appartenant au passé, on utilise les temps suivants : prétérit simple (Remember Unit 5 p. 45), prétérit en *-ING* et *past perfect*.

PRÉTÉRIT EN *-ING*
Formation : *Be* au prétérit + V-*ING*

Formes affirmative et négative			Forme interrogative		
I, she, he, it	was wasn't	V-ing	Was	I, she, he, it	V-ing ?
we, you, they	were weren't		Were	we, you, they	

- **Le prétérit en *–ING* permet de décrire une situation ou activité ayant lieu dans le passé.**
→ It was snowing; two children were making a snowman...
Il neigeait ; deux enfants étaient en train de faire un bonhomme de neige...

- **Il permet de dire qu'une action était en cours à un moment précis du passé.**
→ What were you doing yesterday at 9.30? I was waiting for my train to London.
Que faisiez-vous hier à 9h30 ? J'attendais mon train pour Londres.

- **Le prétérit en *–ING* se rencontre souvent avec le prétérit simple : il permet de présenter le cadre de la situation, une action déjà en cours, dans laquelle un ou plusieurs autres événements se sont produits (prétérit simple), pouvant interrompre cette action.**
→ We were chatting when the boss came into the office, so we stopped our conversation.
Nous étions en train de discuter quand le patron est entré dans le bureau, alors nous avons arrêté notre conversation.

Il se traduit le plus souvent par un imparfait ou par l'expression « était en train de ».

Pour indiquer qu'une action, un événement a eu lieu avant une autre action, elle même située dans le passé (au prétérit simple) on peut employer le *past perfect*.
→ She became a famous actress because she had married a film producer.
→ Before they manufactured surfwear, they had made surfboards.
→ Europe discovered chewing gum after the American soldiers had landed in France.

PAST PERFECT (ou ***pluperfect***): Formation à toutes les personnes

Forme affirmative	Forme négative	Forme interrogative
sujet + ***had*** + participe passé	sujet + ***hadn't*** + participe passé	***had*** + sujet + participe passé

Vocabulary

Verbs / verbes
bleed* *saigner*
conceive *concevoir*
discover *découvrir*
expand *prendre de l'expansion*
found *fonder*
grow* *cultiver, pousser, grandir*
land *débarquer*
launch *lancer, sortir (produit)*
look for *rechercher*
pack *emballer*
plan *projeter, prévoir*
share *partager*
water *arroser*

Nouns / noms
an apprentice *un apprenti*
baking powder *de la levure*
canvas *de la toile*
consumption *consommation*
an earphone *une oreillette*
an environmentalist *un écologiste*
a greenhouse *une serre*
an incentive *une incitation, une prime*
a premium *une prime, un bonus*
a sewing machine *une machine à coudre*
soap *du savon*
rubber *du (en) caoutchouc*
a wetsuit *une combinaison (plongeur, surfeur...)*
a warranty *une garantie*

Adjectives / adjectifs
available *disponible*
efficient *efficace*
functional *fonctionnel*
torn *déchiré*

unit 12

Making future plans

contact

B1

1 **Listen to the first part of the dialogue and give the missing information about the young man:**

Name: ...... Age: ...... City of origin: ......
Occupation: ...... Next experience: ......

2 **Listen again and choose the right answers.**

a. There are (9% – 5% – 19%) male au pairs in Britain.
b. His departure day is: (Tuesday 10 – Sunday 10 – Monday 10).
c. He will travel by: (Eurostar and coach – Eurostar and plane – Eurostar and high-speed train).
d. His contract is (5 months – 9 months – 18 months) long.
e. When he arrives, he will (register – work) at the university, for a language course.

3 **Listen again and answer the questions:**

a. Why has the boy become an au pair?
b. Why has he chosen Nantes?
c. What is specified in his contract?

fOcus

How are you going to travel? I am going to take Eurostar.
Will you travel by plane? No, I won't. I will travel by train.
I am leaving next week.

- *Les actions se passent-elles au présent, au passé ou au futur ? Relevez les différentes constructions possibles. Traduisez les énoncés.*
- *Comment se construisent les formes interrogatives, négatives ?*
- *Relevez un marqueur de temps du futur. Citez-en d'autres.*

Action

1 **Turn these sentences into the future tense with *will*.**

a. New devices (influence) our daily life for sure.
b. Some old people (not be able) to adapt to new technology.
c. We may suppose people (live) a better life.
d. Visioconference (replace) teachers in the classrooms.

2 **Listen to the second part of the dialogue and choose in the list what tasks Steve will do:**

ironing – washing the car – feeding the baby – taking the children to school – doing the family shopping – cooking – doing everyday shopping – hoovering *(passer l'aspirateur)* – cleaning the windows – painting – preparing tea – sewing – making beds.

B1

3 **Listen again and say what Steve is planning for the future, after his experience.**

4 **Reorder the words to make correct sentences and translate them into French.**

a. / probably / next year / I'll / to Paris / move /
b. / going / engineering / he / study / at / to / university / is /
c. / won't / work / much / be / next month/ there / the factory / in /
d. / job / he / for / need / English / will / his / new /
e. / job / going / quit / she / her / next / is / week / to /

5 **Here is Linda and Tom's activity programme for next weekend. Ask and answer questions as in the example.**

Question: *What is Linda going to do on Thursday?*
Answer: *She is going to have a ballet class; it starts at 1.30 p.m.*

Thurs 14	ballet class 1:30 (Linda)	**Sat 16**	meet friends 2:00 (Linda) / shopping early afternoon (Tom); disco 8:00 (Linda and Tom)
Fri 15	tennis match 6:15 pm (Tom and Linda)	**Sun 17**	picnic+ seaside (Linda) / rugby match (Tom)

6 **Say what is going to happen in these situations.**

a. There are many black clouds in the sky (rain).
b. It's 7.40. Jane is leaving her house; school starts at 8.00 and the journey takes 30 mn. (late)
c. Paul hasn't handed back his homework in time; his teachers are angry (punish).

Chat time

B1

Some English friends of yours are going to spend a few days in your region next summer. It will be their first visit; you want them to have a good time and see as much as possible. With your partner, discuss and decide what they will do. Talk about where you will go, what you will see, what you will do.

Write your daily plans:

	Morning	Afternoon	Evening
Day 1	Arrive 10:45		
Day 2			
Day 3			
Day 4			
Day 5			
Day 6	Depart 11:15		

B1

When will he do it finally?

The Frenchman Michel Fournier was supposed to skydive from an altitude of 130,000 feet (40 kms) in August 2003. Now the question is: "When will he do it?"

Altitude	
40,000 m	- Michel Fournier
20,000 m	- military plane
18,000 m	- Concorde
12,000 m	- passenger aircraft
8,848 m	- Mount Everest

(...) When he skydives above the plains of Saskatchewan, Canada, Fournier will contribute to the development of future technologies and the safety of stratospheric flight. Four world records will be beaten: altitude record for freefall, altitude record for human balloon flight, time record for longest freefall, speed record for fastest freefall.

(...) The Jump equipment is composed of the balloon and the gondola, the spacesuit and helmet with the ground equipment, the launch equipment, the rescue equipment. The gondola is the main part of the equipment and shelters navigation instruments, bottles of oxygen, radio, movie cameras, videorecorders and GPS... After the separation of the balloon the gondola will descend by parachutes in order to be recovered with its instruments. The balloon has an envelope of 600,000 m^3 and is approximately 200-meter high. A pyrotechnic device will separate the balloon from the gondola after the jump; this will tear the top of the balloon which will deflate itself and fall back to earth.

(...) Michel Fournier will be equipped with a pressurized spacesuit, a helmet and special gloves allowing him to be exposed to temperatures of -110°C for 10 minutes. His physical preparation has been based on a work in endurance, jogging, swimming, stretchings plus a specific work of cold resistance, for nearly twenty years.

(...) The rise of the balloon will take about 2.30 hrs. As soon as he arrives at his top altitude, Michel Fournier will decompress his gondola and compress his spacesuit. When he opens the door of the gondola, he will have a few minutes before he free falls. Thirty seconds later, he will cross the sound barrier in free fall for the first time in human history and will reach 255 km/h.

(...) During the climbing phase of the balloon the flight can be interrupted at any moment in case of emergencies (Fournier's life, the aerial security or the civil populations). During the free fall phase (6 mn 30 s), if Fournier loses conscience, the relief* parachute will be activated. It possesses an oxygen tank* of 48 minute-autonomy. The descent of the gondola and of the balloon will also be totally controlled from ground.

(...) This project is for humanity: it will help push ahead the limits in aeronautics, space, and medicine. It will prove that astronauts in high altitude emergencies can use the proper equipment and survive. The astronauts will be able to escape in the critical phases of their spaceflight, which became capital after the accidents of the American space shuttles "CHALLENGER" and "COLUMBIA". Studies for this world premiere have mobilized unknown techniques and devices for experimental observation.

Adapted from *www.legrandsaut.org*

help

relief *de secours*
a tank *un réservoir*

Anticipating

1 Look at the title and the photo; then answer the questions.

a. What sport is the text about?
b. What will Michel Fournier try to do?

Comprehension

2 Match each paragraph with the correct title.

a. The man
b. The means of security
c. The project
d. The equipment
e. The jump
f. The record collection

3 What's the English for...?

a. dégonfler (§2)
b. le mur du son (§ 4)
c. des urgences (§5)

4 What's the French for...?

a. freefall (§1)
b. rescue (§2)
c. be recovered (§2)

5 Answer the questions.

a. What is the most important part of the equipment for the experience?
b. What is Michel Fournier equipped with?
c. What will happen if Fournier loses conscience?
d. What do these figures precisely correspond to: 200 – 255 – 2.30?

6 Correct theses statements with elements of the text.

a. The balloon can never be stopped during its climbing.
b. The gondola will disappear in the stratosphere after the jump.
c. Michel Fournier's clothing equipment will allow him to survive for 110 minutes.
d. His free fall will last forty-eight minutes.

fOcus

**As soon as he arrives at his top altitude, Michel Fournier will decompress his gondola.
When he opens the door, he will have a few minutes before he free falls.**

- *Quel est le temps employé dans la proposition principale ?*
- *Quel est le temps employé après* when *et* as soon as *?*
- *Traduisez ces deux phrases en français. Que remarquez-vous par rapport à l'emploi des temps en anglais et en français ?*

>> Training n°3

nOw in French

7 Répondez en français aux questions suivantes.

a. Quels records Michel Fournier a-t-il l'intention de battre ?
b. Que prouvera Michel Fournier avec ce saut ?
c. Donnez deux objectifs de ce projet.
d. Quel genre de préparation suit Michel Fournier ? Depuis combien de temps ?

Writing

B1

8 Use the following information to write a summary of the text.

Who?	Where?	When?
The jump: altitude? speed? temperature? duration?		
The equipment: balloon? gondola? clothing?		
Why?		

9 Write about the sport you like practising or would like to practise. Or give your opinion about Michel Fournier's trial and say if you think it will succeed or not.

Will you or will you not?

A2

1 YOU WILL BE MY VALENTINE

Our eyes met across
a crowded room,
You gave me the
love I've always wanted,
And filled my
heart with joy.
I will wrap my
arms around you,
Keep you safe,
never let you down.
I will love you
everyday forever,
If you let me be
your Clown.
Gus

1. **When is Valentine's day? What do people do on that special day?**
2. **Which message do you prefer? Why?**
3. **Write a message to your Valentine, or to any person of your choice, using the future form.**

outlook

A2

2 WHEN WILL MY TIME COME?

When will the time come when I ...
learn how to drive
star in the lead role
make the first move
have him to myself
make my own choices
stand up for me.
My time will come.

Nicole. P., Woburn, MA
www.teenink.com

4. **What does Nicole expect?**
5. **Why?**
6. **Finish up the question "When will the time come..." for yourself.**
7. **What will you do: next fall? next year? in two years' time?**

WHEN I'M SIXTY FOUR

3

B1

When I get older losing my hair,
Many years from now,
Will you still be sending me a Valentine,
Birthday greetings, bottle of wine?
If I'd been out till quarter to three
Would you lock the door?
Will you still need me, will you still feed me,
When I'm sixty-four?

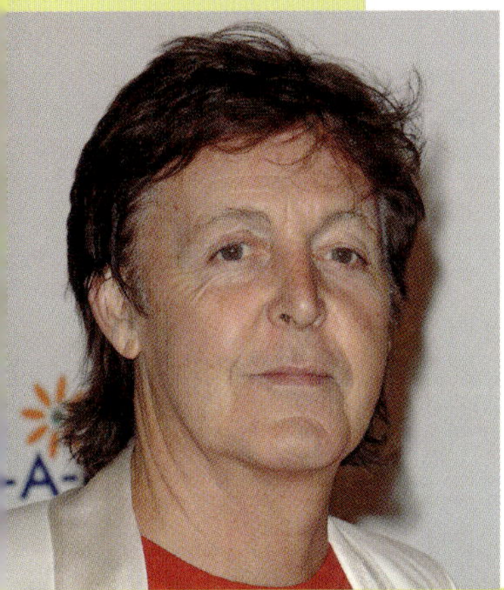

You'll be older too,
And if you say the word,
I could stay with you,
I could be handy, mending a fuse*
When your lights have gone.
You can knit a sweater by the fireside,
Sunday morning go for a ride,
Doing the garden, digging the weeds*,
Who could ask for more.
Will you still need me, will you still feed me,
When I'm sixty-four?
Every summer we can rent a cottage,
In the Isle of Wight, if it's not too dear
We shall scrimp* and save
Grandchildren on your knee
Vera, Chuck and Dave.
Send me a postcard, drop me a line,
Stating point of view,
Indicate precisely what you mean to say
Yours sincerely, wasting away
Give me your answer, fill in a form
Mine for evermore.
Will you still need me, will you still feed me,
When I'm sixty-four?

Words and music by John Lennon and Paul McCartney

* mend a fuse *réparer un fusible* – dig the weeds *enlever les mauvaises herbes* – scrimp *lésiner, être chiche.*

8. What actions will take place soon? What actions will take place later in the future?
9. What will the narrator do? What will his girlfriend do? What will they do together?
10. Do you think this letter / poem is a love declaration? Justify your answer.
11. What will you do ... when you are sixty-four?

hot line

B1

Arranging to meet

1. Listen to the telephone conversation between Dan Monroe, a businessman and Liz, the secretary of Nancy Douglas, a marketing manager. Fill in the blanks.

Liz, the secretary	Dan Monroe, the businessman
Hello. Nancy Douglas' s office.	Hello, could I speak to Nancy Douglas, please? This is Dan Monroe.
I'm afraid she's out at the moment. She .... a factory.	What time ....?
Well, I don't know how long she .... there.	Right. What about lunchtime? Is she free then?
Just one moment. I .... No, she .... with a sales representative.	Until what time? Do you know?
Er... She .... a customer here in her office at 2.00.	Ah! So what time can I try again?
Any time after 2.45.	Are you sure?
Definitely. She .... in her office for the rest of the afternoon.	OK. I .... then. Thank you.
That's all right. Good bye.	

B1

2. Practise similar telephone conversations with your partner. Dan Monroe wants to meet John Jarman first, then Nora Smith and phones their secretaries. Use the prompts below.

a. **John Jarman 's diary** / 9.30 : visit workshop – 12.15 : lunch outside – 2.30 –3.00 : meeting with the production manager – 5.00 : dentist.

b. **Nora Smith 's diary** / 10.00 : meeting with representatives – 12.30 : lunch with a designer – 3.00 : sample testing – 5.30 : art gallery reception.

say it

Présent ou futur ? Qu'entendez-vous ?

a. I do it / I'll do it.
b. I call you / I'll call you.
c. I show her / I'll show her.
d. We love that / we'll love that.
e. You like it / you'll like it.
f. They learn English / they'll learn English.

1 D'après les situations suivantes, dites ce que font Mr et Mrs Brown, puis ce qu'ils vont faire.

2 Complétez ce que dit Gordon avec *will('ll)* ou *won't*.

a. Wait for me ; I ... be very long.
b. There is no need to take an umbrella. It ... rain.
c. If we walk fast, we ... be on time for the meeting.
d. Don't ask the new accountant for advice. She ... know what to do.

3 Mettez le verbe au temps qui convient : (futur ou présent simple) pour dire ce que vous ferez (+) ou non (–) lors d'un séjour aux États-Unis.

a. As soon as we (arrive) at San Francisco, we (go) on a tour by cable cars. (+).
b. We (spend) one day at Universal Studios when we (stay) in Los Angeles. (+).
c. We (take) the ferry to go to Ellis Island when we (be) in Manhattan. (+).
d. When we (visit) Washington, we (have) time to visit Arlington Cemetery. (–).

4 Dites quel temps il fera demain dans ces capitales européennes. Puis faites les prévisions météorologiques de votre région pour lundi et mardi de la semaine prochaine. (showers, snow, fog, wind ...),

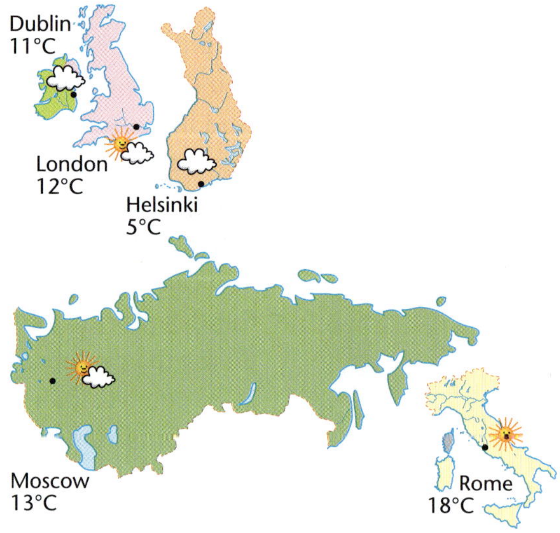

5 Traduisez les énoncés suivants en anglais.

a. Il est tôt ; les magasins ne seront pas ouverts.
b. J'achèterai le livre demain.
c. Le week-end prochain, j'irai dans les magasins spécialisés en informatique car nous allons changer d'ordinateur.

6 Complétez les expressions avec un des marqueurs de temps suivants : *tomorrow, next, in, last, yesterday, ago.*

a. We are going to have a training period ... month.
b. The visitors did some sightseeing ... afternoon.
c. She hopes she won't have too much work ... week.
d. The new sales manager was born ... 1982.
e. They are going to spend 5 weeks abroad ... six months' time.
f. Thieves visited the new warehouse ... night.

7 Vous êtes voyant(e). Prédisez l'avenir de votre voisin(e).

Studies: pass your exams – fail your exams – go on your studies – change courses
Job: interesting – demanding – find a job for two months – be unemployed for a year – find a job immediately – successful career – go abroad
Health: ill – many headaches – a long and healthy life
Family: single – married – an only child – many children – many love affairs
Home: a house with a large garden – a small flat – rent – buy – move often

remember

Pour parler de l'avenir, prédire la réalisation d'une action future, d'un événement futur, on peut utiliser *will*.

→ Tomorrow will be sunny and warm. *Il fera beau et chaud demain.*
→ What time will she be back? *À quelle heure reviendra-t-elle ?*
→ I'll phone back later. *Je retéléphonerai plus tard.*

Forme affirmative	Forme interrogative	Forme négative
S + *will* / *'ll* + V...	*will* + S + V ... ?	S + *will not* / *won't* + V ...

On utilise le présent simple, et non le futur, dans la subordonnée introduite par *when* ou *as soon as* pour exprimer une prédiction ou un souhait, ou dans la subordonnée introduite par *before, while, after, until* pour exprimer un futur.

→ We'll buy a new car when we have the money for it.
Nous achèterons une nouvelle voiture quand nous aurons l'argent.

Pour exprimer la certitude que quelque chose va se produire, on peut utiliser *be going to* + V.

→ My son is going to study biology at Oxford University.
Mon fils va étudier la biologie à l'université d'Oxford.
→ We are going to buy a new car. *Nous allons acheter une nouvelle voiture.*
→ Look at those clouds; it's going to rain. *Regarde ces nuages ; il va pleuvoir.*

Pour dire ce qui est prévu dans un avenir proche, on utilise le présent en *-ING*, en particulier avec les verbes comme *go, come, see, visit, meet, have (a party), leave*. (Voir Unit 1, page 13).

Pour parler d'un événement programmé, on peut utiliser le présent simple.

→ I leave tomorrow. *Je pars demain.*
→ The plane takes off at 5:30 pm. *L'avion décolle à 17h30.*

Pour exprimer que quelque chose est sur le point de se produire, on utilise *be about to* + V.

→ He is about to cry. *Il est sur le point de pleurer.*

Vocabulary

Verbs / verbes
deflate *dégonfler*
free fall *tomber en chute libre*
hoover *passer l'aspirateur*
iron *repasser*
mend *réparer*
recover *récupérer*
shelter *abriter*
skydive *sauter en chute libre*

Nouns / noms
cooking *la cuisine*
a decade *une décennie*
a device *un appareil*
a jump *un saut*
a rescue *un sauvetage*
the sound barrier *le mur du son*
a tank *un réservoir*

Adjectives / adjectifs
foggy *très brumeux*
rainy *pluvieux*
upper *supérieur*
windy *venté, venteux*

Time markers / marqueurs de temps
in the future *à l'avenir*
in a year *dans un an*
in the year 2020 *en l'an 2020*
in three months *dans trois mois*
in the coming weeks *dans les semaines à venir*
in one century *dans un siècle*
next week *la semaine prochaine*
next Sunday *dimanche prochain*
tomorrow *demain*
tomorrow afternoon *demain après-midi*
the day after tomorrow *après-demain*

unit 13

Applying for work

contact

B1

1 **Make two sentences describing the photos above. Use elements from each column.**

job-seekers tourists	are admiring are reading	- job-offers on an employment-agency window. - a beautiful shop-window. - job advertisements in a job centre.

2 **Listen to Roman Hamilton and Matt Lawson. Then start the questions you hear with: *how – how far – how long – how many – how much – how often – how old*.**

a. ... are you?
b. ... have you been taking tiling at school?
c. ... practice do you have?
d. ... have you already been on work placement?
e. ... days did you work per week?
f. ... is it from Doncaster?
g. ... will you get here early every morning?

fOcus

How will you get back home in the evening?
How far are the jobs?
How long will you stay with us?
How many persons do you employ?
How much are the meals?
How often will I have to work on Saturday?
How old are they?

- *Quel mot interrogatif questionne sur une distance ? une fréquence ? une manière ? une durée ? un âge ?*
- *Que signifient* how much *et* how many *? Lequel est toujours suivi d'un nom au pluriel ? Quand l'autre interrogatif est-il employé ?*
- *Quel verbe conjugué suit obligatoirement* how old *?*

Action

1 Listen again to Matt and Roman. Then answer the questions.

a. How old is Matt?
b. How long has he been taking tiling at school?
c. How often has he already been on work placements?
d. How long will he work at Hamilton Tiles?
e. How far from Doncaster does he live?
f. How will he get to work every day?
g. How many tilers, plasterers and painters does Roman Hamilton employ?

2 Ask questions corresponding to the underlined words. Use the 'how' question-words.

a. Mr Hamilton's employees are between 30 and 45 years old.
b. The jobs are in a radius of 30 miles.
c. The meals are paid with luncheon vouchers.
d. Matt will have to work once or twice on Saturdays.
e. The new trainee will earn €150.
f. A training period usually lasts four or five weeks.
g. The factory employed 220 people in 2004 and they are 300 now.

B1

3 Listen to Matt and Roman's second conversation and fill in the blanks with the words below.

assessment grid – attendance certificate – insurance cover – letter of application – professional school leaving certificate – qualification – qualified – training agreement – working hours.

a. I have brought my ...., my CV and my ....
b. I see you are a .... plumber too!
c. What .... are you preparing? A .... in tiling and plaster work.
d. You will have to fill in an .... with the details of my .... and an ....
e. My school has an .... for all the students.

4 Read again the vocabulary given in exercise 3 and find the English for:

a. une assurance : ....
b. un diplôme : ....
c. une attestation de présence : ....
d. une grille d'évaluation : ....
e. une convention de stage : ....
f. une lettre de motivation : ....

Chat time

Mrs Haywood wants to hire a baby-sitter. Matilda is applying for the job. Make a dialogue with your partner, using the 'how' question-words.

A2

Mrs Haywood	Matilda Stevenson
1 spell / name?	2 S.T.E.V.E.N.S.O.N
3 age?	4 21 years old
5 live from here?	6 1 mile
7 two children / a boy and a girl	8 number / children?
9 5 and 7 years old	10 age?
11 2 hrs per evening	12 will look after them / duration?
13 4 / from Monday to Thursday	14 number / evenings / per week?
15 £12 / evening	16 will pay me?
17 practise baby-sitting / duration?	18 for 4 years

unit 13

B1

How to apply for a job

A letter of application and a CV are important documents when you apply for a job. Employers use them to decide if they will give you an interview.

Julien LORMIER
5, rue Marchand
57000 Metz - France

Laura HIGGINS
23, Birkenhead Street
LONDON WC1H8BA
Great Britain

25 July 2007

Dear Madam,

Re: job-ad ref N° EE/UN02

In reference to your advertisement in *the Guardian* of 21 July 2007, I wish to apply for the position of waiter in the bar you will open in St Pancras International in November.

I have completed a 4-year course in catering with a French hotel school in Metz and I am qualified in the food and beverage service.

As you will see from my CV, I had several training periods abroad, including England, Ireland and Luxembourg. These work placements have helped me gain a real fluency* in English and good language skills in German. As French is my mother tongue, I feel that I would be able to deal efficiently with the European travellers who will make a stop in your bar before taking the Eurostar.

I am confident my skills, my previous work experience and school studies will enable* me to perform* in the post you are offering. I am available for an interview at anytime and I look forward to hearing from you soon.

Yours faithfully.

Julien Lormier

ST PANCRAS INTERNATIONAL
LONDON

NOW HIRING FULL-TIME & PART-TIME

2 WAITRESSES
2 WAITERS
2 CASHIERS

For a bar opening next November in the new Eurostar Station. Must be fluent in English and French. Must have basic professional skills in any other European language. Must be qualified and have experience.

Flexible schedule* and shift work*.
EXCELLENT PAY AND BENEFITS.

Send a CV and a letter of application to:
Laura Higgins
23, Birkenhead Street LONDON WC 1H8BA
Great Britain

help

fluency *l'aisance à s'exprimer*
enable *permettre*
perform *être performant*
schedule *horaires*
shift work *travail posté (2x8 ou 3x8)*

Anticipating

1 Look at the documents and complete the sentence with the appropriate words.

Julien – British – written – letter of application – read – CV – job-offer.

...... has ...... an interesting .... He has ...... a ...... to a ...... employer named L. Higgins. He has enclosed his ..... .

Comprehension

2 Find the following information in the beginning of the letter.

a. The sender's address and the date.
b. The job Julien is applying for.
c. The employer's address.
d. The location of the place of work.

3 Match the words.

a. the addressee
b. the closing formula
c. Re
d. the sender
e. the opening formula
f. la formule de politesse
g. l'expéditeur
h. la formule d'appel
i. objet
j. le destinataire

4 Look at the layout of the letter and correct the statements if they are wrong.

a. The sender's name and address are in the top left-hand corner.
b. The addressee's name and address are under the sender's.
c. The date is at the bottom of the page.
d. The opening formula is composed of two words.
e. The closing formula is as long as on a French letter.

5 What's the English for...?

a. votre annonce (§1)
b. j'ai effectué (§2)
c. en restauration (§2)
d. des compétences (§3)

6 What's the French for...?

a. French hotel school (§2)
b. my mother tongue (§3)
c. deal with European travellers (§3)

fOcus

my mother tongue
a French hotel school
good language skills
a 4-year course

- *Combien de mots comporte un nom composé ? Combien de noms ?*
- *Où se trouve le terme le plus important ? Et son déterminant ? Y en a t-il toujours un ?*
- *Traduisez les noms composés ci-dessus et trouvez-en d'autres dans la lettre et le CV.*

>> Training n°4, 5 et 6

now in French

7 Répondez aux questions en français.

a. Dans quels pays européens Julien a-t-il déjà travaillé ? Quel était son statut ?
b. En quelles langues peut-il communiquer ? Pourquoi désire-t-il travailler dans un bar à St Pancras International ?
c. Quelle a été l'évolution professionnelle de Julien au cours de ses trois stages ?

Writing

B1

8 Write full answers to the questions.

a. How did Julien know about the job-offer?
b. How long did he study catering and where?
c. How old is he? Is he married?
d. Why has he completed his training periods in foreign countries?
e. Will he have opportunities to use his language skills in Laura's bar? Why?

9 You have just read an interesting job ad. Write your CV and a letter of application. Then, type them.

B1

Looking for a job

SENDING A CV

1

Julien LORMIER
5, rue Marchand
57000 METZ
France

Tel : (00 33) 3 87 85 42 07
Mobile : 06 02 50 34 81
e-mail : j.lorm@orange.fr

Date of birth: 20.9.87
Marital status: single
Nationality: French

EDUCATION & QUALIFICATIONS

2003-2007	Lycée Mondon 57000 METZ BEP hôtellerie (equivalent Technical School Certificate) **Baccalauréat hôtellerie et restauration** (equivalent School Leaving Certificate)
1999-2003	Collège R.Aubry 55000 LIGNY **Brevet** (equivalent GCSE)

WORK EXPERIENCE

March-April 2007
6-week period in the Shamrock hotel in Cork. Duties as a bar person including cash handling, serving customers and keeping the bar well-supplied and clean.

October 2006
4-week period in Caesar Pizzeria in Luxembourg. I took the customers' orders and served them. I also kept the place clean and tidy.

May 2006
4-week period in the "Yorkshire Barrel", a pub in Sheffield. I worked at the bar with three other barmen.

PERSONAL INTERESTS

I play basketball in a club and I train children from 10 to 12. I like communicating in foreign languages and I like to learn foreign traditions and local history.

1. How long did Julien stay in each foreign country?
2. Can you locate Cork?
3. What did Julien's work consist in at the Irish hotel? At the pizzeria?
4. Where is Sheffield? (country and county) What did Julien do there?
5. What does he do in his free time?
6. Why is he attracted by foreign countries?

2 JOB ADVERTISEMENTS

NOW HIRING FULL TIME & PART TIME

SECURITY OFFICERS

$7.00 / Hr

ALL SHIFTS AVAILABLE FOR the following locations: Lexington, Mt Sterling, Somerset

mg. Murray Guard
1029 Industry Rd,
Lexington, Ky 40505

Applicants must be at least 18 years old and have clean criminal background.

FOR IMMEDIATE INTERVIEW, apply in person between 9am-11am and 2pm-4pm, Mon-Fri

---

$10.25/hr — $11.65 on Su.

SALES POSITIONS NATIONWIDE RETAIL GIFTSHOP

has positions available :
full time: 40 hrs/wk
part time: 24 hrs / wk
One year retail / restaurant exp.

- opportunity for advancement
- vacation pay
- employee discounts
- holiday pay
- free employee parking
- profit sharing
- health and dental ins.

Send a resume and covering letter to:
THE PARADIES SHOPS
Blue Grass Airport - 4000 Terminal Drive
LEXINGTON, Ky 40510

FAYETTE COUNTY SCHOOLS
Lexington, Ky

SCHOOL BUS DRIVERS
needed now

$11.68 - $13.68
Starting salary, depending on exp.

Applicants must be at least 21, have a good driving record, be able to pass a criminal records check, pass a drug and alcohol test, possess a High School qualification.

FREE HEALTH INSURANCE

Apply on line
www.FCPS.net or call Mona Serrat

✆ 381 45 34

---

7. Give the names of the companies offering jobs. Where are they all located?
8. What jobs are offered? Are they all full time?
9. How can the applicants contact the companies?
10. Which company employs people day and night?
11. Which request never appears on French ads?
12. In the second advertisement, what do 'vacation pay' and 'holiday pay' mean?
13. Read the three ads again and find the abbreviations for: Kentucky - hour(s) – Monday – Friday – Sunday – week – experience – insurance.
14. Which American words correspond to a 'letter of application' and a 'CV' ?

hot line

B1

I have found a job!

1. You are student A. Listen to the telephone conversation and write Astrid's questions. Then check on page 154.

Astrid	Julian
a.	In a restaurant called 'the Manor'.
b.	Only ten miles.
c.	I drive. I've bought a car.
d.	For two weeks.
e.	There are eight cooks and twenty waiters and waitresses.
f.	Between 22 and 40 years old.
g.	Eight hours a day.
h.	It's closed on Sunday evenings and Mondays.
i.	The cheapest menu costs £15 and the most expensive is £35.

B1

2. Make dialogues with your partner.

say it

La terminaison « *sion, ssion, tion* », des noms se prononce : [ʒ] comme dans « *television* », soit [ʃ] comme dans « *invention* » ou « *mission* ».

Écoutez et classez les mots dans la bonne catégorie puis répétez.

invasion – division – option – obsession – emission – decision – profession – instruction – adhesion – fiction – admission – erosion – immersion – supervision – attention – revision – corrosion – evaluation – fusion – lotion – pronunciation.

1 Préparez 5 questions (*where* et *how*) et interrogez votre voisin sur son dernier stage.

Ex: *Where did you work?*

2 Rétablissez l'ordre des mots dans les questions suivantes.

a. application / did / how many / letters / John / send /?
b. for / will / Stella / earn / this / how much / job /?
c. was / how old / grandfather / your / when / retired / he /?
d. Paul / has / been / how long / working / factory / the / in /?
e. have / called / how often / you / the / already / job-centre /?
f. they / company / from / live / how far / do / the /?
g. work placements / find / how / would / the / students / their / teachers / without /?

3 Retrouvez les mots cachés correspondant aux définitions.

C	L	O	S	I	N	G	J	P
O	P	E	N	I	N	G	F	R
V	C	B	E	N	I	J	O	B
E	A	C	D	A	T	E	R	N
R	E	S	U	M	E	S	M	O
I	X	K	C	E	A	J	U	I
N	P	I	A	D	D	S	L	T
G	E	L	T	Y	D	E	A	A
L	R	L	I	R	R	R	K	V
E	I	S	O	A	E	E	M	I
T	E	D	N	L	S	T	O	T
T	N	E	G	A	S	N	L	O
E	C	F	H	S	E	I	N	M
R	E	F	E	R	E	N	C	E

a. beginning of a letter (2 words)
b. document that goes with a CV.
c. the jobs you've had before.
d. a synonym of 'competence'.
e. details about school and diplomas.
f. curriculum vitae.
g. synonym of profession.
h. synonym of 'job offer'.
i. on your identity-card.
j. money a worker gets.
k. the reasons why you want the job.
l. the person who receives a letter.
m. a synonym of 'hobbies'.
n. the person who can recommend you.

4 Choisissez le nom composé correspondant à chaque dessin.

a radio-car / ice-water / water-ice / a car-radio.

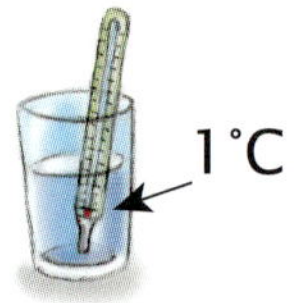

....

....

....

....

5 Retrouvez le nom composé correspondant à :

Un immeuble d'assurances / un cheval de course / un grand magasin / un externat / une course de chevaux / une assurance immobilière / une chaîne de magasins / un jour d'école.

a horse race / a race horse / a day school / a school day / a chain store / a store chain / an insurance building / a building insurance.

6 Formez les noms composés correspondant aux termes ci-dessous.

un stage – un agent de sécurité – des postes de vendeurs – une agence d'intérim – des tickets repas – une ANPE.

a job	vouchers
a work	centre
luncheon	agency
a security	positions
sales	officer
a temp	placement

remember

Pour demander des informations, on débute la question ouverte par un mot interrogatif: les pronoms en *wh* ou *how* et leurs composés.

what	*que / quel ?*	**how**	*comment ?*
what time	*(à) quelle heure ?*	**how far**	*(à) quelle distance ?*
what...for	*pour quoi / dans quel but ?*	**how long**	*(depuis) combien de temps ?*
what...like	*comment ?* (description)	**how many**	*combien de ?* (+ dénombrable au pluriel)
when	*quand ?*	**how many times***	*combien de fois ?* (nombre)
where	*où ?*	**how much**	*combien de ?* (+ indénombrable)
which	*quel / lequel ?*	**how often***	*tous les combien ? combien de fois ?* (fréquence)
who	*qui ?*	**how old**	*quel âge ?*
whom	*qui / à qui / de qui ?* (COI)	**how deep** (is it?)	*quelle est la profondeur ?*
whose	*à qui ?* (possession)	**how fast** (is it?)	*à quelle vitesse ?*
why	*pourquoi ?*	**how heavy** (is it?)	*combien pèse... ?*
		how high (is it?)	*quelle est la hauteur ?*
		how long (is it?)	*quelle est la longueur ?*
		how tall (is he?)	*combien mesure-t-il ?*
		how wide (is it?)	*quelle est la largeur ?*

→ how often do you see them? I see them every evening. *Tu les vois tous les combien ? Je les vois tous les soirs*. How often have I warned you? Very often! *Combien de fois t'ai-je prévenu ? Très souvent !* How many times has she already called? Five times. *Elle a déjà appelé combien de fois ? Cinq fois.*

Pour former un nom composé, on place le nom le plus important à la fin du groupe nominal. C'est ce dernier terme que l'on devra d'abord considérer si l'on veut comprendre l'ensemble. La lecture doit donc s'effectuer de droite à gauche, à l'inverse du français.

→ a horse race *une course de chevaux* / a race horse *un cheval de course*.

- **Les noms composés anglais peuvent comporter plus de deux termes. Le déterminant du nom principal se place en premier.**

→ Two 6-month fixed contracts. *Deux CDD de 6 mois*. Full-time and part-time security officers. *Des agents de sécurité à temps complet ou à temps partiel.*

Vocabulary

Verbs / verbes

be assessed *être évalué*
plan *prévoir*
tile / tiling *carreler*

Nouns / noms

the addressee *l'expéditeur*
an advertisement *une annonce*
an assessment grid *une grille d'évaluation*
an attendance certificate *une attestation de présence*
a business *une entreprise*
education *la scolarité*
a letter of application / a covering letter *une lettre de motivation*
a job-ad / a job-offer *une offre d'emploi*
a job-centre / an employment agency *une agence pour l'emploi*
a luncheon-voucher *un ticket-repas*
a plasterer *un plâtrier*
a position *un emploi, une place, un poste*
a qualification *un diplôme*
a raise *une augmentation*
a resume (US) /a CV (GB) *un CV*
the sender *l'expéditeur*
temp(orary) work / temping *le travail intérimaire*
a temp *un intérimaire*
a tiler *un carreleur/ un couvreur*
a training agreement *une convention de stage*

Expressions / expressions

I'll put you through to him *Je vous le passe (tél.)*
Is he in? *Est-ce qu'il est là ?*

unit 14

Complaining and criticizing

contact

B1

1 Listen to the first part of the dialogue. Answer the questions.

a. How long have they been waiting?
b. When did he buy his DVD player?
c. How many times has he charged the battery this week?
d. What must they bring back for the exchange?

2 Listen again. Choose the right answer.

a. They (should / could) realize it's Christmas time.
b. They could (employ / have employed) more staff.
c. You could (charge / have charged) the battery.
d. You should (keep / have kept) the packaging.
e. We have (the guarantee coupon / the receipt).
f. Let's say she was stressed and (overworked / underworked).

3 Listen again and complete the following sentences.

a. What's the .... ?
b. It doesn't .... any more.
c. You can .... it.
d. Then we'll do an ....
e. I .... you have kept the .... coupon.
f. Yes, it's all right. There's the right ....
g. Don't .... to bring back all the accessories for the exchange.

focus

... salespeople should be more polite.
We could inform the manager ...
They should have told us about the box.
They could have printed it on the packaging.

- *Lesquelles de ces critiques font référence à des situations passées ? des situations présentes ?*
- *Quels énoncés correspondent à « pourraient »,« auraient pu » « devraient », « auraient dû » ?*

Action

1 React to these present situations. Criticize the people. Say what they should / shouldn't do and /or what they could do. Use the prompts.

a. Sally will never find a summer job watching TV all day long! *(look for – employment agency – letters of application – interviews – local supermarkets...)*
b. Our children never help us. *(the housework – their beds – shopping – the car – the grass...)*

2 React to these past situations. Criticize the people. Say what they should / shouldn't have done and / or what they could have done. Use the prompts.

a. Ted forgot his girlfriend's birthday. *(calendar – phone – flowers – a present – a restaurant – a good meal...)*
b. Fred didn't go to work because his car didn't start yesterday. *(warn – taxi – bus – friend – walk – garage – late...)*

B1

3 Listen to the second part of the dialogue and complete the sentences.

a. You can choose another player worth £...
b. But I paid £... for it.
c. He gets a £... voucher.
d. You can choose a DVD player worth £...

4 Listen again and answer the questions.

a. What are the accessories?
b. How much does the DVD player cost now?
c. According to the father, what should the saleswoman have done?
d. What could the salesman have told the boy?
e. Who does the saleswoman call to find a solution?
f. Finally, what does she suggest to do?
g. For the father, what should they have done when he bought the DVD player?

Chat time

Criticizing and finding excuses. Student A criticizes with the help of the pictures. Student B gives excuses with the vocabulary help on appendix page 154. Change roles.

B1

Situation 1. Your friend was on holiday in London but he completely forgot you... . Tell him what he should(n't) have done, and what he could have done.

Situation 2. Your friend was late for the Sunday morning match.

Situation 3. A friend has been caught by the police for speeding and drunk driving after a night at the disco.

unit 14

B2

Crisis in the rainforest

Just imagine that every second the surface of a football ground is cut down... Over the years, more than half of the world's rainforests have been destroyed to make life in our industrialized countries more comfortable.

Tropical forests are the oldest and most complex ecosystems on earth, containing half of the world's wildlife and at least two thirds of its plant species. In Central and South America, western Africa and south eastern Asia, rainforest tribes have been living there for thousands of years, depending on it for their medicines, food and shelter*.

Yet, incredibly, half of Central and South American rainforests have been cut down and burnt to make cattle farms and supply American hamburger fast-food chains or China and Russia with cheap beef. The second cause of deforestation is logging*. Exotic trees such as mahogany* or teak are cut down to make costly furniture. Besides, rainforests have also been removed to extract metals and minerals like diamond, copper* or gold. Recently, with oil research, forests have also been damaged by the construction of extraction sites, roads and pipelines.

Together with deforestation, many tribes have been forced to move away. The worst happened in the 1990s, when Yanomami Indians were massacred by gold miners to take their land, shooting them and introducing diseases such as small pox and tuberculosis.

Finally, on the one hand, intensive agriculture for export of tropical fruit, makes the soil poorer, forcing farmers to create new plantations, while on the other hand, indigenous people are destroying their forest to grow food simply to survive.

Consequently, with the destruction of their habitat, thousands of species of plants and animals have already disappeared. Moreover, scientists estimate that by 2030, 20 % of them will become extinct if nothing is done to stop the process.

As a result, with less forest to absorb carbon dioxide, deforestation has still increased the threat posed to the world's climate because of the greenhouse effect.

To conclude, we should keep in mind that a quarter of our modern medicines originate from tropical forests even though we use hardly one percent of those amazing plants to fight leukaemia, malaria or hypertension… And whenever you consume cola, chocolate, bananas, coffee, spices or use products like rubber or deodorants, don't forget they were originally found in "virgin forests". So take action and join ecology and conservation groups like "Greenpeace", "Friends of the Earth", "Rainforest Action Network" …

adapted from *The Disappearing Rainforest*
www.pokemonultimate.wanadoo.co.uk and http://ran.org

help

shelter *abri*
logging *abattage*
mahogany *acajou*
copper *cuivre*

Anticipating

1 Look at the pictures. Read the title and the introduction

a. Where are these forests?
b. Why is there an environment crisis?
c. Is deforestation significant?
d. Why are these forests cut down?

Comprehension

2 Read the text and find the 3 different words or expressions to name these forests.

3 Find a title for the introduction and each of the paragraphs.

a. The main reasons for the crisis. §:...
b. Global warming. §:...
c. The other victims. § : ....
d. Different kinds of agriculture. §: ....
e. Old living communities. §:.....
f. Grown in rainforests. §:...
g. Murders in the forest. §: ....
h. The present situation. §: ...

4 What's the English for...?

a. faune (§ 1)
b. bovins (§ 2)
c. des maladies telles que la petite vérole (§ 3)
d. la menace posée (§ 6)

5 What's the French for...?

a. species (§ 1)
b. tribes (§ 1)
c. costly furniture (§ 2)
d. the greenhouse effect (§ 6)

6 Find which facts match these figures.

1/2 – 2/3 – 1990s – 1/4 – 1%

7 Right or wrong? Justify your answer.

a. Rainforest Indians cut the grass of football grounds in one second.
b. Most plants and animals of the world originate from rainforests.
c. Indians killed gold miners in the nineties.
d. We know the benefits of all the rainforest plants to fight diseases.

Focus

like – together with – such as – on the one hand – while – on the other hand – consequently – because of – to conclude – even though – like

- *Comment appelle-t-on ces mots ou expressions ?*
- *Relisez le texte et retrouvez pour chacun sa signification :* à cause de, d'autre part, en conséquence, comme, d'une part, en même temps que, en conclusion, même si, tandis que, tel que.
- *Rappelez le sens des mots de liaison suivants déjà étudiés :* yet, as a result, besides, moreover.

>> Training n°5 et 6

now in French

8 Répondez en français à ces questions.

a. Qu'apportent les forêts tropicales à leurs habitants ?
b. Quel rapport y a-t-il entre ces forêts et la restauration rapide américaine ?
c. Le sous-sol est-il également exploité ? Pourquoi ?
d. Quels sont les points communs entre l'agriculture industrielle et celle des Indiens ?
e. Quelles sont les différences ?

Writing

B2

9 Answer these questions.

a. Why should rainforests be protected?
b. Where could the fast-food chains have settled their farms instead?
c. Where can you currently see teak furniture? When?
d. What unforgivable facts should never have happened in the nineties?
e. What is the role of rainforests on carbon dioxide? What if they disappear?
f. Which rainforest products do you use?

10 In your opinion, what should / could we do to stop this process? Suggest and develop solutions (protected areas / reforestation / help to the third world / boycott / public pressure...).

unit 14

Crisis...

... IN THE GARAGE

B1

1

In October, 1998, Terrence Dickson of Bristol, Pennsylvania, was leaving a house he had just finished robbing* by way of the garage. However, he was not able to get the garage door to go up, because the automatic door opener was malfunctioning. Moreover, he couldn't re-enter the house because the door connecting the house and garage locked* when he pulled it shut. As the family was on vacation, Mr. Dickson found himself locked in the garage for eight days. He subsisted on a case of Pepsi he found in the garage and a large bag of dry dog food. Consequently, Mr. Dickson sued* the homeowner's insurance, claiming the situation caused him undue mental anguish. The jury agreed to a compensation of a half million dollars...

rob *cambrioler* – lock *fermer à clef* – sue *intenter un procès à*.

1. Who was Terrence Dickson? What was he doing?
2. What happened? How long did he stay in the garage? How did he survive?
3. Why is his attitude surprising?
4. How could you criticize Terrence Dickson?

2

B1

... IN THE STREET

Man arrested for OWI after hitting dog, six parked cars and house.

DES MOINES, Iowa (AP) — A Des Moines man was arrested on suspicion of driving while intoxicated Saturday after crashing into six parked cars, running over* his dog and hitting his own house. Witnesses told police that Matthew John Payne, 30, hit "a couple of parked cars and some mailboxes" before ramming* into an oncoming car, leaving his front fender* and license plate on the street. Witnesses said Payne then drove around cars stopped at a four-way stop, ran down* the stop sign and rear-ended another car. Payne reportedly got out of his car, checked the damage and then returned to his car and drove it home, hitting two more mailboxes on the way. Witnesses said Payne hit his dog in his driveway* before crashing into his house. Payne told the responding officers that he had not been drinking. Payne submitted to several sobriety tests, which police said he failed, and was charged with operating while intoxicated and four counts of hit-and-run*. Payne was laughing when police found him. He told them he had recently changed his brakes*.

www.siouxcityjournal.com/

ram into = crash into = hit *heurter* – a fender *un pare choc* – run down *renverser* – run over *écraser* – a driveway *une allée de garage* – hit-and-run *accident avec délit de fuite* – the brakes *les freins*.

5. Why was Payne arrested? Find what OWI means.
6. Did he only hit cars?
7. What damages did his car have? When?
8. For the police, what shouldn't he have done? What should he have done instead?

outlook

... ON TOP OF THE WORLD

3

B1

9. Why is the Himalayan Region very touristy? Why are there environmental problems in the region?
10. Explain the expression "the highest junkyard in the world".
11. Are the Everest climbers nature lovers? What should they do?
12. List the rubbish. Explain why they have been left. What should climbing teams have done?

In recent years, tourism and climbers expeditions in the Himalayan Region have increased drastically. During peak tourist season, there are about 700,000 tourists; and twenty to forty thousand of them attempt to ascend the mountains. However, there is no infrastructure to cope with the solid waste* or pollution these people generate.

American climber Barry Bishop, leader of 'Sagarmatha Environmental Expedition', who first publicized the environmental problems, labelled the mountain "the highest junkyard* in the world." For him, the situation on Mount Everest is "a major ecological scandal by men and women who believe their personal conquests are more important than preserving the integrity of a unique natural site."

Garbage* on the mountain includes climbing equipment, foods, plastics, tins, aluminium cans, glass, clothes, papers, tents, and dead bodies. Their trash is scattered everywhere, at different altitudes, but is most prominent on the most popular route to the summit. It has been estimated that every team leaves, on average, five hundred kilograms of trash* behind after each expedition. Moreover, S.E.E have even reported finding medical waste such as bloody syringes. Oxygen bottles are also a big problem because they do not decompose, are heavy, and expensive to remove. Another problem is the practice of tossing rubbish* into the crevasses where it is ground up* by the action of the ice.

Adapted from
www.associatedcontend.com/

a junkyard *un depôt d'ordures* – trash, garbage, rubbish, waste *déchets, ordures* – grind up *broyer*.

hot line

A2

Apologizing for being late

1. Listen and complete the telephone conversation.

Britannia Plastics, ... ! .... ?	Yes, John Peters speaking. I work in the ....
Hello, Mr Peters. What ....?	Well, ... you put me through to Mr Craig, the ....?
Of course, ...	All right...
Hello, Mr Craig .... What's ....?	Hello Mr Craig. .... John Peters. I'm calling because ....
OK. But you .... have .... your	I did. But my ....
Then you .... have ....No, it's a joke. Don't .... When are you ....?	I'll be there in ....
Good. See you then.	OK. Good bye, Mr Craig.

2. Practise dialogues with your partner.

A2

Situation 1: You work in the Marketing Dept. Call Mrs Berk. Explain that you missed your bus (get up earlier!) because your alarm clock didn't ring (change the batteries!) and that you'll arrive in $1/2$ an hour.
Situation 2: You work in the Accounts Dept. Call Mr Parker. Explain that you forgot the morning meeting (enter it in your e-book!) because you left it at the office (sleep in the office!) and that you'll arrive in $3/4$ of an hour.

training

say it

Prononciation de ou : [ʊ] comme *wood*, [aʊ] comme *cow*, [ɔ:] comme all, [ʌ] comme *cut*. Classez ces mots. Puis écoutez et vérifiez.

court – pound – counter – should – foul – bought – could – country – course – voucher – thousand – double – would – fourth – south – ground – thought – foundation

[ʊ]	[aʊ]	[ɔ:]	[ʌ]

1 Pour chaque situation, dites ce qu'ils devraient faire ou pourraient faire pour régler leur problème.

a. He has had a toothache for two days. (... dentist /... some aspirin).
b. We have invited some friends for dinner but there's no bread left (... baker's / ... neighbour).
c. It's raining but they have no umbrella. (... another umbrella / ... in a shop).
d. She has a flat tyre. (... the wheel /... a garage)

2 Pour chacune des situations précédentes (ex. 1), dites ce qu'ils (n')auraient (pas) dû faire et ce qu'ils auraient pu faire pour éviter cela.

a. eat less sweets / buy sugar-free chewing gum.
b. get more bread this morning / keep some in the freezer.
c. take an umbrella / watch the weather forecast.
d. learn to change a wheel / check her car before leaving.

3 Mauvaise journée. Lisez le paragraphe et critiquez Mike Cheeky.

Yesterday, Mike had an interview for a travelling representative's job in London.
As he was driving to it, he was caught in a traffic jam, then he got lost in London and arrived one hour late without warning. Unfortunately, he panicked and forgot to take his file with his C.V. and his references. During the interview, he didn't say anything about his training periods. He asked only one question about the company but wanted to know his future holiday dates. He also remarked that the starting salary was a bit low. He was very surprised to learn that he was refused for the job.

4 Voici Mike pendant son entretien. Observez l'illustration et formulez d'autres critiques sur son attitude.

5 Choisissez le mot de liaison qui convient afin que chaque énoncé soit logique.

a. (because of / as) the weather was bad, the climbing team didn't leave the camp.
b. (although / despite) it was still snowing, they decided to climb.
c. The weather was too bad to climb safely; (moreover / however) the team was badly trained, (consequently / yet) an expedition was sent to rescue them.
d. Rubbish pollutes the snow; (nevertheless / as a result) cleaning expeditions are organized to collect trash (such as / whereas) clothes, tents or empty oxygen bottles.
e. Local authorities hope to limit the number of climbers (thanks to / for instance) expensive climbing taxes.
f. (finally / in my opinion), those dirty climbers should bring back their garbage (in spite of / instead of) leaving them in the montains.

6 Complétez cette lettre de réclamation avec les mots de liaison suivants : *thanks to, but, although, as, moreover, first, like, nevertheless, because, then, on top of it all.*

Dear Sir,
I am writing to complain about the poor sales service in your shop. ... I had a problem with a DVD player I recently bought, I took it back for exchange ... I had to deal with an incompetent salesman.
... , I had to wait for 20 minutes. ... , this person was hardly polite, and ... I was nearly insulted.
... I had paid €150 for this player, he wanted to give me one worth €120. ... he could give me a 6-month guarantee ... it was a promotion article and not a brand product ... JVC or Sony. Fortunately, ... to the dept. manager the problem was settled. ... I wanted to inform you of my unpleasant experience.

Yours faithfully,

7 Rédigez une autre lettre de réclamation.

remember

Pour critiquer, émettre des reproches dans un contexte présent, on peut utiliser les modaux *should* (idée de « devrait ») et *could* (idée de « pourrait »).

L'emploi de *could* permet d'envisager une action, d'évoquer une possibilité non réalisée.

→ He should look for a job; he shouldn't watch TV all day. He could go to an employment agency. *Il devrait chercher un emploi; il ne devrait pas regarder la TV toute la journée. Il pourrait aller dans une agence pour l'emploi.*

Pour critiquer ou dire que quelque chose n'a pas été fait correctement dans un contexte passé, on emploie *should / shouldn't have* + participe passé : aurait / n'aurait pas dû + infinitif

→ He should have arrived on time; he shouldn't have been late. *Il aurait dû arriver à l'heure, il n'aurait pas dû être en retard.*

Pour envisager une solution ou une possibilité non réalisée, on utilise *could have* + participe passé : aurait pu + infinitif

→ She didn't phone me; she could have written a letter ... she could have sent a postcard. *Elle ne m'a pas téléphoné ; elle aurait pu m'écrire une lettre... elle aurait pu m'envoyer une carte postale.*

Pour présenter des idées, des arguments, et les articuler de manière ordonnée et logique, on utilise les mots de liaison (ou liens logiques). **(Voir également unit 9)**

- **Pour énumérer :** first of all (*avant tout*) – first (*d'abord*) – firstly (*premièrement*) – secondly (*deuxièmement*) – then (*puis, ensuite, alors*) – finally (*finalement*) – to conclude (*pour conclure*).
- **Pour ajouter :** moreover / in addition (*de plus*) – besides (*en outre*) – on top of it all (*en plus de tout cela*).
- **Pour opposer, faire une objection :** but (*mais*) – however (*cependant*) – yet (*pourtant*) – nevertheless (*néanmoins*) – although / though (*bien que*) – instead of (*au lieu de*) – instead (*à la place*) – on the one hand (*d'une part*) – on the other hand (*d'autre part*) – despite / in spite of (*malgré*) – whereas / while (*alors que, tandis que*).
- **Pour exprimer une conséquence :** so (*ainsi, alors*) – as a result / consequently (*par conséquence*) – hence (*d'où*).
- **Pour exprimer la cause :** as (*comme*) – because (*parce que*) – because of (*à cause de*) – thanks to (*grâce à*).
- **Pour introduire un exemple :** such as (*tel que*) – like (*comme*) – for example / for instance (*par exemple*).
- **Pour donner son avis :** in my opinion / to my mind (*à mon avis*) – for me (*pour moi*) – according to .... (*selon ...*) – personally (*personnellement*) – as for me (*quant à moi*) – as far as I am concerned (*en ce qui me concerne*).

Vocabulary

Verbs / verbes

advise *conseiller*
blame *accuser*
breakdown *tomber en panne*
bring back *ramener*
cut* down *abattre (forêt)*
climb, ascend *escalader*
complain *se plaindre*
insult *insulter*
joke *plaisanter*
rob *cambrioler*
run into, crash into, ram into, hit *heurter, tamponner*
sue *poursuivre en justice*
toss *jeter*
work *fonctionner, marcher*

Nouns / noms

cattle *des bovins, du bétail*
a climber *un alpiniste*
copper *cuivre*
a disease *une maladie*
an earphone *une oreillette*
garbage, trash, rubbish, waste *déchets, détritus*
a guarantee, a warranty *une garantie*
furniture *des meubles*
logging *abattage* (a log *une bûche*)
mahogany *acajou*

Adjectives / adjectifs

major *majeur, important*
peak *de pointe, haute (saison)*
prominent *visible, en vue*
worth *valant, d'une valeur de...*

unit 15

contact

Advertising products and services

B2

1 Listen and answer the questions.

a. What type of business have Lilly and Harold just created? What do they need?
b. What does Lilly want to launch? What can she ask her boyfriend to do?
c. What does she want to inform people about?
d. Why is a good slogan very efficient? What slogan does Harold propose?

2 Listen again and give the following information.

a. One advantage and one drawback of TV commercials.
b. Two advantages of advertisements (ads) in local newspapers.
c. Two advantages of posters (which could be pinned all over the town).

focus

I want to inform people
I want you to find a good slogan.
We don't want people to forget our company name.

- *Quel est le verbe qui indique une notion de volonté ? Comment se construit le verbe qui le suit ?*
- *Qui est la personne qui exécute l'action de « trouver » / d'« oublier » ?*
- *Quel est l'ordre des éléments suivants :* to / someone / V / want / S *(pour indiquer que l'on veut que quelqu'un fasse quelque chose) ?*

Action

1 Tell what Lilly and Harold want to do or want people to do using the following elements.

a. Lilly / want / launch an advertising campaign.
b. Lilly and Harold / want / give details about their services in local newspapers.
c. They / want / people / telephone them when they have computer problems.
d. Lilly / not / want / Harold / call the local radio tomorrow.
e. They / not / want / their clients / pay too much.

2 Complete the following sentences as in the example.

Ex: *People don't call when they have computer problems. Lilly and Harold want ....*
➡ *Lilly and Harold want* *them* *to call when they have computer problems.*

a. People don't know the technicians are available 24 hours a day. Lilly wants ...
b. Helen, the local reporter doesn't know there is a new computer assistance business. Harold and Lilly want ...
c. The slogan must be easy to memorize. Harold wants ...
d. We have no information about their services and rates. Harold and Lilly would like ...
e. Her boyfriend can create a TV commercial for OK Comput. Lilly can ask ...

B2

3 Listen to the interview (part 2) and answer the questions.

a. What is the name of the radio? Who is Helen? What time is Helen's interview?
b. How old are Lilly and Harold? Where did they work before creating their own firm?
c. What do they love doing? What type of computer can they repair?

4 Listen again and complete the sentences.

a. Your target audience is ...
b. We wanted ... to become a job.
c. If ..., we'll be there within 10 hours.
d. First they want to know ...
e. We'll publish ads in the newspaper ...
f. We want our clients ...
g. We'd like them to be sure ...

Chat time

You have just created your own company. You want to launch an advertising campaign. First choose the products or services you want to advertise and complete the chart. Then explain how you want to advertise this product.

B2

Product or service	
Name of the company	
Important information	
Prices / rates	
Target audience	
Slogan	
Media: **newspapers, posters, TV commercials...**	

Ex: *I want to inform people about ...*
I'd like my clients to be sure...
My target audience is ... because...
I want my clients to ... because ...
I want to launch ... because ...
My company slogan is...
I'd like my ads to ...

unit 15

Brand-name schools

B2

Imagine going to a school where the uniforms are made by Nike, the cafeteria food comes from Pizza Hut, and the math lessons involve adding and substracting M&M's, then eating the answer.

That may sound like a cool school to you, but it's a big nightmare* for many parents and teachers. They are worried that bringing brand-name products and advertisements into schools will distract kids from learning and turn classes into all-day commercials. But that's not stopping many schools from making deals* with big companies.

Pepsi-only Schools

Public schools get most of their money from state and local governments, which collect it from taxpayers. That money pays for books, buildings and teachers' salaries, but schools are often looking for extra funds.

More and more of them are turning to companies that sell products to kids. These companies, such as Pepsi and Pizza Hut, agree to pay schools for the right to advertise and sell their products in school cafeterias, classrooms and stadiums. The companies figure* that if kids start buying their stuff today, they will continue buying it when they're grownups.

Big companies are willing to pay big bucks* to promote their brands in schools. Last month Pepsi paid $5.75 million to the school system of Denver, Colorado. For the next five years, all Denver public schools will carry only Pepsi-brand drinks in vending machines. The deal also gives Pepsi the right to splash its logo throughout the school. In another Colorado district, Coke paid $5.5 million to be the only soda in school.

What's The Cost?

Television, magazines, movies – they all aim ads at kids. So why shouldn't schools have ads too? Many people say such advertising encourages kids to think about spending money rather than doing schoolwork. They are also worried that kids will be brainwashed* into preferring certain brands. Says Dave DiGiacomo, a school-board member in Jefferson County, Colorado: "Schools shouldn't sell minds to the highest bidder*."

Other school officials, like John Bushey of Colorado Springs, argue that school advertising "doesn't interfere with education." His district signed an $8 million deal with Coke in November. The money will help pay for musical instruments, athletic equipment and other expenses. School districts in California, Florida and Maryland are also considering joining up with big companies.

http://www.timeforkids.com
Time for kids on line

help

a nightmare *un cauchemar*
make deals *faire des affaires*
figure *(ici) penser*
bucks *dollars (familier)*
be brainwashed *subir un lavage de cerveau*
the highest bidder *le plus offrant*

Anticipating

1 Read the title and the introduction. Then answer the questions.

a. What is the general topic of the document?
b. In your opinion, what's the advantage for these schools?

Comprehension

2 Read lines 1-31 and answer.

a. Do parents and teachers agree with school advertising?
b. What do the schools need?
c. What are Pepsi-only schools?
d. Why do big companies want the kids to start buying their products?

fOcus

If kids start buying their stuff today, they will continue buying it ...

- *Quel est le sens de* start / continue *? Indiquent-ils le début / la fin / la continuité d'une action ?*
- *À quelle forme est le verbe qui suit* start / continue *?*
- *Relevez au début du texte d'autres verbes suivis d'un verbe en* -ING.
- *Dans cette liste de verbes :* want – involve – persuade – would like – end – finish – agree – encourage – consider – enjoy, *lesquels sont suivis d'un infinitif ? Lesquels sont suivis d'un verbe en* –ING *?*

>> Training n°5 et 6

3 Read lines 32-50 and complete.

a. Ads for kids are found on ..., in...
b. Many people think school advertising is worrying because ...
c. Yet, ad money can pay for ...

4 What's the English for...?

a. les contribuables (§2)
b. les distributeurs automatiques (§4)
c. réfléchir à, envisager (§6)

5 What's the French for...?

a. splash (§4)
b. a school-board member (§5)
c. joining up (§6)

6 Right or wrong? Justify your answer.

a. Many American schools make deals with big companies.
b. Public school buildings and teachers are paid for with private funds.
c. Big companies want to persuade the students to buy only their products.
d. Coca-Cola and Pepsi-Cola are ready to pay a lot to be the exclusive soda.
e. Some people think advertisers shouldn't buy students' minds.
f. Other people think that school advertising is educative too.

nOw in French

7 Répondez en français aux questions.

a. Donnez trois exemples permettant de mieux imaginer les écoles sponsorisées.
b. Quel genre d'entreprises sont susceptibles de sponsoriser les écoles ?
c. Pourquoi Pizza Hut et Pepsi versent-ils des fonds aux écoles ? (objectifs à court terme et à long terme).
d. Pourquoi peut-on dire que la publicité achèterait les esprits ?
e. Le Colorado est-il le seul État américain intéressé par la publicité à l'école ?

Writing

B2

8 Write a summary of the text by filling in the blanks below.

a. This article taken from ... explains that some American schools ...
b. It explains that public schools get their money from ..., but they often need ...
c. Big companies want to ...
d. Many parents and teachers are worried because ...
e. However, more and more school districts are considering ...

9 Give your opinion about school advertising.

What are the effects of school advertising on students? Do you think that there should be restrictions? What should be permitted and not permitted?

How to analyse an ad

TWO INTO ONE DOES GO!

1. Match each number with one of the following words:

❍ the product
❍ the brand name
❍ the picture / the setting
❍ the focus*
❍ how to get more information
❍ the text

* the focus *l'accroche.*

2. Describe the ad.
(cf. vocabulary p. 125)

Ex: *This ad is about ... The brand name is ... The picture, which is at the top of the page, shows ... The focus is on ... The text insists on ... It says... The product is also shown at the bottom of the page in a line of photos which show ... You can get more information if ...*

2

B1

THE NEW IPOD

3. Answer these questions, then write a paragraph about this ad. You can also choose other ads and present them to the class.

a. What sort of product / service / idea is advertised? What's the brand-name?
b. Describe the ad: brand name, slogan, picture, focus, colour ...
c. What is suggested by the atmosphere, the colours...?
d. Who is the target audience?
e. Do you like or dislike this ad? Justify your opinion.

hot line

B1

Asking for more information about ads.

1. Listen to the dialogue and complete the chart.

Salesperson	Buyer
Hello.	Hello, I'm .... I've just read your ad. .... and I'd like to have ....
Oh, it's a	Is it ....? How long ....?
Only .... but	Is there a ....?
No, we only had	How much ....?
Only	I think ....
I can propose .... It's really	If I'm interested, ...
Don't wait too long because	OK ....

REFRIGERATOR
like-new condition,
very good quality,
a real bargain
Call 952-817-1455

WASHER / DRYER 5 yrs old, great condition, delivery available, good price, $275 pair
Call 962-829-2365

COMPUTER,
Power Mac G3266 desktop, 2 years old, fantastic condition
Call 651- 859-4892

27" COLOR TV,
only $175,
absolutely new!
Famous brand name
Call 612-440-3725

2. Practise more dialogues. You are the buyer and you ask for more information about another ad. Your partner is the salesperson and tries to persuade you to buy. Then change roles.

say it

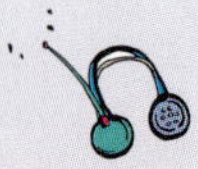

Distinguez le son [tʃ] comme dans *teach* ou *picture* du son [ʃ] comme dans *shoes* ou *fashion*.

a. Écoutez les mots suivants et classez-les dans le tableau ci-dessous.

children – choose – commercials – vending machine – conventional – future – should – manufacturer – each – brainwashed – officials – chocolate – chewing gum – shampoo

[tʃ]	[ʃ]

b. Écoutez pour vérifier et répétez.

1 Construisez des énoncés à partir des éléments ci-dessous et retrouver ce que veulent ou voudraient Lilly et Harold.

a. Lilly / want / launch an advertising campaign.
b. They / would like / draw / people's attention to their services.
c. They / want / have more clients.
d. Harold / want / people / call them when they have computer problems.
e. They / 'd like / persuade the local radio to interview them.

2 Vous assistez à une conférence sur la publicité. Expliquez ce que les publicitaires veulent / ne veulent pas / voudraient.

Ex: *Commercials must attract consumers.*
➡ *Advertisers want commercials to attract consumers.*

a. Ads can be more efficient. ➡ They'd like...
b. Advertising must create new needs.
c. Magazines can inform about new products.
d. Television must not be switched off during commercials.
e. Teenagers must not be bored by ads.

3 Vos voisins sont très autoritaires. Vous expliquez ce qu'ils veulent ou ne veulent pas.

Ex : *David says: "Paul, wash my car!"*
➡ *David wants Paul to wash his car.*

a. David shouts: "Jenny, switch off your TV!"
b. Jenny says: "Paul, don't be late!"
c. David and Jenny cry out: "Hey, kids, come here immediately!"
d. They say to their children: "Don't invite your friends to our house!"

4 Complétez les phrases ci-dessous en fonction de ce que vous voulez ou voudriez.

a. I want my family to ....
b. I'd like my friend(s) to ....
c. I want to persuade ... to ...
d. I'd like my future job to ...
e. After my exams, I want to ...

5 Ajoutez le verbe entre parenthèses à la forme qui convient (infinitif ou V-*ing*).

a. He started (drive) when he was 18.
b. He enjoyed (discover) new places.
c. His wife wants (work) as an advertiser.
d. She continues (study) at the university.
e. They expect (find) new clients.

6 Complétez les énoncés ci-dessous pour parler de votre expérience personnelle.

a. When I was young, I wanted (work) as a(n)... But I finally started (study) in a ... school.
b. Now, I'd like (find) a job in a ... because I enjoy (work) in a ...
c. I don't wish (live) in .... because I dislike ...

7 Analysez cette publicité. Vous pouvez utiliser les éléments ci-dessous.

Ad featuring ... / foreground / background / The focus is on ...
The brand name is ... / ... right-hand ... / at the top ... / aimed at ... / In my opinion ...

remember

Pour indiquer ce que l'on veut faire, on utilise *want + to* + V

→ I **want to** come with you. *Je veux venir avec toi.*
→ He doesn't **want to** leave. *Il ne veut pas partir.*

Pour indiquer ce que l'on veut que quelqu'un fasse, on utilise *want + someone + to* + V

→ I **want you to** come. *Je veux que tu viennes.*
→ He doesn't **want me to** leave. *Il ne veut pas que je parte.*

- **D'autres verbes, exprimant la volonté, se construisent comme *want* :**
Verbe exprimant la volonté + *someone* + *to* + V, comme par exemple :
ask (*demander*), **encourage** (*encourager*), **expect** (*s'attendre à*), **persuade** (*persuader*), **wish** (*souhaiter*), ainsi que la forme **would like / 'd like**.

→ I'd like my friends to help me. *J'aimerais que mes amis m'aident.*
→ They persuaded me to buy a new one. *Ils m'ont persuadé d'en acheter un nouveau.*
→ Advertising encourages kids to spend money. *La publicité encourage les enfants à dépenser de l'argent.*

Pour indiquer le début, la fin ou la continuité d'une action, on utilise souvent la construction Verbe + V-*ING*

→ They **will stop offering** gifts. *Ils cesseront d'offrir des cadeaux.*
→ She **goes on working**. *Elle continue à travailler.*

À noter : les deux formes sont possibles indifféremment avec **begin** et **start**.
→ He begins to eat. / He begins eating. He started eating. / He started to eat.

RAPPEL : Pour exprimer la préférence, on utilise également la construction :
Verbe + V-*ING* avec, par exemple, les verbes :
like (*aimer*), **enjoy** (*apprécier*), **love** (*adorer*), **hate** (*haïr*), **dislike** (*ne pas aimer*), **can't stand / can't bear** (*ne pas supporter*), **be fond of** (*aimer beaucoup*), **be keen on** (*être passionné de*) …
→ They **enjoy playing** video games. She **loves shopping**. He **likes watching** TV.

Vocabulary

Verbs / verbes

advertise *promouvoir, faire de la pub*
aim at *viser à*
back up *soutenir*
feature *représenter*
involve *nécessiter, inclure, toucher*
motivate *motiver*
remind *rappeler*
stop from *empêcher de*

Nouns / noms

an advertiser *un publicitaire*
an advertising agency *une agence publicitaire*
a bargain *une bonne affaire*
a campaign *une campagne (de pub)*
a discount *une réduction*
an executive *un cadre, un responsable*
the focus *le centre, le point de focalisation*
an official *un (représentant) officiel*
a rate *un tarif*
a setting *un cadre*
a target audience *un public cible*
a warranty *une garantie*

unit 16

Reporting facts and words

contact

B2

1 Listen to the conversation and answer the questions.

a. Who is Debbie? How old is she?
b. What is she doing in the agency?
c. Did she have work experience abroad?
d. Does she know about shift work?
e. What is her opinion about it?
f. How long is her contract?

2 Listen again and choose the right answers.

a. The agency is in (Milwaukee / Norwich / Ipswich).
b. After this experience, she can get a (permanent / long term / three-term) contract.
c. Debbie got ("GSCE" / "Scottish Higher" / "A Levels") at Norwich High School.
d. She went to (Sweden / Finland / Denmark) for one of her training periods.

3 List all the information required at the job centre.

focus

Mr Jarman: "You will be paid as a beginner".
➡ Mr Jarman said I would be paid as a beginner.
"Did you enjoy it?" "Yes, I did, it was great." ➡ He wanted to know if I enjoyed it. I answered I enjoyed it very much.
"How old are you?" ➡ He asked me how old I was.

- *Quelle partie de chaque énoncé est au discours direct, au discours indirect (ou rapporté) ?*
- *Quels verbes introduisent les propos rapportés (= verbes introducteurs) ? À quel temps sont ces verbes ?*
- *Comment se transforment les verbes du discours direct dans le discours rapporté ? Quelle(s) autre(s) transformation(s) remarquez-vous ?*

Action

1 Report Cameron's words as in the example.

Ex: *"I am a student at Perth College".* ➡ *She said she was a student at Perth College.*

a. "I work part-time in a local pub".
b. "I am going to France in summer".
c. "I will pass my driving test soon".
d. "My parents work in New Zealand".

Ian

Debbie

Peter

Vivian

2 Report what the different members of the Cowing family said yesterday morning. Introduce their sayings with "say" or "ask".

B2

3 Listen to the second part of the conversation and choose the right answers.

Debbie: They told me to start next Monday with the (evening shift / afternoon shift / morning shift).

Ken: That would be great! Did they tell you how much you will get for (meal compensation / transport compensation)?

Debbie: They told me that I would share my time between (the production department and the finance department / the marketing department and the sales department / the marketing department and the finance department). I think that it's going to be (interesting / fascinating / impressive).

Ken: Yes, sure. Well, Debbie, I have to go now! And don't forget... We are having (a party tomorrow afternoon / a party on Sunday night / a party tomorrow night). It's Brenda's birthday!

4 Write the different words said by the staff members of LTC Catering.

Ex: *The watchman asked every one to show their identification cards. He said: "Show your identification cards, please."*

a. The new trainee said he was exhausted at the end of his first working day! He said: "..."
b. Mrs Miller asked if the applicant could go to the secretary's office. She asked: "..."
c. One of the cooks said he would quit the company by the end of next month. He said: "..."

Chat time

Ask your partner to choose 4 numbers between 1 and 12. Then ask the questions which correspond to the numbers your partner has chosen. Record your partner's answers and report them orally. Then change role.

B1

HAVE YOU EVER THOUGHT ABOUT...

1 moving house?
2 giving up smoking?
3 going to America / Britain?
4 getting new and different qualifications?
5 becoming a vegetarian?
6 doing humanitarian work?
7 where you will be in ten years' time?
8 travelling round the world?
9 leaving home?
10 going to college?
11 going to work abroad?
12 becoming a professional sportsman?

unit 16

B2

From machinery* to boat building

Mike Broome, 37, left a computer job designing machinery to train as a traditional boat-builder. He lives in Lyme Regis with his girlfriend, Liz and has been working as a boat-builder with Kayla Simmons for a few years now.

Mike Broome grew up in the Midlands with parents who were not really interested in boats but he said he loved sailing and admiring the wooden ships that he had seen when he was a child on seaside holidays. Six years ago, when he traced for his birth mother – he was adopted – he realised that his mother and his birth father used to race catamarans.

In his previous career he designed machinery* using Computer Aided Design. He says: *"Although it was a stimulating work, sitting in front of a computer for forty hours a week was too much. I decided it was time to try a new direction, and boatbuilding seemed natural."* He adds: *"In 2002, I took a £8,000 career development loan to help pay for my course at the Boat Building Academy in Lyme Regis and I sold my house to fund myself."*

He met his business partner Kaila Simmons on the course. They decided to build a boat together, and began *Prima*, a beautiful 22-foot sailing sloop* built of mahogany on oak*, with copper and bronze fastenings*. "Prima" is still unfinished because Mike and Kaila are waiting for a careful owner before they fit out* the interior. But the ship gained them recognition from the industry when the couple showed her at the Beale Park Thames Boat Show in 2003. At the end of this year Mike and Kaila were asked to build a sailing sloop named *Wee Seal*. The profits helped them to set up their workshop and buy equipment. Mike says that they have also worked as sub-contractors since then and that they are one commission away from paying themselves.

For now, they are funding the business from other work. *"I teach part-time at the Boat Building Academy"* Mike says *"and Kaila does computer work"*.

Drawing a boat's lines full-size is a more intimate process than designing on a computer. Mike tells his students that working with wood is a lot more organic than engineering with steel*. *"Wood is a natural material so there are inherent stresses* that only become apparent when you are sawing it. But you can mould it using steam* and fit it into wonderful curves"* he says.

Adapted from John Lewis's free magazine

help

machinery *des machines*
a sloop *un voilier*
oak *du chêne*
fastenings *l'accastillage*
fit out *aménager, équiper*
steel *l'acier*
an inherent stress *une contrainte particulière*
steam *la vapeur*

Anticipating

1 Look at the title, the photos and the introduction; then, answer the questions.

a. Give personal details about Mike Broome (age, marital status, home...).
b. What was his previous job?
c. What is his present job?

Comprehension

2 Read the text and match the paragraphs with the titles.

a. working with wood.
b. reasons for a change.
c. first ships.
d. a love for boats.

3 What's the English for...?

a. les bénéfices (§3)
b. des sous-traitants (§3)
c. vous êtes en train de le scier (§4)

4 What's the French for...?

a. his birth mother (§1)
b. gained them recognition (§3)
c. you can mould it (§4)

5 Answer the questions.

a. What does Mike think about his previous job?
b. What did he do to get money for his studies?
c. What are the technical characteristics of the sloop "Prima"?
d. What was the consequence of the presentation of "Prima" at the Boat Show in 2003 for Mike and Kaila?
e. What does Mike say about working with wood?

6 Right or wrong? Justify all your answers with elements from the text.

a. Mike Broome has always loved boats and ships.
b. He changed job because he did not like his previous job.
c. He works alone in his company.
d. For Mike, working with wood is more realistic than designing on a computer.

fOcus

Mike tells his students that working with wood is a lot more organic... Mike says that they have also worked as sub-contractors.

- *Dans ces deux phrases, quels sont les deux verbes, introducteurs du discours rapporté ?*
- *Comment se construit chacun d'eux ?*

>> Training n°5

nOw in French

7 Répondez en français aux questions suivantes :

a. Qu'a découvert Mike Broom sur ses parents naturels ?
b. Pour quelle(s) raison(s) Mike et Kayla n'ont-ils pas terminé leur voilier « Prima » ?
c. Quelles autres activités Mike et Kayla exercent-ils pour s'assurer des revenus complémentaires ?

Writing

B2

8 Complete the text in order to write a summary.

This text is about .... who had a computer .... and decided to ....
He went to .... in 2002 to train ....
Kaila and Mike started .... This boat gained them .... In 2003, they built a .... To make a living, Mike .... and Kaila ....
Mike says that working with wood ....

9 Do you think you will keep your job for life? What other job(s) would you like to do?

What did they all say ...?

B1

1 LIONEL RICHIE'S INTERVIEW

Q. What do you find frightening?
L. R. Walking through an airport is more frightening than stepping on a stage. For me that's my home.
Q. What brings you more down to earth?
L. R. Having kids.... They are our best judges. I have got three: adopted Nicole, Miles and Sophia.
Q. What do you like doing when you want some rest?
L. R. I walk in the woods; it clears my head. And I'm lucky to have a little forest in my property.
Q. What did you like doing in your spare time?
L. R. I used to play tennis... Now meditation helps me to unwind*. I am travelling constantly, I need to find a home for myself.
Q. What have you learnt from life?
L. R. Many things... But the most precious lesson was from my friend Milton. He made me understand that everybody can be there for you when you're winning, but it's the true friends who want to hang around* when you're not. (...)

Adapted from *Woman & Home*, January 2007

* unwind *décompresser* – hang around *être présent*.

1. Write a paragraph reporting Lionel Richie's answers.
2. Who is Lionel Richie? Find as much information as possible to write a portrait.

B2

2 VOLUNTEERING MAKES A DIFFERENCE

PAMELA WILLIAMS, a section manager at John Lewis's, Norwich, elected to work at a rehoming Centre of Dogs Trust (for abandoned or lost dogs).

"Trying a different job was like a breath of fresh air. I've always loved dogs. My role at the centre was to help clean out the kennels*, prepare dog food, take the dogs out for walks and sit in on vets' visits. I really enjoyed that aspect of being at the kennels. It was great to be outdoors for one day every week and lovely to mix with people who were passionate about the work. And knowing you are helping an organisation that relies totally on charity gives you great satisfaction. (...) I would recommend a scheme like this to every one; it broadens your experience. (...)"

* a kennel *un chenil* –
an earthquake *un tremblement de terre*.

SOBIA RAHMAN, from London, took a two-month sabbatical to work with the Pakistani earthquake survivors.

"I needed something more. So I went to work with U-GOOD, an organisation involved in helping survivors of the Pakistan earthquake* of October 2005, a real human disaster. I had to take unpaid leave, but I was determined.

I was working at the camp from eight in the morning until 10 at night with very traumatised people who had lost everything. My favourite part of the day was running a class for around 100 children; it was a way for them to start communicating and play games again. When you have a bad day at work, you can relax at home. A bad day at the camp is different; you must be patient and accept you can't help everybody. (...) If you do something like this, you will always want to go on helping (...)"

Adapted from *Source*, a John Lewis magazine

3. Why did Pamela and Sobia go for volunteering?
4. Where did they do it? What was their work there?
5. After their experiences, what do they think of volunteering?
6. Would you go for volunteering? Why?
7. Do you know names of charities dealing with volunteering? Give information about them.

3 B1 "WE FIXED IT ON-LINE"

"I upped my qualifications in my own home. Although I wanted to improve my qualifications, I didn't want to go to college for an adult evening course. So..."
Phyllis S. (Perthshire)

"I applied for my daughter's secondary school place. Applying for school places is always a difficult affair. So..."
Margaret P. (Perthshire)

"Tracing my family tree was surprisingly easy. We all come to a point in our lives when we want to know more about our family history. So..."
Suzanne H. (Norfolk)

"We bought a car. I can't stand car dealerships and we knew exactly which car we wanted to get. So..."
Christiane J. (Norfolk)

"We planned our whole wedding abroad on-line. Mel and I are living in England but we both come from Melbourne where we wanted to get married. So..."
Nicola R. (Hampshire)

Interviews in UK.

8. What do all these persons have in common?
9. Report what every person says in different paragraphs.
10. Would you do the same way? Justify your answer.

hot line B2

National Plastics Limited
Court Road
NEWCASTLE NC1 6H2

April 12th, 2008

To AB Packaging
24, Brucefield Road
BLAIRGOWRIE PH10 6LA
Ref. PP/LB/03/46

Dear Sir,
As previously arranged, I will be able to come over to Edinburgh on May the 5th. I will fly with BMI; my flight number is BM592 and the plane leaves at 11.15 a.m. On arrival, I am going to take the airport bus to Waverley Bridge. Can we meet there at 3.30?
Looking forward to meeting you soon,
Yours sincerely
Pauline Parr

Reporting what you read on a letter.

1. Listen to the telephone conversation between Alex Murray, the R'nD manager and Linda McMillan, a secretary in the same company. Correct the statements below.
   a. Mr Brown said he would arrive on the 7th.
   b. The airport is Gatwick, terminal 1.
   c. The arrival time is 3.50 p.m.
   d. He said he was going to get on the airport bus.
2. Listen again and write the questions Alex is asking.

B2

3. Practice more telephone conversations with your partner.

Conversation 1
Student A: you are a secretary at AB Packaging and you answer the manager's questions with the help of Pauline Parr's letter.
Student B is the manager(ess). (See p. 155.)

Conversation 2
Student A: now, you are a manager(ess) at R. C. S. &C° and ask your partner questions about Miss Templeton's venue.
Student B is the secretary. (See p. 155.)

say it

a. **Repérez la consonne muette des mots suivants puis prononcez-les mots.**

would – walk – answer – what – theatre – knock – night – neighbour – ought – write.

Écoutez et vérifiez.

b. **Entourez le mot au son différent puis répétez chaque série de mots.**

a. murder – turned – learn – sure – but
b. around – encounter – journey – house – now
c. wait – scarce – shared – fair – age
d. peak – cheap – piece – wear – meat
e. good – food – trout – group – boot
f. building – picnic – convinced – stripe – notice

Écoutez et vérifiez.

1 Hier, vous avez rencontré Brad, un de vos amis qui vous a donné des nouvelles. Plus tard dans la journée, vous rencontrez Andrew, un autre ami, et vous lui rapportez les propos de Brad.

Ex: *Brad: "I'm living in Manchester now."* ➡ *Brad said that he was living in Manchester now.*

a. "My mother isn't very well."
b. "Sophie and Mel are going abroad this summer."
c. "I saw Mary at a party in May."
d. "I haven't seen Ann recently."
e. "Meg has had twin babies."
f. "I want to go on holiday but I can't afford it."

2 Terry parle de Will à Pam. Pam n'a pas entendu les mêmes informations que Terry. Complétez la conversation.

Ex. *Terry: Will doesn't like his new job.*
Pam: But he told me he loved it (love).

a. T: He loves living in Kent. – P: but he told me ... (hate).
b. T: He is moving to Ontario, next fall. – P: (British Columbia).
c. T: He'll be forty next month. – P: (thirty-five).
d. T: He can speak a little French. – P: (German).
e. T: He hasn't been to cinema for ages. – P: (last week)

3 Retrouvez les questions que l'officier de l'immigration a posées à Joan, à son arrivée à Chicago International Airport.

Joan: "The officer asked me what my name was, then how old I was. Next, he asked where I came from. After that, he wanted to know where I was going to stay. And then, he asked me to show him my job contract. In his next question, he asked if I had relatives in the States. Finally, he asked how much money I had brought with me."

4 Rapportez les propos de Cameron et Ruppert à propos de leur séjour à San Diego en Californie.

Cameron:
a. "I have never been to San Diego before."
b. "I may come back again before 2012."
c. "I'll stay in a different hotel, next time."

Ruppert:
d. "I don't like the city at all."
e. "I didn't like my stay there."
f. "I will stay at home next time."

5 Complétez par *say* ou *tell* à la forme qui convient.

a. "... us about your last promotion".
b. She ... it was pure luck.
c. We ... her it wasn't, it was due to her talent.
d. We also ... she had to give a party for that.
e. She ... yes to the proposal.
f. We ... everyone in the company, then.

6 Utilisez les verbes proposés pour compléter les informations correspondant aux dessins : *remind – ask – warn – order –suggest – tell*

Ex: *The man asked the hairdresser to shave his head.*
a. The waiter ... the customer .... b. She .... her daughter ...
c. The guide ... the tourists ... d. The man ... his son .... /
e. The manager ... his secretary ...

remember

Pour rapporter des faits, des ordres, des suggestions, des questions, des paroles dans des phrases simples ou complexes, on emploie le discours rapporté ou indirect.
Le passage du discours direct au discours indirect peut entraîner des modifications.

- **Le verbe introducteur est au présent, (au *present perfect* ou associé à *will*) :** il n'y a pas de changement de temps dans la deuxième partie de l'énoncé par rapport au discours direct.
"It's cold and I've nowhere to stay." → She says (that) it's cold and she has nowhere to stay.

- **Le verbe introducteur est au prétérit, (au *past perfect* ou au conditionnel) :** cela entraîne des modifications importantes.
– Le verbe de la phrase rapportée « recule dans le temps » :
Présent simple → prétérit simple
Présent en *-ING* → prétérit en *–ING*
Present perfect → *past perfect*
Prétérit → *past perfect* (ou prétérit)
He said: "I'm leaving" / "I have passed my exams." / "My mother died last year".
→ He said he was leaving, that he had passed his exams and that his mother died / had died last year.
– Certains modaux changent :
can → *could*, *will* → *would*, *may* → *might*.
– Le vocabulaire relatif au temps et à l'espace change :
"I saw **this** girl here two days **ago**."
→ She said she **had** seen **that** girl **there** two days **before**.

- **Autres transformations indépendantes du temps du verbe introducteur :**
– Pronoms personnels, adjectifs et pronoms possessifs :
Selon le contexte, plusieurs modifications peuvent intervenir : "My mistake is real, but I am your son!" → He said that his mistake was real, but he was his son!"
– L'impératif
Un ordre à l'impératif devient un infinitif.
"Stay there!" → She told him to stay there.
"Don't ask me!" → She told me not to ask her.
– L'ordre des mots
Dans les questions, l'ordre des mots redevient celui de la forme affirmative. S'il n'y a pas de mot interrogatif, on utilise ***if*** ou ***whether***.
"Sir, can you help me?" → She asks him if he can help her. / She asked him if he could help her.

- **Les verbes introducteurs *say*** (s'il n'y a pas mention de l'interlocuteur) et ***tell*** (s'il y a mention de l'interlocuteur) sont les plus fréquents. ***Explain, refuse, order, warn, promise***, etc. expriment des notions plus précises.

Vocabulary

Verbs / verbes
add *ajouter*
beg *supplier, prier*
explain *expliquer*
fund *financer*
fit out *équiper, aménager*
mould *mouler*
order *commander, ordonner*
promise *promettre*
saw *scier*
trace *rechercher*
warn *avertir*

Nouns / noms
a birth mother *une mère biologique*
copper *du cuivre*
a curve *une courbe*
an earthquake *un tremblement de terre*
fastenings *accastillage*
a kennel *un chenil*
a loan *un prêt*
machinery *les machines*
oak *du chêne*
a profit *un bénéfice*
a sloop *un voilier*
steam *la vapeur*
a sub-contractor *un sous-traitant*
volunteering *du bénévolat*

Adjectives / adjectifs
confident *confiant*

Expressions / expressions
can't stand *ne pas supporter*

Exam: 1 training

A 300 millionth American. Don't ask who!

Yesterday was the birth day of Emanuel Plata in Queens, of Zoë Emille Hudson in Manhattan, of Kiyah Lanaé Boyd in Atlanta and of a number of other babies. Each of them might be the 300 millionth American.

The babies were born at 7:46 am Washington time, when, the Census Bureau* estimates, the nation's population reached 300,000,000.

Theoretically, the 300 millionth US inhabitant may have arrived at an airport from overseas at that hour, or been smuggled* at night across an unguarded section of the Southwestern border. However, hospital publicists and proud new parents were still claiming for the title of 300 millionth American.

In Queens, NYC, Emanuel Plata weighed 6 pounds 15 ounces at Elmhurst Hospital Center, where he was not different from the 4,400 other infants born there each year except for a tiny white cap, provided by hospital officials, that proclaimed in blue letters, "America's 300 millionth baby."

His mother, Gricelda Plata, 22, was draped in an oversized T-shirt that announced, *"I delivered America's 300 millionth baby."* She and the boy's father, Armando Jimenez, 25, a cook who works in Forest Hills, are immigrants from Puebla, Mexico, and live in East New York, Brooklyn.

Asked by reporters if he considered himself lucky to be the father of a celebrity, Mr Jimenez replied: *"My baby is healthy. My wife is fine. What more luck do I want?"*

At New York-Weill Cornell Hospital in Manhattan, Zoë Hudson was born, the daughter of native New Yorkers. Zoë's father, Garvin, 29, an investment banker, is the son of a couple from Jamaica, and her mother, Maria Diaz, 28, a teacher in Harlem, is of Puerto Rican heritage.

In Atlanta, Kiyah Boyd of Mableton, Georgia, was welcomed by a TV crew from "Good Morning America". Kiyah's father, Kristopher Boyd, 28, is in the Navy and had been stationed in Bahrain, but came home on leave* to join his wife, Keisha, also 28, whom he met in the service. Both are American-born.

At the Census Bureau headquarters in Suitland, Maryland, a crowd broke into cheers* at 7:46 when the digital population clock* flashed 300,000,000. This clock is calculating that an American is born every 7 seconds; one dies every 13 seconds and the nation gains an immigrant from abroad every 31 seconds.

[The United States is now one of three countries with more than 300 million people, ranking behind China and India. In contrast to most other industrialized nations, America has a population that is still growing, propelled by immigration and higher fertility rates.]

Statistically, demographers generally agreed, the person who pushed the national population to 300 million was most likely a Hispanic boy in the Southwest.

Adapted from *The New York Times*, October 18, 2006

Word box

the Census Bureau *le Bureau de recencement*
smuggle *entrer clandestinement dans un pays*
on leave *en permission*
break into cheers *se mettre à acclamer*
population clock *compteur public permanent indiquant la population américaine.*

Compréhension

A Répondez en français aux questions suivantes en utilisant uniquement les informations contenues dans le texte et en justifiant vos réponses.

9 points	A1 = 0,5 pt	A2 = 1pt	A3 = 1pt	A4 = 1pt	A5 = 3pts	A6 = 1,5pt	A7 = 1pt

1. D'après le Bureau de recensement des États-Unis, que s'est-il produit à 7h46 (heure de Washington) le 17 octobre 2006 ?
2. Le 300 millionième habitant des États-Unis est-il forcément un bébé ? En théorie, qui pourrait-il être également ?
3. Au centre hospitalier d'Elmhurst (Queens, NYC), qu'est ce qui distinguait un certain bébé des autres ? Que portait sa maman ?
4. Qu'est-ce qui est le plus important d'après le père de ce bébé ?
5. Recopiez le tableau ci-dessous et complétez-le pour donner toutes les informations concernant les trois bébés candidats au titre de 300 millionième Américain et leurs parents.

Bébé :			Parents :			
Prénom	Nom	Lieu de naissance	Noms	Ages	Professions	Origines

6. Comment le compteur de population (*Population clock*) calcule-t-il le nombre d'habitants aux USA ?
7. D'après les statistiques des démographes, quelles sont les caractéristiques probables du 300 millionième Américain : sexe, origine, région d'habitation ?

B Traduisez en français l'avant-dernier paragraphe du texte. (3 pts)

[*The United States is now .... higher fertility rates.*]

Compétences linguistiques

C Posez des questions sur les éléments soulignés. (2 pts)

1. The babies were born at 7:46 am.
2. Emanuel Plata weighed 6 pounds 15 ounces.
3. At Elmhurst Hospital Center, 4,400 babies are born each year.
4. The nation gains an immigrant from abroad every 31 seconds.

D Recopiez le texte suivant en mettant les verbes entre parenthèses à la forme exigée par le contexte. (2 pts)

The US Census Bureau *(to count)* exactly three hundred million people on October, 17, 2006. "Well, we *(not to know)* who the 300 millionth is," a demographer said, "but we think this person could *(to be)* Hispanic". He estimates the US population *(to reach)* 350 million in 2020.

Expression écrite

E Answer the following questions in English (80 words minimum). (4 pts)

1. **Secteur tertiaire :** In your opinion what are the advantages and drawbacks of living and working in the USA or another foreign country?
2. **Secteur industriel :** Would you like to visit the USA? Where would you like to go? What would you like to see? Why? Would you like to live and work in the USA? Would you prefer to stay in France? Why?

Exam: 2 training

Try telling the ladies of Chelsea a stylish 4x4 is 'not cool'!

Yesterday, drivers of sports utility vehicles (also called SUVs or 4x4s) in the wealthy area of London were the target of 'The Alliance Against Urban 4x4s'.

The environmental protesters gathered outside a Chelsea Land Rover dealer, to inform motorists and potential 4x4 buyers of the safety and climatic dangers associated with the vehicles nicknamed "Chelsea tractors".

Holding a banner with the slogan "Not safe, not clean, not cool", campaigners handed out fake parking fines*, issued by "the climate", to "your conscience". Local mothers, driving their children to the nearby Natural History Museum in a Range Rover, Shogun or Cherokee, were urged to think "how our children and grandchildren will pay for our dependence on fossil fuels".

For Susie Edwards, 34, an environmental leader, these mothers — or at least, their vehicles — are a menace. "They present a unique danger: it's a combination of size, weight and emissions of carbon dioxin". But it isn't just their effect on the environment, she added. "Their kids are less safe in a 4x4. Moreover, other children are also at risk."

According to the 'Insurance Institute for Highway Safety', a 4x4 is twice more likely to be involved in a fatal rollover* than an ordinary car. The blind spots* extend more than 20 feet behind the vehicle and in America, about 60 parents a year reverse* over and kill their own children.

"SUVs are also gas-guzzlers: driving a 4x4 in town for a year will waste more energy than leaving the television on for 32 years. Besides, the 4x4 is a status symbol, a fashion item, and there is no reason to have one unless you live in farming communities or rural areas where you need to go off-road."

A lot of their drivers realise some disadvantages — the difficulty of manoeuvring, for instance, but believe that the cars are safer and more practical. Others are very defensive. There's a sort of fortress mentality when you climb into one of these things. [Their drivers just think they can do what they want. Not only does a 4x4 contribute to a feeling of superiority by being physically higher than almost everything else, but the vehicles are roomy enough to accommodate most family members and pets. Besides, driving something called 'Discovery', or 'Defender', or 'Explorer', makes people feel much more exotic than braving motorways at the wheel of a smaller vehicle.]

Recent figures showed that more than 100,000 SUVs are now registered to London addresses.

Adapted from *www.telegraph.co.uk/core/Content*

Word box

fake parking fines *de fausses amendes de stationnement*
a rollover *un tonneau*
a blind spot *un angle mort*
reverse *reculer*

Compréhension

A Répondez en français aux questions suivantes en utilisant uniquement les informations contenues dans le texte et en justifiant vos réponses.

8 points	A1 = 1 pt	A2 = 1pt	A3 = 1,5pt	A4 = 1,5pt	A5 = 1,5pt	A6 = 1pt	A7 = 0,5pt

1. Quelle organisation a manifesté hier à Londres ? Où précisément ?
2. Quel était le but de cette manifestation ?
3. En quoi cette manifestation a-t-elle consisté ?
4. Que reproche Suzie Edwards à ces mères et leurs véhicules ?
5. Qu'indiquent les rapports du 'Insurance Institute for Highway Safety' ?
6. Ces véhicules sont-ils économiques en ville ? Pourquoi ?
7. Quel est l'inconvénient de la conduite de ces véhicules en ville ?

B Traduisez en français ce passage de l'avant-dernier paragraphe du texte. (4 pts)

[*Their drivers just think ... of a smaller vehicle.*]

Compétences linguistiques

C Recopiez le texte suivant en mettant les verbes entre parenthèses à la forme exigée par le contexte. (2 pts)

1. Yesterday, drivers of 4x4s (*stop*) by environmental protesters.
2. Ecologists regularly campaign against SUVs that (*pollute*) the air with high dioxin emission.
3. If we don't react soon, the air (*become*) unbreathable within a decade or two.
4. Statistics show that 60 American children (*kill*) every year by reversing 4x4s.

D Recopiez les phrases suivantes en les complétant par l'élément qui convient. (2 pts)

who	which	than
as	whose	that

1. Those Chelsea ladies, ... cars are stylish and expensive, don't realise the potential danger of their vehicles.
2. Many male drivers are persuaded .... they are invincible at the wheel of their 4x4s.
3. Driving a hybrid fuel car doesn't consume as much petrol .... an expensive diesel SUV.
4. My husband cycles to work, ... is more ecological and cheaper.

Expression écrite

E Answer the following questions in English (80 words minimum). (4 pts)

1. **Secteur tertiaire :** Do you think that a car is necessary? Why?
In your opinion, what means of transport are better for our environment? Why?
(Give 3 or 4 examples of transport).

2. **Secteur industriel :** How do you go to school? Why? Are you satisfied with this transport?
In your opinion what are the advantages and drawbacks of driving to work?

Exam: training

3 Wind power: energy from the air

Human beings have used the wind as an energy source for a long time. The Babylonians and Chinese were using wind power for irrigating 4,000 years ago. Wind was also used for grinding grain in Persia in 200 BC* and for draining the Dutch soil by the fourteenth century.

Yet, the first windmill for electricity production was built in Cleveland, Ohio, in 1900. Eight years later, they had 72 wind-driven electric generators. The largest machines were 24-meter high towers with four enormous blades* and they produced 25KW* per hour.

Those towers are now called 'wind turbines' and are gathered on sites called 'wind farms' which produce electricity. Their energy does not come from oil or from nuclear power and it is renewable. The more wind, the more wind farms; the larger they are, the more electricity we can make. The best places for wind farms are in coastal areas, at the top of hills, in open plains and gaps in mountains. In fact, any place where the wind is reliable with an average speed of 25km/h. Many of them are also built offshore because the wind is constant and strong.

Nowadays, there are wind farms everywhere – in the US and in Canada, in Argentina, in Japan, in New Zealand, in South Africa and in India. The list is endless. Germany has the largest number of wind farms in the world. France is far behind and its wind power represents only 1% of its consumption. The UK has a target* for 10% of domestic energy to be generated from renewable sources by the year 2010.

However, wind farms are not approved by everybody. The investment is higher than for generators functioning with oil and wind farms are often located far from cities where electricity is needed. They deface the countryside and are noisy. The turbines can affect television reception if you live nearby and they kill birds. [But the advantages are numerous: wind farms don't pollute the air and don't produce greenhouse gases such as carbon dioxide.

The land under the turbines can still be used for farming and brings money to the farmers who let their fields to the turbines owners. Moreover, wind farms need no fuel, they just need wind and wind is free.

Winds will keep on blowing and it makes sense to use them.]

Adapted from Energy resources

Word box

BC (Before Christ) *avant Jésus-Christ*
a blade *une pale*
KW *kilo-Watt*
MW *méga-Watt*
a target *un objectif, une cible*

Compréhension

A Répondez en français aux questions ci-dessous en justifiant vos réponses par des éléments contenus dans le document.

8 points	A1 = 0,5pt	A2 = 2pts	A3 = 0,5pt	A4 = 1pt	A5 = 0,5pt	A6 = 1,5pt	A7 = 2pts

1. Quel est le thème abordé dans le document ?
2. Quels peuples utilisaient la force du vent avant le 19e siècle ? Pour quels travaux ?
3. À quoi sert-elle surtout maintenant ?
4. Où se trouvent les meilleurs sites d'implantation d'éoliennes ?
5. Quelle est la principale condition de fonctionnement d'une éolienne ?
6. Quel pays européen a la plus grande puissance éolienne ?
   Quel est l'objectif poursuivi par le Royaume Uni ?
7. Citez quatre inconvénients engendrés par l'énergie éolienne ?

B Traduisez en français ce passage de la fin du texte. (4 pts)

[*But the advantages are numerous... to use them.*]

Compétences linguistiques

C Complétez les phrases par le comparatif qui convient (supériorité, égalité ou infériorité). (2 pts)

1. Offshore wind turbines function (good) .... inshore turbines because the wind is (reliable) ....
2. Wind power is (polluting) .... oil power and it is not (dangerous) .... nuclear power.

D Complétez par *ago*, *for* ou *since*. (2 pts)

1. Windmills have been used as electric generators .... the beginning of the 20th century.
2. Most western governments have been worrying about pollution .... 30 years.
3. Some decades .... , renewable energy became a new topic in ecology.
4. My neighbours have been supporting *Greenpeace* .... their teenage.

Expression écrite

E Write a paragraph in English about renewable energies (80 words minimum). (4 pts)

Is wind power the only renewable energy that exists? Are there other natural ways to produce electricity? In which ways are they interesting for the environment and for the economy? Why should all the countries make efforts to develop them?

help

solar power – the sun heat – solar panels – hydraulic energy – barrage – hydro-electric turbine – to turn – to transform – water energy
tidal power station – to use the tide power – geothermal power – to drill – hot groundwater – hot springs – forest

Exam: training 4 A green village in Europe

[The town of Güssing, in south eastern Austria, was one of the poorest regions of the country, marked by high unemployment and migration. In the 90s, its *burgmeister** set up a new energy concept for its 4,000 inhabitants, with the aim of coverage of the total demanded energy by means of ecological processes. Therefore a bio-diesel plant and a district heating system, based on biomass*, were installed.]

95% of the heat demand and more than 100% of the fuels, needed in the region, are now produced from the local renewable energy sources. The different units comprise heat, fuel and electricity. The resources come from agriculture (colza, sunflower, corn, lucerne) as well as from forestry (wood), from households (old edible oil), from industry (sawmill residue) and also directly from the sun (solar energy).

At the beginning of the experience, only 29 households were connected to the first small plant. Today, they are about 90%. For heat and electricity, the city is totally autonomous and in the future wishes to become independent for car energy. Farm tractors are using a bio-diesel made from old edible oils and colza oil. Within a few years, if car manufacturers accept to transform the car engines, millions of litres of bio-diesel could be produced to meet demand.

As a result of these efforts in favour of renewables, a "European Centre For Renewable Energy" was established in Güssing. Every week, the centre welcomes 400 visitors; the counsellors of this centre study the feasibility of the projects and they control their completion.

Ernst Kedl, the landlord of a hotel restaurant presented his project to these specialists. He and his neighbours had decided to build a heating plant in Ubersdorf and had created a cooperative in 1995. They obtained funding from Brussels, the Land* and the Austrian state for more than half of the total cost of the plant and its network. The 43 members of the cooperative paid for the difference, which means 7,200 euros; this sum includes the connection to the network and the purchase of a special boiler that produces heat and hot water for 40% less than the usual fuel bill. Ernst Kedl says: "our station is working with wood coming from our members' own forests; the district is totally autonomous today. Ten new households could even join us..."

The green policy of Güssing has been extremely positive. The heat bills of its inhabitants have decreased. Within 10 years, 1,100 new jobs have been created and fifty new companies have been set up. The city is an ecological example and is giving ideas to other cities in Western Europe for an environment-friendly life.

Word box

burgmeister *le maire*
Land *équivalent autrichien d'un conseil régional*
biomass *biomasse*[1]

1. La biomasse est l'ensemble des énergies provenant de la dégradation de la matière organique, utilisées soit directement (bois énergie), soit après une méthanisation (biogaz) ou de nouvelles transformations chimiques (biocarburant).

Compréhension

A Répondez en français aux questions suivantes en utilisant uniquement les informations contenues dans le texte. Rédigez des phrases complètes et justifiez toujours vos réponses.

9 points	A1 = 1pt	A2 = 2pts	A3 = 1pt	A4 = 1pt	A5 = 1pt	A6 = 1pt	A7 = 1pt	A8 = 1pt

1. Qu'a voulu faire le maire de Güssing dans les années 90 ?
2. D'où proviennent exactement les ressources des énergies renouvelables ?
3. Quelle transformation serait nécessaire pour que Güssing soit entièrement autonome dans la production de carburant automobile ?
4. Quel est le rôle des conseillers du Centre Européen pour les Energies Renouvelables ?
5. Qui a financé la station de chauffage du quartier d'Ubersdof ?
6. Quelle est sa ressource énergétique ?
7. Combien de foyers sont raccordés à cette centrale ? Combien pourraient y être raccordés au total ?
8. Quelles sont les conséquences économiques de la politique environnementale de Güssing ?

B Traduisez en français le premier paragraphe du texte. (3 pts)

[*The town of Güssing ... were installed*].

Compétences linguistiques

C Mettez les phrases suivantes à la forme passive. Commencez chaque phrase par les mots soulignés. (2 pts)

1. The counsellors study the feasibility of the projects.
2. Brussels will give more and more money for environment-friendly European projects.
3. The burgmeister of Güssing started a green policy more than twenty years ago.
4. All the inhabitants can control the local policy for energy.

D Un journaliste a enregistré les avis de passants sur l'avenir de la planète. Recopiez les propos de ces passants en mettant les verbes à la forme exigée par le contexte. (2 pts)

1. "I think water *(disappear)* if we don't save it."
2. "Many years ago, we *(can)* breathe clean air in the cities; today, there (*be*) only fumes and exhausts..."
3. "Global warming *(increase)* for a few years; we must do something about it".

Expression écrite

E Answer the questions. (4 pts)

1. **Secteur tertiaire :** Where can we get energy from? What must we do to protect our resources of energy: at home? at work? in the countryside? when travelling?
2. **Secteur industriel :** What can we do in our daily lives to protect our environment? Give three or four precise examples. (80 words)

Exam: training

5 Setting up on your own* is a serious business

When Tracey left school, she wanted to have her own pottery business. Instead of this, as she was obliged to earn her living, she took a job as a receptionist. After she got married, she started going to pottery classes in the evening. Everyone admired her pots, and one day, when she came back home from her class, she told her husband Bill that she would like to give up her job and start a pottery in the garage.

They worked out that she would save £700 a year on fares to work, £3,000 on child minder's fees and another £900 on lunches and clothes that she would no longer have to buy. In addition, her tax bill* would certainly be lower and with the pots she would sell, they would be just as well off.

They decided to spend their savings of £10,000 on pottery equipment. Tracey worked hard and soon had a stock of pots to sell. She took some samples* round to local shops but failed to get a single order. She hired stalls* at markets and fairs but she sold very few pots.

One day, she forgot to switch off the kiln* and her small garage caught fire. [The insurance company refused to pay because Tracey had not told them that she had converted her garage into a pottery workshop. Fortunately, the blaze* did not spread* to the house.

Tracey sold her pottery equipment at a loss and took a job as a receptionist again. Her pots and her savings were lost and there were no profits.]

Bill and Tracey understood that she shouldn't have given up her job so quickly, that they shouldn't have spent their savings, that they should have made a market study before starting the business and that they should have declared that the use of the garage had changed. But things could have been far more serious: the fire could have burnt their home and could have spread to the neighbours' houses, and as Tracey and Bill did not have permission from the Council to start the pottery, they would be in prison now.

Word box

to set up on one's own *créer une entreprise / se mettre à son compte.*
the tax bill *les impôts à payer*
a sample *un échantillon*
to hire a stall *louer un stand*
a kiln *un four*
the blaze *l'incendie*
to spread *s'étendre / se propager*

Compréhension

A Répondez en français aux questions ci-dessous, en utilisant uniquement les informations contenues dans le texte. Justifiez toujours vos réponses.

9 points	A1 = 1pt	A2 = 1,5pt	A3 = 1,5pt	A4 = 1,5pt	A5 = 2pts	A6 = 1,5pt

1. Quel est l'emploi de Tracey après ses études ? Est-elle satisfaite ?
2. Quelle entreprise Tracey crée-t-elle ? Où et quand ?
3. Citez trois éléments sur lesquels le couple se base pour avoir des revenus viables ?
4. L'entreprise est-elle un succès ? Pourquoi ?
5. Indiquez quatre actions que Tracey et son mari auraient dû faire ou ne pas faire pour mieux réussir.
6. En quoi la situation aurait-elle pu être plus grave ?

B Traduisez en français ce passage, lignes 24 à 30. (3 pts)

[*The insurance company… there were no profits.*]

Compétences linguistiques

C Transformez les phrases suivantes à la forme passive. (2 pts)

1. Many people admire Tracey's pots.
2. Tracey created a new business two years ago.
3. She thought she would make a lot of profit.
4. Unfortunately, she will sell her equipment at a loss.

D Recopiez les phrases suivantes sur votre copie en les complétant à l'aide des mots choisis dans la liste ci-dessous. (2 pts)
enough – too much – too many – a few – a little – no.

1. You can't start a business if you have .... permission from the authorities.
2. Do you have .... money or do you need more?
3. .... problems bring stress and illness.
4. I would like to work with .... friends; it would be great!

Expression écrite

E Answer the following questions in 80 words minimum (4 pts).

1. Secteur industriel : Sum up Tracey's story. Use the following questions as a guide.

a. What was Tracey's first job? Why did she drop it?
b. What did she decide to do then? Where and when?
c. How did she buy her equipment?
d. Did she make profits. Why?
e. What happened one day? Why?
f. How did the insurance company react? Why?
g. What did Tracey have to do afterwards?

2. Secteur tertiaire : A friend of yours has just sent you a letter, saying he would like to open a shop. He asks you for advice.

Write him back and list the advantages and disadvantages of setting up on one's own. Tell him what he should do or shouldn't do to succeed.

Exam: training

6 Turning a passion into business

> ALEXANDER HALL, from Lincolnshire, started his garden design business after a year-long course.

"I'd always been interested in growing plants and thought I'd like to work in a nursery. In 2000, I inherited some money and decided to do a course at The English Gardening School in London. I found the course interesting but it was a lot of work. After I finished the course I was not sure what I wanted to do. A local school asked me to design its centenary garden. That's how it began. [You don't need a big amount of money in garden design, just a drawing board, a pencil and a ruler. But you worry about doing wrong when you are self-employed and are afraid the phone won't ring. Working from home means you must be disciplined, even if you can do your own hours."]

> JANET ELLIOT set up her successful decorated papers business in Durham in March 2001.

"I started painting and drawing a long time ago because I had always loved making things like marbling*. I read a lot about marbling. Then I thought I could work for myself. I had £2,000 in savings and the Prince's Trust* helped me with a £3,000 loan. I leased a shop. But I had no customer order! I am still doing everything myself, which means fifteen separate operations by hand. The British Library is one of my clients, and many experts, worldwide, consult me. In the future, I hope to develop new techniques. Going into business means being prepared to work hard, but I feel lucky: I've found something I enjoy."

> PAM JARMAN is the managing director of It's Nut Free, a Norfolk-based company which makes and supplies nut-free* cakes, biscuits and desserts.

"I have always loved making special cakes because my daughter had a nut allergy, like some other children. In October 2001, I decided it was time to do something about it. Initially, I made birthday cakes for people I knew and found quite a market. Later, with a friend, we registered as a limited company, and now we have about 600 clients. We run the business from my friend's kitchen and my office at home. The Anaphylaxis Campaign – a charity providing information and support to people with serious allergies – has helped us a lot, making sure that we're meeting health and safety regulations; they gave us a £1,000 grant. We want to have our nut-free products in every restaurant and supermarket in Britain. At the moment we're making a profit, but it's not enough, and we're not paying ourselves, but we need and want to expand. We'll get £50,000 from the bank to get a workshop and employ ten or fifteen staff."

Word box

marbling *la marbrure*
The Prince's Trust *Organisme d'aide à la création d'entreprises*
nut-free *sans arachide*

Compréhension

A Répondez en français aux questions suivantes en utilisant uniquement les informations contenues dans le texte. Rédigez des phrases complètes et justifiez toujours vos réponses.

9 points	A1 = 3pts	A2 = 2pts	A3 = 0,5pt	A4 = 1pt	A5 = 0,5pt	A6 = 1pt	A7 = 1pt

1. Recopiez ce tableau et complétez-le en FRANÇAIS avec des informations extraites du texte.

	Zones géographiques (ville ou région)	Passe-temps (hobby)	Métiers actuels	Lieux d'exercice de leur métier
Alexander HALL				
Jane ELLIOT				
Pam JARMAN				

2. Dites en français, à quelles informations correspondent ces données chiffrées.
a. £3,000 **b.** 2000 **c.** £50,000 **d.** 600
3. Quel événement a donné l'envie à Alexander Hall de transformer sa passion en métier ?
4. De qui Pam et Janet ont-elles reçu une aide financière pour démarrer leur entreprise ?
5. Que veut faire Janet à l'avenir ?
6. Qu'envisage Pam pour l'avenir de son entreprise ?
7. D'après Alexander et Janet, quelles sont les qualités nécessaires pour travailler à son compte ?

B Traduisez en français le passage suivant, lignes 14 à 19. (3 pts)

[*You don't need a big amount... you can do your own hours.*]

Compétences linguistiques

C Posez des questions sur les éléments soulignés. (2 pts)

1. She made special cakes <u>because her daughter had a nut allergy</u>.
2. The Prince's Trust gave them <u>£1,000</u>.
3. In the future, they <u>will employ more staff</u>.
4. You need <u>a drawing board and a pen</u> to be a garden designer.

D Recopiez les énoncés suivants en les complétant à l'aide de mots choisis dans la liste suivante : *unless – since – so – in order to – although – in case* (2 pts)

1. Alex went to London .... do a course in gardening.
2. Pam and her friend haven't been paid .... they started their business.
3. Janet is still doing everything by hand .... there are special machines for marbling.
4. Pam needs to expand her business .... she will raise £50,000 from the bank.

Expression écrite

E Answer the following questions in English (80 words minimum). (4 pts)

1. **Secteur industriel :** What sport(s) do you practice? Where do you practice it? How often? Would you like to become a professional sportsman?
2. **Secteur tertiaire :** Have you got a hobby? How long have you had it? Would you like to turn it into a job? Justify your answer.

Exam: 7 training

We have become a fast food nation

How many people ate at a fast food restaurant last night? Come on, be honest. Chances are it is a lot of people.

America truly is turning into a fast food nation, echoing the title of a current best-selling book. People are inundated with work, family obligations, sports and other activities. They often prefer having a quick meal at McDonald's, Arby's, Burger King, Wendy's or Taco Bell. The food tastes good. It's cheap. It's fast. But what does this mean for people's health and for society at large?

"Fast food is now so commonplace that it has acquired an air of inevitability, as though it were something unavoidable, a fact of modern life" Eric Schlosser wrote in *Fast Food Nation*, published last year. He goes on to point out* how this attitude has invaded society in more places than just the food industry.

In 2000, Americans spent more than $110 billion on fast food. McDonald's now provides nearly 90 percent of the country's new jobs, and operates* 28,000 restaurants nationwide. It is the largest purchaser* of beef, pork and potatoes.

["Americans are enjoying the rewards produced by several generations of sweat, hard work and steadily mounting wealth", said Tom Majeski of the *Pioneer Press* in his recent article about the health risks of a fast food nation. In short, people feel they deserve it, as a result of a highly automated society.] Everywhere people go, they are greeted by automatic doors, elevators and enclosed parking ramps two feet from the buildings. The message they get is that exercise and health are not valued; convenience is.

"People don't have time anymore," said Christine (student). "They're all in a hurry so they eat fast food. Then they go to the office and sit all day."

As a result, 69 percent of adults and 13 percent of children are overweight. This is not the only consequence. The "McRestaurant" attitude of Americans is spreading* throughout the world. American fast food restaurants are spreading through Europe and Asia and crowding out independent businesses. In the process of creating all this food, the employees at meat-processing plants are some of the most underpaid and badly treated in the country, paying the price for a fast food nation.

There is a lot more under that Big Mac wrapper* than just a hamburger.

By Claire Shefchik,
Poney Express (Stillwater Area High School Magazine)
March 2002

Word box

point out *mettre en évidence*
operate *gérer*
a purchaser *un acheteur*
spread *(ici) s'étendre*
a wrapper *un emballage (une feuille de papier d'emballage)*

Compréhension

A Répondez en français aux questions suivantes, en utilisant uniquement les informations contenues dans le texte. Rédigez des phrases complètes.

8 points	A1 = 0,5pt	A2 = 1,5pt	A3 = 0,5pt	A4 = 1,5pt	A5 = 1,5pt	A6 = 0,5pt	A7 = 2pts

1. Quel est le titre du livre qui a inspiré cet article?
2. Pour quelles raisons les Américains préfèrent-ils la restauration rapide ?
3. Combien les Américains dépensent-ils en restauration rapide ?
4. Citez trois éléments du texte qui indiquent que Mc Donald's est la chaîne de restauration rapide la plus importante aux États-Unis.
5. Quelles autres facilités permettent aux Américains de limiter leurs efforts partout où ils se rendent ?
6. Quelles sont les conséquences de ces habitudes sur la santé des Américains ?
7. Quelles en sont les conséquences économiques et sociales ?

B Traduisez en français le début du cinquième paragraphe du texte, lignes 26 à 31. (4 pts)

[*"Americans are enjoying...highly automated society."*]

Compétences linguistiques

C Vous vous adressez à des amis américains qui souhaitent perdre du poids. A partir des énoncés ci-dessous, rédigez 4 ordres ou conseils différents à la forme affirmative ou négative. (2 pts)

1. They often eat fast food.
2. They don't like eating fruit or vegetables.
3. They prefer taking elevators or parking ramps to walking.
4. They drink soda all day long.

D Recopiez les énoncés ci-dessous en mettant le verbe entre parenthèses au temps qui convient. (2 pts)

1. Claire often *(have)* a quick lunch at a fast food restaurant.
2. Today, she *(prepare)* a soup and a salad for her dinner.
3. If she *(eat)* less fast food, she will lose weight.
4. If she lived in another country, she *(walk)* more.

Expression écrite

E Secteurs tertiaire et industriel.
Write a letter in English to a new American pen-friend. (4 pts)

Tell him / her about your studies, explain how French students live: time-tables, meals, sports, free time... Ask your friend some questions about his / her habits (80 words minimum).

unit 1 pages 6 à 13

Chat time

Student B, you are interviewing Sam. Then you are Peter or Jane and answer student A's questions.
Then write a paragraph about them.

NAME	Sam	Peter RABBIT	Jane KECK
AGE		22	18
OCCUPATION		representative	mechanic trainee
COMPANY / SCHOOL		Nokia phones in the Marketing department	Ford car factory in the electric workshop
JOB / STUDIES		visit clients / show new models	check lights / test electric circuits
PRESENT ACTIVITY		take appointments	change a faulty part
OPINION ABOUT JOB		++ very interesting good salary	– rather boring / always same job
SALARY		£ 20,000 / year	0 / only a trainee
WORK OVERTIME		often / come back home late	never / in my contract
HOME		rent a flat in the suburb of Bristol	with mother / flat in the town centre
TONIGHT		watch TV / go to bed early	meet friends at the pub

hot line

You're phoning to enrol for the Students' Union. You are one of the following students.
Listen to your partner's questions and answer according to the role card information.
Here is the beginning of the telephone conversation.

CLUB RECEPTIONIST/OPERATOR	ENROLLING STUDENT
1. Students' Union Galway, ...?	Yes, I'm phoning to enrol in the Students' Union. Is it possible by phone?

> Vous êtes Lola (F) ou Jose (M) GOMEZ > Vous êtes étudiant ESPAGNOL à Galway au : Commercial College. > Votre numéro de carte d'étudiant: 50942 > Votre adresse en Irlande est: 105 Moycullen Road à Galway. > Vous choisissez le code personnel (PIN code): EG 3978	> Vous êtes Maria (F) ou Gianni (M) MARINETO. > Vous êtes étudiant ITALIEN à Galway au : Civil Engineering College. > Votre numéro de carte d'étudiant: 21093 > Votre adresse en Irlande est : 98 Abbeygate Road à Galway. > Vous choisissez le code personnel (PIN code): IM 4047
> Vous êtes Martina (F) ou Igor (M) PUSHKINOF > Vous êtes étudiant RUSSE à Galway au : Catering Institute College. > Votre numéro de carte d'étudiant: 18763 > Votre adresse en Irlande est: 68 Loughrea avenue à Galway > Vous choisissez le code personnel (PIN code): RP 2185	> Vous êtes : vous-même > Vous êtes étudiant FRANÇAIS (ou autre nationalité) à Galway au : (*choisissez :* Commercial College ou Catering Institute College ou Civil Engineering College.) > Votre numéro de carte d'étudiant: *(imaginez-en un de 5 chiffres)* > Votre adresse en Irlande est:.......... *(imaginez-en une à Galway)*. > Vous choisissez le code personnel (PIN code): ....

unit 2 pages 14 à 21

Chat time

You are student B. Student A has problems and asks you to advise him / her. Give a minimum of 3 tips.

Example: **A:** - *I'm always late at school. What can I do? Can you advise me? . . . .*
B: - *Always get up early. You should . . . . / Be careful. Don't . . . .*

Help: **a.** use an alarm-clock – get up early in the morning – watch TV at night – go to bed early/late
b. go out – meet friends – have a walk – exercise – talk about your problems with your parents/friends
c. ask your friends to help you – see a doctor – buy cigarettes – exercise – wear a patch
d. improve your English – talk during English classes – learn your lessons – watch O.V. films

Then change roles. Explain your problems (pictures e, f, g, h) and ask student A to advise you. Student A will give you tips to help you. Note down the 3 tips he gives you.

e

You are in love.

f

You have put on weight.

g

You spend too much money.

h

You have got bad marks.

You can also imagine other problems and give other advice.

hot line

You work at the tourist office and you answer your partner's questions (p. 19). You can use this grid.

Tourist Office	Miami Tourist Office	Edinburgh Tourist Office	Madrid Tourist Office
Country / State	Florida	Scotland	Spain
Places to visit	Disney World Universal Studios	Edinburgh Loch Ness	Madrid: Prado Museum Barcelona
Other activities	Sailing, swimming	Fishing, cycling	Dancing, swimming
Climate			
Food	Beef / salads / ice creams / fast-food	Salmon / trout / mutton / Haggis	Paella / fish / fruit / salads / ice creams
Special events	Many tourists all year round	Edinburgh Tattoo (in August)	Bullfights (corridas)

unit 3 pages 22 à 29

hot line

2. Practise more dialogues. You are the travel agent. Listen to your client and give the details of the trip he wants. Note the date of the trip and the client's name.

Destination	PARIS	
Transport	plane	Eurostar
Departure from	8:15 am / 2:45 pm / 6: 20 pm London Heathrow	7:30 am / 9:10 am / 11:30 am / 1:10 pm / 3:30 pm / 5:10 pm St Pancras International
Arrival at	10:00 am / 4:30 pm / 8:05 pm Paris-Charles de Gaulle Airport	10:45 am / 12:25 am / 2:45 pm / 4:25 pm / 6:45 pm / 8:25 pm Paris-Gare du Nord
Time for journey	45 minutes / 3/4 hr	2 hrs 15 mn
Return fares	economy class : £120 / business class : £250	standard class : £110 / 1 st class : £180

Date .... Name ....

Destination	MADRID	
Transport	plane	
Departure from	7:40 am / 11:20 am / 03:30 pm Heathrow Airport	
Arrival at	10:55 am / 2:35 pm / 6:45 pm Madrid Airport	
Time for journey	2. 1/2 hr	
Return fares	economy class: £220 / business class: £450	

Date .... Name ....

unit 4 pages 30 à 37

Chat time

You are student B.

1. You ask questions to your partner to complete your plan. You will also answer his questions to complete his plan. Be as precise as possible. (Student A : see page 31)

GROUND FLOOR

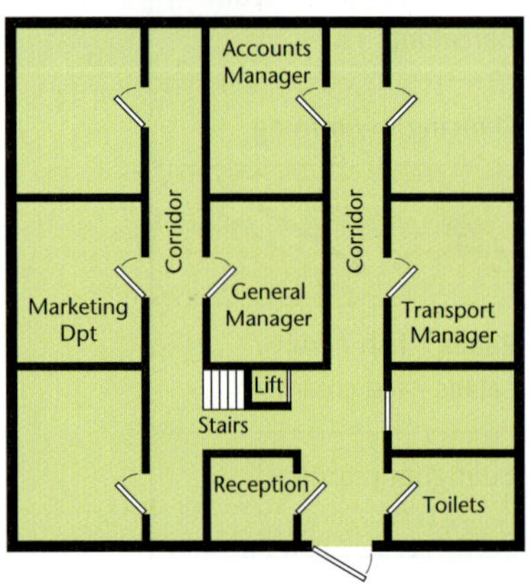

FIRST FLOOR

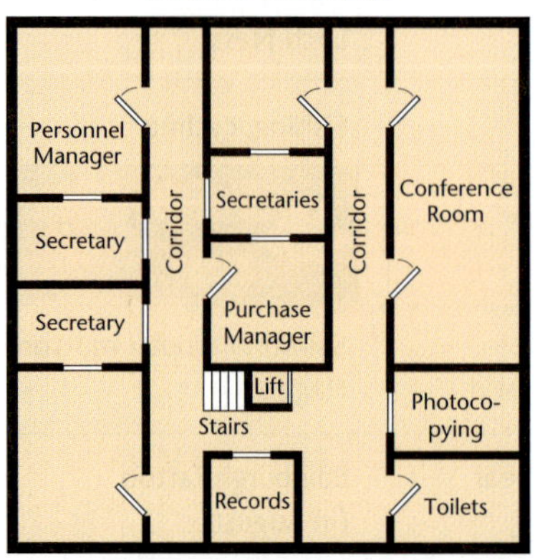

You must find where :
- the sales manager's office,
- the marketing department,
- the research and development manager's office,
- the accounts department,
- the showroom,
- the legal department are.

2. Then choose a position *(un poste)* or a room and tell your partner how to go there. Student A must find it.

unit 6 pages 46 à 53

Chat time

Student B. Look at the pictures. Choose the right order to proceed and explain student B what must or can be done for printing photos.

Ex: *First, the photos must / can be taken. Then...*

a. Insert photo paper into your printer.

b. Transfer your photos to your computer.

c. Take photos.

d. Adjust the size.

e. Connect your camera to the computer.

f. Choose the best photo.

g. Display the photos on the screen.

h. Print the photo.

Student A: Listen to the advice and write down the order to proceed.

hot line

Here is some help for your dialogue on the telephone (you can practise the dialogue in groups of two or three students). Complete this dialogue with the questions you'd like to ask. / Answer with what you know of the recycling programme in your town.

You can also ask and answer questions about other wastes, for example: catalogues, phone books, advertising leaflets, plastic bags, motor oil, batteries, old clothes, automobile tyres...

B: Good morning, City of . . . Town Hall.
A: Oh hello, could I speak to . . ., please?
B: Just a moment. . . . I'm afraid . . . 's line is busy.
A: Could you put me through to his secretary?
B: Wait a minute, please. . . .
C: Hello, Recycling Office . . . speaking.
A: Hello, this is . . . . I'd like to ask you a few questions about recycling. I don't know what to do with . . . (the old catalogues / plastic bags / old batteries...)
C: They can be placed in . . . (a special bag / box). It's collected every . . . / They are not collected. You have to take them to a special container / a recycling site *(une déchetterie)*.
A: And what about . . .?
C: They can be . . . .
A: What about . . . ? Are there special bags or boxes for the . . .?
C: Yes, you will be given . . . / No, sorry, you have to take them to . . .
A: How can I get the special bags / boxes for the . . .?
C: You can come here or ask . . .
A: Where's your recycling office located exactly?
C: It's . . . .
A: What can I do with . . .?
C: . . . .
A: Thank you.
C: You are welcome. Have a nice day. Goodbye.
A: Good bye.

unit 7 pages 54 à 61

Chat time

Student B. Play the role of the caller. BUILD CORRECT ANSWERS.

Police	Caller
Emergency Service / I / help / you / can /?	Yes, I've just had ....
what / it / sort of / is / breakdown /?	two tyres / blow up / only one spare wheel.
have / control / you / lost /?	fortunately / not / no.
is / your / where / car / parked /?	hard shoulder.
warning lights / are / on / your /?	yes + open bonnet.
anyone / there / is / inside / vehicle / your / ?	yes / my girlfriend / my boyfriend.
get out / they / must / of / car / the /. and / keep away / they / traffic / must / from / the / .	OK / walk back to the car. Stay with them.
is /car / what / your / make /the / of /?	Volkswagen / blue Golf / 3 doors.
the / will / there / breakdown service / be / 20 minutes / in /.	Thanks. Good bye.

unit 9 pages 70 à 77

Chat time

Student B: You play the salesman / girl and you ask questions and give information.
Student A: see page 71.

Ex: *Can I help you? What size ...? What colour would you like? Would you like a special pattern ...? Does it fit? .... I think it's... . How are you paying?*

Your role	You sell jeans	You sell shirts	You sell bags
Item	?	?	?
Size	?	?	?
Colour / Pattern	?	?	?
Price	€109.45	€22.50	€39.50
Fitting	?	?	?
Opinion	in fashion / first-quality	nice and not expensive at all	very convenient / strong material
Payment	?	?	?

hot line

2. Practise more dialogues. You are the receptionist. If you are the caller, see p. 75.

Mail-order catalogue	The House of Bruar	The Green Shop Home	Collection	Liberty by post
Item				
Reference				
Size				
Price	£45	£59.75	£39.90	£28.25
Colour / material	dark blue / cotton	green / plastic	white / porcelain	light grey /silk
Postage and packing	£3.45	£12.90	£6.50	£5.80
Delivery	4 days	1 week	3 working days	6 days

unit 10 pages 78 à 85

hot line

2. Make dialogues with your partner.
Student B: you are Meg or Jack and you answer the receptionist's questions.
Then you play your own role.

Characters	Meg Dowling	Jack Murphy	You
Sports practised	aerobics	scuba diving	
New club	Manchester Fitness	the Brighton Big Blue	
Former club	Liverpool Elastica	the Portsmouth Coral	
New residence	Manchester	Brighton	
Former residence	Liverpool	Portsmouth	
Experience	2 years	3 years	
Preferred training days	Tuesday + Thursday	Monday + Wednesday	

unit 11 pages 86 à 93

hot line

2. Practise other surveys. Answer the interviewer's questions.

1	.... Hello!
3	Yes. What can I do for you?
5	Yes. What about?
7	All right, I'm ready.
9	I ....
11	Yes , I ....
13	Well, I .... it ....
15	I ....

Quelqu'un vous téléphone pour un sondage. Décrochez, présentez vous par votre numéro (1).
- La dernière fois que vous avez vu la pub pour "BIG BONE Dog food" vous alliez au supermarché (9). Vous aviez déjà vu cette pub quelques fois (13). Vous étiez en train de cuisiner quand le téléphone a sonné (15).
- La dernière fois que vous avez vu la pub pour "SUPERGUY Vitamin cocktail" vous étiez en train de prendre le petit déjeuner (9). Vous l'aviez vue de nombreuses fois (13). Vous étiez en train de réviser pour votre examen quand le téléphone a sonné (15).
- La dernière fois que vous avez entendu la pub pour "VAMPIRE Amusement Park" vous étiez en train de lire un magazine (9). Vous l'aviez déjà entendue une ou deux fois. Vous étiez en train de regarder la TV quand le téléphone a sonné (15).

unit 13 pages 102 à 109

hot line

1. You are student B. Listen to the telephone conversation and complete Julian's answers. Then, check on page 107.

ASTRID	JULIAN
a. Where do you work?	a. .... called ' the Manor'.
b. How far is it?	b. Only ....
c. How do you get there?	c. I .... I've bought a car.
d. How long have you been working?	d. ....
e. How many employees are there?	e. ....
f. How old are they?	f. Between .... years old.
g. How long do you work every day?	g. ....
h. When does the restaurant close?	h. It's closed on ....
i. How much do the meals cost?	i. The cheapest menu costs..... and the most expensive is.....

unit 14 pages 110 à 117

Chat time

You are student B.
Student A is criticizing you in one of the following situations :

A: You were on holiday in London but you forgot to send news from you.
B: You had a football match on Sunday morning but you were late and arrived after the match had begun.
C: The police stopped you because you were driving too fast and you had drunk too much alcohol.

Reply to his remarks by choosing one of these arguments to make sentences:

A	B	C
– (have) no writing paper – (have) no pen – (not have) enough money – (be) too expensive	– (watch) TV late – (not hear) the alarm clock – my telephone (not ring) – parents (be away) for the weekend	– (there be) no traffic – (be) alone on the road – (be) at a birthday party – (there be) only beer or wine. – she (not have) her driving license – she (be) too young

unit 16 pages 126 à 133

2. Practise more telephone conversations with your partner.

Conversation 1:

Student B: you are a manager(ess) at AB Packaging and you ask questions to the secretary about Mrs Pauline Parr's venue. Note down the answers. Student A is the secretary (see page 131).

Conversation 2:

Student B: Now, you are a secretary at R.C.S. and C° and answer the manager's questions with the help of Miss Templeton's letter. Student A is the manager (see page 131).

WALLACE and Sons Ltd
16, Culloden Crescent
STIRLING ST5 9Y2

To R.C.S. and C°
Laundry Lane
Blomfield Health
Croydon SE2 8Z4

Stirling, September 3rd, 2008

Ref. B.T./AB/03/85

Dear Sir,

We have finally decided the conference should be next month. The production manager and myself will fly over to London Stansted, on October 1st. Our flight number is GO502, with Easyjet and arrives at 12.00. We'll take the airport bus to Liverpool St Station. We'll go by taxi to Croydon and arrive at about 5.

Looking forward to hearing from you soon,
Yours sincerely,

B. Templeton

The British Isles

+ 5 million inhabitants

500 000 to 1 million inhabitants

250 000 to 500 000 inhabitants

GREAT BRITAIN
230 000 km²
55.9 million inhabitants
(236/km²)

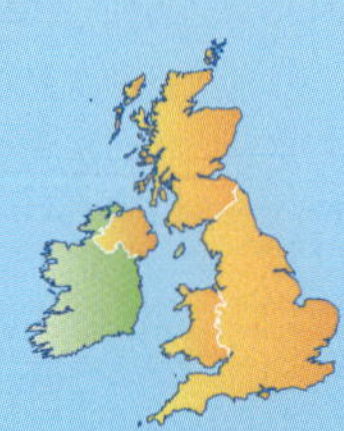

THE UNITED KINGDOM
244 100 km²
60.6 million inhabitants
(228.8/km²)

IRISH REPUBLIC
70 300 km²
4.2 million inhabitants
(50/km²)

The United States

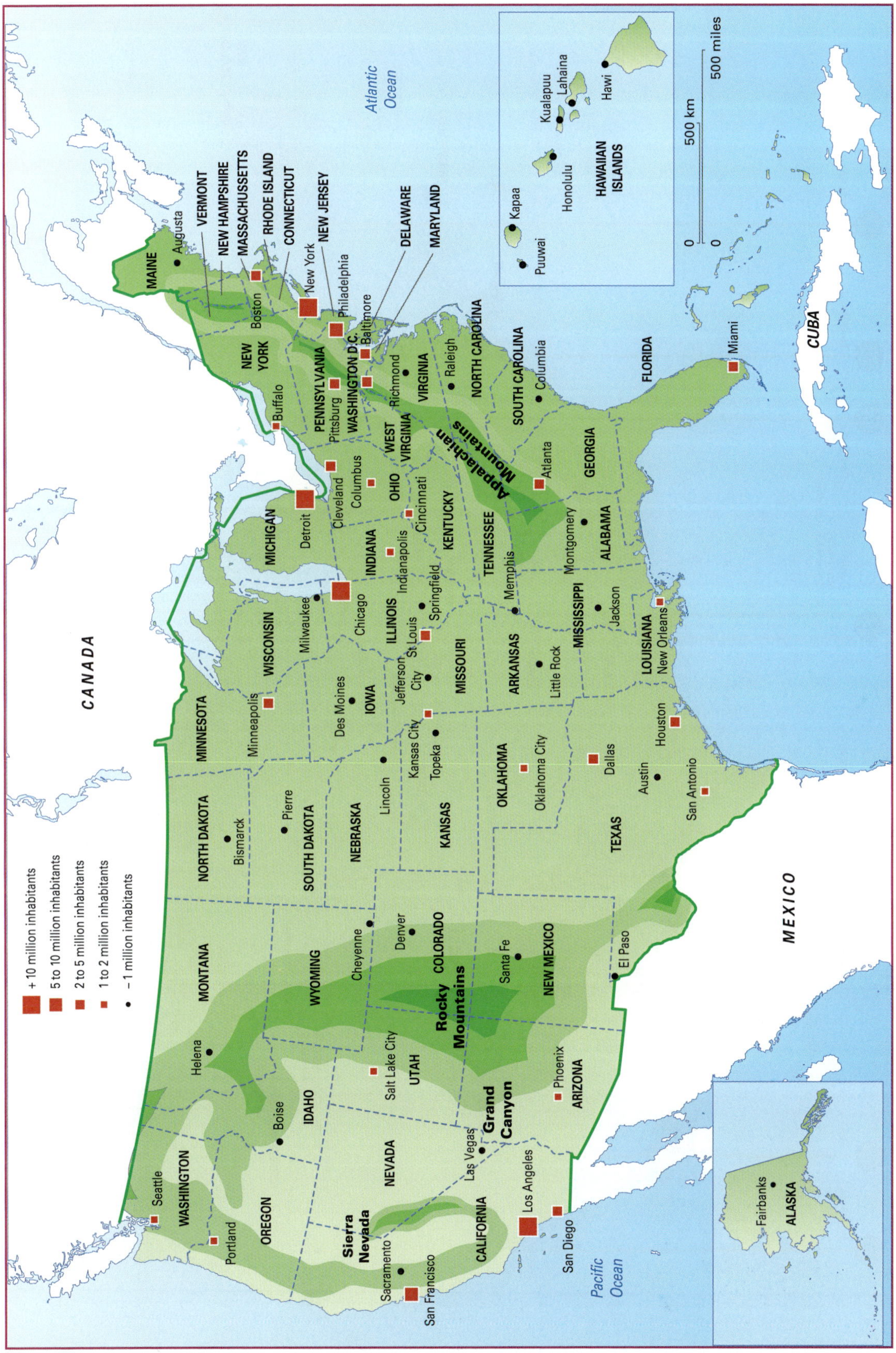

The English speaking world

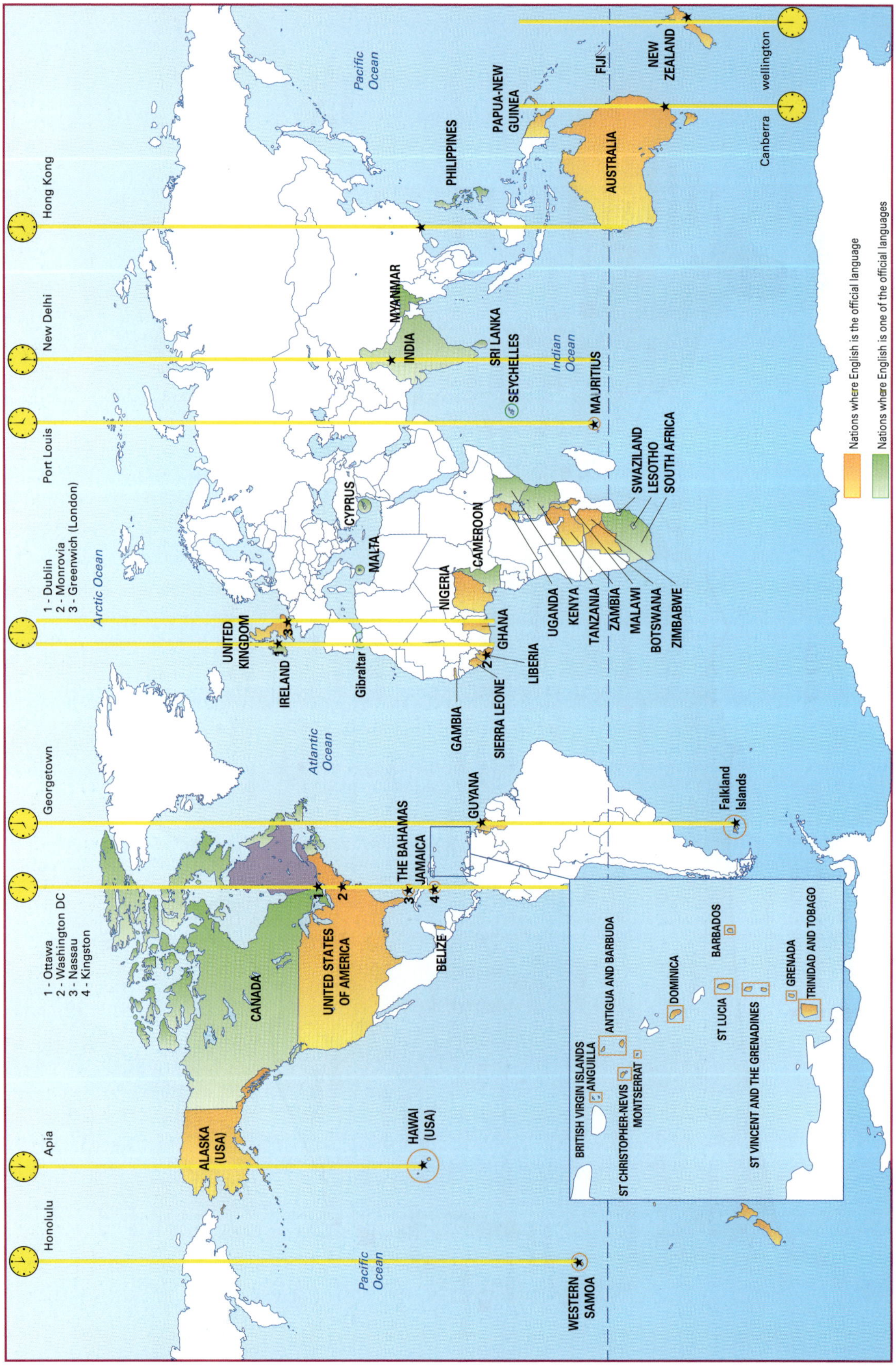

Measures

INCHES AND MILLIMETERS

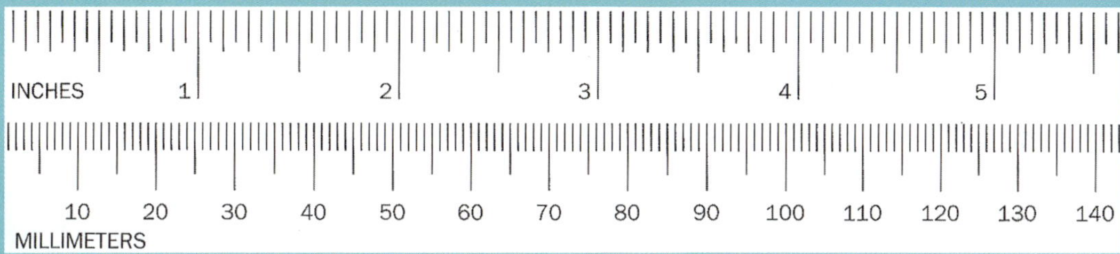

DEGREES

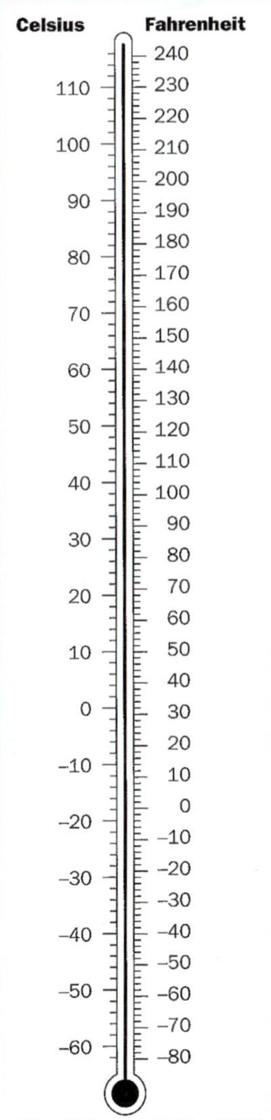

0 °C = 32 °F 100 °C = 212 °F

$\left(°C \times \frac{9}{5}\right) + 32 = °F$

$\left(°F - 32\right) \times \frac{5}{9} = °C$

METRIC CONVERSIONS

APROXIMATE CONVERSIONS FROM METRIC MEASURES

LENGTH

When you know	Multiply by	To find
millimeters (mm)	0.04	inches
centimeters (cm)	0.4	inches
meters (m)	3.3	feet
meters (m)	1.1	yards
kilometers (km)	0.6	miles

MASS

When you know	Multiply by	To find
grams (g)	0.035	ounces
kilograms (kg)	2.2	pounds
tonnes (t)	1.1	short tons

APROXIMATE CONVERSIONS TO METRIC MEASURES

LENGTH

When you know	Multiply by	To find
inches (in)	25.4	millimeters
inches (in)	2.54	centimeters
feet (ft)	30	centimeters
yards (yd)	0.9	meters
miles (mi)	1.6	kilometers

MASS

When you know	Multiply by	To find
ounces (oz)	28	grams
pounds (lb)	0.45	kilograms
short tons (2,000 lb)	0.9	tonnes

Table des illustrations

Page	
8	Corbis/Robert Harding World Imagery
9	Sipa Press/Florence Durand
10	The Environmental Press Agency/David Higgs
14 haut	Panos/Hughes Crispin
14 bas	Rea/Nicolas Tavernier
15	Sipa Press/Bruno Bebert
18	Photodisc
24	Gettyimages/Altrendo Travel
26 haut	Hoa-Qui/ Age Fotostock/José Fuste Raga
26 milieu	Hoa-Qui/Age Fotostock/Bruno Morandi
32 gauche	Corbis/Kevin Fleming
32 droite	Corbis/David Turnley
34 haut	Corbis Sygma/R. Ressmeyer
34 bas gauche	Photo12.com/Alamy
35	Corbis Sygma/Eye Ubiquitous/P. Thomson
40	Sipa Press/Tom Hood
46	Corbis/Andrew Fox
48, 49	Sipa Press/Interfoto Usa
56	Corbis Sygma/Duomo
58	Photodisc
62 gauche	Stockfood/Damir Begovic
62 droite	Stockfood/David Loftus
64	Sipa Press/Alfred
65	Corbis Sygma/B. Zaunders
67	Hoa-Qui/Age Fotostock/Graham Ken
70	Rea/Tom Craig
72	Gettyimages/Frank Herholdt
74	Sipa Press/Ching Nelson
75	Gettyimages/Robert E. Daemmrich
78 gauche	Abacapress.com/Startaks/Bill Davila
78 milieu	Corbis/Andrew Holbrooke
78 droite	Abacapress.com/William Gratz
79	Corbis Sygma/ChromoSohm Inc./J. Sohm
80	Reuters/Jack Dabaghian
81	Gamma/Camerapress/David Dyson
82 haut	Gamma/Van Tine Dennis
82 bas	Reuters/Jeff Christensen

Page	
83 gauche	UMA/Ray Giubilo
83 milieu gauche	Abacapress.com/ImagineChina
83 milieu droite	UMA/PCN/Paul J. Sutton
83 droite	Abacapress.com/DPA/Bernd Thissen
88	Photo12.com/Alamy
90, 122, 123, 124	Image courtesy of the Advertising Archives
91	Corbis/NewSport/Jeff Flindt
96	Gamma/Philippe Poulet
99	Abacapress.com
102 gauche	Corbis/Eye Ubiquitous/John Hulme
102 droite	Sipa press/Rex Features/Peter Brooker
104	Photo12.com/Alamy
112	Hoa-Qui/Explorer/Jean-Louis Dubois
113	Sunset/Philippe Blanchot
115	Sipa Press/Alexandra Boulat
118	Photo12.com/Alamy
120	Sipa Press/AP/Mike Hutmacher
126	Sipa Press/Rex Features/Peter Brooker
130	Abacapress.com/LFI/Michael Williams
130 bas gauche	Corbis/Paul A. Souders
130 bas droite	Gamma/Jean-Luc Luyssen
131	Photodisc
134	Corbis/Annie Griffiths Belt
136	Photo12.com/Alamy
138	Photo12.com/Alamy
142	Corbis Sygma/R. T. Nowitz
146	Gettyimages/Stone/Robert E. Daemmrich

Conception graphique : Laurence Durandau
Adaptation graphique et mise en pages : Catherine Roussel
Couverture : Piero Brogi, Delius
Illustrations : Delius, Nicolas Julo, Catherine Lasnier, Isabelle Rullier.
Infographies / cartographie : Philippe Bouillon
Iconographie : Marie-France Naslednikov

C. Roussel - IGS - CTP
Éditions Foucher - Vanves - Août 2010 - 06 - DL/EG/DC-EG

Imprimé en France par Loire Offset Titoulet.